Democratic Algorithms

Nikolaus Poechhacker is Post-Doc senior scientist at the Digital Age Research Center (D!ARC), University of Klagenfurt and research fellow at the Department of Innovation and Digitalisation of Law, University of Vienna. He received his PhD in Sociology at the Technical University of Munich. In his work he researches the relationship between democratic institutions, law, social order, and algorithmic systems in various domains, bringing together perspectives from media theory, STS, computer science, and sociology.

Democratic Algorithms: Ethnography of a Public Recommender System

Nikolaus Poechhacker

 meson press

This book is based on the PhD thesis "Rule(s) of Recommendation: What the making of a recommender system can tell us about the difficult relation between social order and machine learning," submitted to the Technical University of Munich in 2021.

The author acknowledges the financial support by the University of Klagenfurt.

Bibliographical Information of the German National Library
The German National Library lists this publication in the Deutsche Nationalbibliografie (German National Bibliography); detailed bibliographic information is available online at http://dnb.d-nb.de.

Published in 2024 by meson press, Lüneburg, Germany
www.meson.press

Design concept: Torsten Köchlin, Silke Krieg
Cover image: alexander_ant@Unslpash
Copy editing: Marc Weingart and Hugh Schmidt

The print edition of this book is printed by Lightning Source, Milton Keynes, United Kingdom.

ISBN (Print): 978-3-95796-224-9
ISBN (PDF): 978-3-95796-225-6
DOI: 10.14619/2249

The digital editions of this publication can be downloaded freely at:
www.meson.press

Contents

Introduction

This is a book about social order. More specifically, it is about the complicated relationship between machine learning algorithms and the formation of democratic order. And there are good reasons for such a book. Algorithms appear to become a defining moment in the digitized societies of the 21st century – and it seems that no domain of life is spared from the rational and seemingly powerful influence of the computational logic of algorithms. At least this is how the "alluring and compelling drama" (Neyland 2016, 51) is being told. And it seems true. Filter bubbles threaten democratic discourse and opinion formation, algorithmic risk scores are being applied in law enforcement and judicial reasoning, and policy is increasingly based on algorithmic evidence. Algorithms specifically, and digital technologies in general, have become deeply embedded in our social life, in contemporary societies, and in the institutions of our democracies (Berg and Hofmann 2021). This fact even provoked the question, whether democracy will survive the rise of AI (Helbing et al. 2017).

The focus of this book is related to these questions, but also inverts them: instead of asking how algorithms are changing our contemporary democracy, I will critically examine the efforts of a democratic institution to make algorithms more democratically aligned. Starting in early 2016, I joined the initiative of a public broadcaster in Germany that sought to develop a new website with a video-on-demand system. To accomplish this, a software development team was gathered to design and implement the new site, and which would "air" the same shows from the linear program – but in a non-linear way. Further, because this website was intended to implement the latest available features, a recommender system was envisioned as a central element of the setup. This, however, created some challenges on the normative side. Public broadcasting entities in Germany have a legal obligation to adhere to the German constitution, which states that such broadcasters must distribute a broad range of information about political, social, and cultural events in Germany. Recommender systems do exactly the opposite of that; they select information pieces based on similarity, not diversity – they tend to create filter bubbles.

The relation between democratic order and algorithmic systems should have now become apparent. However, the specific challenge – not only for this specific broadcaster but for all democratic institutions – is: can we build democratic algorithms? Can we translate our central shared values, beliefs, and norms into machine learning systems and, if so, how? Part of the answer is that we have to go beyond a technical understanding of algorithms, but without losing the technical systems out of sight in the process. Instead, I argue that algorithmic systems are complex socio-technical systems in which the algorithm, as an entity, is enacted. This enactment is a symmetrical process, in which the technical aspects must aligned with their surrounding practices and expectations – and vice versa. Further, algorithmic systems are enacted in multiple ways with different translations and outcomes. In the specific case that I discuss here, the recommender system was enacted in three different ways to form different collectives: a disciplinary enactment of the algorithm as technical object, an institutional enactment of the algorithm as organizational entity, and a political enactment of the algorithm as a normative and legal challenge. Each of these enactments tried to shape the algorithm in its own way, enabling or hindering specific implementations. The challenge for the actual implementation of the algorithm was to align these three different enactments into a broader socio-technical system. The result complicates the notion of the algorithm, because the boundaries of its enactment become a political question as well.

Turning the perspective on democracy and algorithms upside down challenges the notion of the algorithms as it has been discussed thus far in the academic literature. Algorithms act in undeniably powerful ways in many social arenas and produce knowledge, communication patterns and order social relationships. Thus, it is not surprising that this topic has also been taken up within the academic and public debate. The literature that tackles the phenomenon of algorithmic power has grown in recent years to a vast number of articles, books and other resources – including entire research institutes. These studies on algorithms give fascinating accounts of how algorithms act as powerful entities and are essential elements in a system of digital control societies, incorporating a diverse set of values and norms, such as capitalist logic or bias against minorities. These perspectives are more often than not focused on the algorithm as a solid and powerful actor by itself. However, algorithms are not entities that emerge out of nowhere. They are always embedded into, and are the result of, practices, discourses, and rationalities – and therefore we should "consider algorithms as an object of cultural inquiry from a social scientific and humanistic perspective" (Ames 2018, 2). Theoretical and methodological contributions increasingly question this strong focus on algorithms as sole actors and call for a different perspective, studying algorithms as network effects (Ananny 2016) or in their multiplicity (Seaver 2017). What we perceive as the digital entity able to classify, categorize, or act upon our life chances – sometimes even upon our lives – is the outcome of a more or less stable set of interactions brought together in a process of ordering. What the algorithm is, and how it can become powerful is the result of many different choices, elements and discourse coming together. With this book I want to contribute to this ongoing discussion, finding new and different ways to look at the phenomenon of algorithmic agency in socio-technical systems and give some first cautious indications how the enactment of democratic values and the institutionalization of algorithmic systems are related. Paradoxically, such a contribution makes it necessary to start from an algorithm as the central object of attention first because, for one, every story needs a starting point, an entry from where on the journey can develop. And secondly, the notion (and the artifact) of the algorithm, if seen as a process rather than an essence, allows us to observe how different ideas, ideologies, necessities and dependencies come together. Thus, I attempt to create complex (and hopefully interesting) accounts of how power flows through the algorithm, to borrow and adapt an expression of Foucault, instead of assigning them power.

There seems to be a productive tension between the notion of algorithms as powerful and important actors in our digitized societies and at the same time being reluctant to essentialize the concept of the algorithm. However, the argument I make in this book is shifting the perspective from power to social order, asking how the algorithm as a stable actor becomes part of and is stabilized by specific systems of a practically achieved order. Power and processes of social ordering are, as John Law (1994) shows, two sides of the same coin. Powerful entities are able to act and impose their ideas and values upon others – also against resistance to borrow a famous definition from Max Weber ([1922] 1978). However, social order understood as a practical achievement of a system of interactions and practices is the very foundation of this capacity to act. Approaches like Actor-Network Theory (ANT), which is my departure point for the argument of the book and the work behind it, therefore ask what enables powerful actors, opening the metaphorically black box that constitutes them. This perspective can then also be applied to algorithms. Within the scholarly discourse, the notion of networked infor-mation algorithms (Ananny 2016) or algorithms as culture (Seaver 2017) are gaining traction, looking at algorithms as enactments of a socio-technical system or actor-network. Thus, algorithms are emergent effects of a socio-technical order while also acting as ordering devices at the same time. Their agency is an effect of the relational processes of social ordering.

Using the perspective of algorithms as achievements and as being in the making allows us to shift the perspective on the issue. Instead of analyzing the impact of algorithms on our democracy, it is possible to ask the question in a more symmetric way: how are algorithms made in democratic institutions, and how are both changed in the process? Or in other words: what constitutes a democratic algorithm? In this study, I therefore explore the genealogy of a specific algorithm as the result of distributed and coordinated processes in an important institution of contemporary German democracy: a public broad-caster. I thereby explore the question of how the algorithm came into being, what constituted the algorithm as an actor in different arenas and what issues occurred in the governance of such an actor – hopefully neither falling into tropes of social nor technological determinism.

As much as this book is about social ordering, it is also an attempt to order its very object of observation. An attempt to order the empirical material, thoughts and theoretical concepts into something that is convincing to the readers and the scientific community. Throughout the years, many concepts, ideas and versions of this book existed, but at some point, a final version has to be handed in. Therefore, this is a modest attempt to give account on this process and present an analysis of the development of an algorithm. The inquiry into the fragile production of algorithmic agency/power thereby draws on different theoretical and disciplinary backgrounds, including sociology of technology, media theory, and Science and Technology Studies (STS) – but also takes into account considerations and inputs from discussions with computer scientists, legal scholars, and anthropologists. The theoretical background is therefore diverse, and I use and understand theory as a lens that lets us see certain things better – and hides others. Blumer (1954) coined the term 'sensitizing concepts' to describe such an attitude. Also, given the complex and interdisciplinary topic of this book, bringing different approaches and concepts together makes it possible to produce a picture of algorithmic power that is, as Law would call it, fractal, but still coordinated with each other to make a coherent argument. Therefore, I will discuss the topic of machine learning and social order in terms of pragmatism, speech-act theory, ethnomethodology, and media theory. However, what binds these different approaches together is a strong orientation towards post-ANT and its sensitivities for material semiotics and relational ontologies. Thus, the program of ANT functions itself as a toolkit to produce a concept-network that combines interpretative and interactionist social science with computer science and media-sensitive philosophy.

This also makes a reflection on the methods applied necessary. The role of the researcher is always precarious if we take basic assumptions of our own epistemology seriously. For one, there is no such thing as an objective account given by one person, but only an empirically and disciplinary grounded ordering of observations (Law 1994, 2004). The ethnographic research presented here poses a special challenge, as I was not a detached observer but an active project member, bringing in ideas, solutions and, most often, problems. In the chapter on methodology, I therefore critically discuss the role of the embedded researcher and the potential issues it entails. This perspective shifts, however, if we follow the credo often formulated in ANT and ethnomethodology: assuming the actors in the empirical field as knowledgeable and competent (Garfinkel 1984; Latour 1999b). By not pre-assuming given social laws or mechanisms present in the field but to let the field teach and surprise you, going and being native becomes a resource in itself, enabling one to see, experience, and test the different orderings around. The chapter, however, discusses these two perspectives then – in the end – as two sides of the same coin, following Law (2004) in his plea to immerse yourself in the field but to be reflexive about it – and the need to come home (Amann and Hirschauer, 1997).

Throughout the ethnographic study of the making of the recommender system it became obvious that algorithms are enacted in multiple ways. Seaver (2017) argues that the ontological status of an algorithm differs throughout the place and actors we involve in the definition of it. It can be an interface to a library, an abstract idea referred to in meetings, a very material actor calculating job opportunities of unemployed citizens or a racist machine (Angwin et al. 2016). Seaver (2017) thereby bases his argument on post-ANT sensitivities (Mol 2002). The ontology of an object is always an emergent quality of situated practices and the materiality of the object in question. There is no one algorithm but multiple versions of it at the same time. This book is therefore structured by exploring three different enactments of the algorithm from a disciplinary, institutional and political perspective and how they are enacted and mobilized in different settings and situations. And these enactments are fragile in more than one aspect. For one, the making of these different versions in itself calls for an ongoing negotiation and ordering attempts to make a specific version of the algorithm. And each of these versions comes with its own problems and challenges for a system that in the end might be called a democratic algorithm.

There is no such thing as *the* algorithm. An algorithm is a set of instructions solving some kind of problem. Yet, there are different kinds of putting these instructions together. There are graph-theory based algorithms, different kinds of sorting algorithms like bubble sort, quick sort, etc. We can develop algorithms to solve labyrinths or to make sense of DNA sequencing data (basically a problem of combinatorics). Each of these algorithms solves different problems in different ways. And in the formulation of the anticipated problem, the algorithm formulates also an expectation about the world it acts upon and interacts with. There have been several calls to study code in order to understand how they interact with the world, e.g., in software studies. However, the actual code is often unavailable – protected by intellectual property rights (IPRs) – or just makes use of established libraries. And everyone who has debugged or refactored a piece of code written a long time ago or, even worse, written by a different person knows how complex and unforeseeable the actual interactions between the algorithm and its environment can be. At the same time, the question of what the focus of our analysis is or should be when we talk about algorithms in the context of social studies seems to be unresolved (Seaver 2017; Ziewitz 2016). In the chapter *Algorithmic Discipline*, I therefore explore the notion of the algorithm based on my readings of critical code studies and software studies and my observations in the software development project.

The algorithm as a principle and set of expectations does not come from nowhere. Algorithmic techniques (B. Rieder 2017) are circulating within the discipline of computer science, representing generalized solutions to generalized problems. For example, sorting a set of numbers is not a problem that must be solved again and again by computer science engineers. Instead, there exist manifold approaches to solve the general problem of sorting, where the engineers can choose between quick sort, merge sort, or (mostly for educational reasons) bubble sort – amongst others. Thus, the algorithm can be described as a disciplinary object being mobilized in software development projects. These principles can tell us already a lot about the way the reality is enacted by the algorithm and which assumptions about it are formulated in the basic structure of the algorithm. As such, code often refers back to these abstract techniques discussed in textbooks, conferences, and the like. This then also comes closer to what algorithmic work in the computer sciences is normally about. If you visit a lecture about algorithms, you will hardly ever see concrete code implementations but formulations of the idea of the algorithm in pseudo code, making use of theoretical concepts like branches and loops. Through the disciplinary discourse these travelling concepts gain stability by defining different approaches and assumptions around the world. The algorithm gets enacted as a disciplinary and technical object – an abstract solution that requires an abstract problem. In the process of mobilizing these techniques, the concrete problem at hand that should be solved then must be matched and abstracted in a way that meets the available solutions of this discipline (B. Rieder 2017). In describing these mobilization processes, the chapter describes not only how the algorithm gets an initial form but also argues that concrete code also always refers back to an entire collective of engineers, computer machines, networking standards, etc. making the production of algorithms possible in the first place. The algorithm therefore represents an ordering and (digital) world making of a whole discipline.

The algorithm is the result of heterogeneous translations, interactions, and the production of a stable actor-network that gives the algorithm the chance to emerge out of these interactions. What the algorithm is, how it can exert power, to what extent it is able to organize the world is an effect of the relations and translations within the socio-technical structure it is embedded in. If an algorithm is not connected to institutional structures, it cannot do anything. If you deny it access to your database, a machine learning algorithm will produce no model, etc. However, the socio-technical structure, the (potential) actor-network of the algorithm must be provided, built, and maintained – often meeting big obstacles or challenges. At the same time, the social communities and institutions that host algorithms follow their own internal orderings, defining possible ways to implement and deploy algorithms as solutions to newly emerging problems. The problems of the institution must be matched by the algorithms mobilized by the developers, translating the abstract solution of the algorithmic technique into concrete actors able to interact and embedded into the institution's inner workings. *Algorithmic Institutions* therefore describes the issues and problems of integrating two different recommender techniques into the fabric of the organization. The role of engineers thereby shifts, as they become sociologists themselves (Callon 1987), formulating and inscribing expectations into the concrete artifact – in our case the application of the recommender. The making of the concrete algorithm thereby is discussed as constant negotiation of the disciplinary object with the different orderings present in the organization. Thus, the algorithm becomes an actor within the institutional setup, its structure and its order. Understanding an algorithm as an entity that emerges out of a network of interactions and infrastructures (Ananny 2016) always refers back to the social order that makes the production of the algorithm possible – or sometimes also impossible – in the first place.

"Technology is neither good nor bad; nor is it neutral" (Kranzberg 1986, 547). In 1986, Kranzberg formulated this as one of the laws of technology – which has often been cited since. And it refers to the insight that technology always has effects which we may call political. Technological artifacts do have politics (Winner 1980) insofar as they encourage or prevent certain actions. May it be a speed bump (Latour 1990) controlling our driving speed or the height of a bridge regulating access to the beach (Winner 1980). And contemporary instantiations of algorithms have been criticized for their qualities of regulating and surveilling behavior. In other words, algorithms often are installed and discussed as means of social control, e.g., in law enforcement (Gandy and Baruh 2006), HR (Leicht-Deobald et al. 2019), or information provision through search engines (Noble 2018). The criticism thereby is mostly formulated in terms of bias or lack of transparency and is often an extension of a long-going discussion about the social power of statistics (e.g. Scott 1998). Because of these issues of algorithmic politics, several scholars argue for a value sensitive design of algorithms (e.g. Steen 2015; Zhu et al. 2018). However, the political quality of an algorithm poses at least two challenges. First, defining the problem and acceptable forms of solutions is a question of normative frames applied in the discussion and is different in different situations. Therefore, the making of value sensitive algorithms is not located in the formulation of abstract and generalized algorithmic techniques but is formulated and negotiated in the concrete translation of abstract algorithmic solutions into concrete executable code fragments. And secondly, the making of value sensitive algorithms requires the translation of abstract normative principles into technological scripts. Or in other words: the formation and materialization of (political) discourse. *Algorithmic Politics* therefore discusses the translation of normative and regulatory demands into the rationality of the recommender system – and the challenges it poses. What can be observed is that these materializations of discourse interact with other discourse formations, questioning the validity of the problem or the solution – or both. From an analytical perspective, it is therefore interesting to look at the materialized discourses in the form of algorithmic scripts as well as the normative discourse applied to it. Democratic values enacted by and with an algorithm is not just a material effect but also the result of normative claims and the interaction of different – and differing – discourses and different forms of expressing them. The chapter therefore describes how the software development team tried to translate the legal obligation of a public broadcaster, namely, to present a diverse information diet, into algorithmic forms of reasoning available for a recommender system and the challenges that came along with that.

Bringing the three enactments together, I discuss how these different versions of the algorithm relate to each other. While each of the enactments came with its own problems, the coordination of these different enactments into the process making the material object became a challenge in itself. Instead of following a grand narrative of social order, which is enacted or supported by algorithms, I argue that every algorithmic system represents a social ordering in itself, interfering, interacting and competing with other forms of orderings and coordinating different enactments of the same system. Software development projects are thereby not only endeavors to realize a technological solution but must manage these different versions, negotiating changes of or in- or exclude certain enactments to make them compatible with each other. A software development project thereby becomes an ordering effort itself – and a highly political arena of digital world making. This is even more true in democratic institutions such as public broadcasting. What I propose here, as a result, is not to decenter the algorithm as a distinct and stable actor but to decenter the idea of the algorithmic system and embed it in a broader ecology of different modes or ordering from which the stable actor of *the algorithm* emerges. While classical ideas of social order in ANT were based on concepts of delegation and inscription, the aim of this chapter is to discuss how delegation as a means of transsituational order can be understood as the coordination and convergence of different enactments of *the algorithm*.[1] Thus, this chapter contributes to bridging the conceptualization of algorithmic multiplicity (Seaver 2017) and the empirical findings of algorithms as actors of social control – complicating the notion of social order from an interactionist perspective. Only if these different enactments of the algorithm – representing orderings themselves – are able to be put in relation to each other can the democratic qualities of an algorithm be determined. These different orderings, stable or fragile assemblages of actors, materials, and discourses can help us understand where the power of "the algorithm"

---

1   Latour (1990) mentioned the convergence of different enactments quite early in his writings. The scholarly discourse since then, however, shifted towards the multiplicity and messiness of reality, losing the distinct focus on social order of earlier ANT writings.

comes from – and what might stand against it. This, however, also leads to another perspective on algorithms as "weapons of math destruction" (O'Neil 2016), where the way to intervene is not helped by transparency nor by code audits or ethical guidelines alone. What we need to understand is how these algorithmic systems interact with other orders, both to enable them but also to govern them. This is especially complicated, as algorithmic forms of accounting a data-driven reality needs new forms of translating an algorithmic rationality into a democratic or organizational logic. Algorithmic agency is not only a matter of if-then-else statements or neural networks, but also a matter of questioning how other orders lost durability, thus enabling these actors in our digital world and determining who is included or excluded in defining their agency. In a sense, this is a reformulation of issues problematized in deliberative approaches to democratic order (e.g. Habermas 1997). Which collectives and social orderings are being made relevant and who is being left out in the formation of algorithmic systems? In its very core this alone is a democratic question.

By reconstructing different moments of building a recommender system in a public broadcaster, I hope to contribute to the ongoing discussion on algorithmic agency and algorithmic power – especially in relation to contemporary democracy. By framing it through the lens of social order from an interactionist perspective, I seek to describe the problem from a perspective that neither falls into techno-determinist narratives nor a purely social relativist perspective and contributes to the understanding of contemporary digital societies. Decentering the algorithm as the main object of critique might be strange for a book that focuses so much on specific algorithms. Yet, in a world where the observation that "Code is Law" (Lessig 1999, 2006) is no longer contestable, it might be worthwhile to take a look how these digital laws are being negotiated and made in our democracies and how social order(ing) is adapted or re-imagined before the algorithm even calculates a single number. By doing so, we might also find new ways not only to understand how we are governed by algorithms but also how we can govern these actors.

Studying Algorithms in the Making

You have not engaged in our great and gathering conversation, nor did you create the wealth of our marketplaces. You do not know our culture, our ethics, or the unwritten codes that already provide our society more order than could be obtained by any of your impositions. – John Perry Barlow, 1996

In the spring of 2016, I became part of a project on public service media and the development of a new video-on-demand system. This was, however, not an ordinary software development project nor was I a computer scientist or programmer. Instead, I was (and still am) a sociologist who became part of a large development and research team composed of sociologists, communication scholars, project managers, editors, and computer scientists. The project was not only about developing a video-on-demand platform but also taking a value by design approach, taking specific legal and democratic-normative ideas into account. In the following, I will therefore briefly explain the goals and setting of the project on which my empirical observations are based. And since my position was also a specific and demanding one, I will discuss my role in the field and especially the challenges and chances of being part of such a research, intervening in the object of study.

Making a Case: The Development of a Recommender System

In early 2016, a German public broadcaster and research teams of different universities started a research and development project. The aim of the project was to develop a video-on-demand platform for the public broadcaster, not least because this form of media service has been considered as a necessary means of providing media content over the Internet. The public broadcaster already had a video-on-demand website out there, but according to the project leader, it was out of date and was supposed to be updated with newer technologies and a whole new concept. Thus, a software development team was gathered to design and implement the new video-on-demand website, "airing" the same shows from the linear program, albeit in a non-linear way. And, since this new website was supposed to become a state-of-the-art implementation, a recommender system was envisioned as a central element of the setup. For this goal alone, domain experts, i.e., editors, and a software development team would have sufficed. However, the aim of the project was a bit more ambitious.

> Digital services of public broadcasters especially face challenges, as the developed platform strategy is not only oriented towards the demands and feedback of users, but at the same time has to consider the "principles of objectivity and neutrality of media coverage, diversity of opinions, and the balance of their services (Project proposal, 1, my translation).

This quote is taken from the project proposal and demonstrates the general aim of the project. The goal was not only to develop a state-of-the-art video-on-demand system but also to implement it in a way that is compatible with the legal obligations of a public broadcaster within Germany. Being a public media institution, the broadcaster had to adhere to the so-called program mandate, a legal principle demanding the provision of a broad, neutral, and objective selection of information. However, the methods being applied on non-linear online media seem to be at odds with these ideas. The recommender algorithms implemented were identified as especially problematic rather soon in the project. To tackle these issues, a broad and interdisciplinary research team was assembled, including me, the sociologist. I had my own desk in the office of the development team. To get there, I had to pass the entrance control. In the first few weeks, I had to call at the office that someone would come and get me. Later, however, I got my own key card, so that I could enter the facilities whenever I wanted. The development team's office was placed in a separate building. Next to the office was a large meeting room. The room had no central table, was equipped with many books on machine learning, software development, different programming languages, and design patterns, among many other topics. I also contained a large monitor for video conferencing – which was often used to include colleagues from other cities to the local meetings. It also had various seating arrangements, including large and colorful pillows. To a certain extent it reminded me of a Silicon Valley flair, as it was very playful, containing different gadgets – such as a VR set, a gadget the project leader presented to us once – and included no barriers between the participants of the meetings, like a big table. Instead, the space was very open and only small tables were standing around. The setting also reflected the idea of a flat hierarchy. We had several meetings in this room, discussing the next steps, challenges, and the strategy of the development project. I passed this room every time I walked to the project team's office. The office had desks for six to seven people – this number changed over time, as the team grew bigger. After entering the room, the desk of Alice was directly on the left side. Alice was a mathematician and computer scientist responsible for the development of the recommender algorithms. The desk of Bob was located a few steps into the room on the right side. Bob was the project leader and also a computer scientist. Everyone was sitting in front of two big screens, most of the time with headphones on their head. This created a climate of focus and silence within the office, in which everyone was looking at their own two screens, reading, and typing on their keyboards. Even within the office, communication mostly happened via Slack, a web-based chat service mimicking the communication experience of early IRC servers.

> In one instance, I was debating with Alice a question of data production and recommender algorithms, which she could not answer and tried to get some information about it from Bob. Bob, however, did not react to our attempts to catch his attention. And as if it was the most normal thing in the world, she took the nerf gun next to her, aimed, and shot at him. Now we had Bob's attention and could discuss the issue further (from memory).

This scene illustrates an important element in doing ethnographic field work in a software development project. Observations are not continuously or ongoing, and it is simply not enough to just be there. Sitting in a room full of developers meant most of the time that I saw people in front of their computers, silently hacking on their keyboards. The interactions happened somewhere else. Online tools for communication and coordination were essential in the development of the software and the coordination within the project team. Additionally, the project was managed in an agile way, that is, defining small next steps in weekly and daily meetings together, implementing them in so-called sprints, and reporting on the progress made in the meeting afterwards. Sprints are defined as the implementation of small tasks and features in a short amount of time, normally around a week. The meetings therefore framed the activity defined by these sprints. So instead of working all the time alone in front of one's computer, the team heavily relied on physical meetings in a rather high frequency. However, these meetings only included the inner circle of the software development team. Other meetings were also held regularly with the online editorial team, adding their expertise on organizational and editorial processes in the broadcaster to the project. Being part of the team, I had access to all of these different digital and analog communication and documentation facilities. In order to reconstruct how the algorithm was developed and enacted in different situations, I had to follow the developers around, in Slack conversations, edits in Wikis, and to different meeting rooms.

Accounting Accounts

One of the great challenges in doing qualitative empirical research is the ordering of observations into something that resembles a linear argument, while the data collection and participation is based on non-linear and distributed events and observations. This is even more true for such a long ethnography. I was part of the project to develop the new video-on-demand platform for roughly a year, from spring 2016 till summer 2017. During this time, I was able to collect many different forms of data. This list includes conversations via Slack, both directly with colleagues and in the open channels. It also includes conversations via email, fieldnotes from meetings and the analysis of documents. In addition, I was able to analyze interviews that were being conducted with team members and producers of meta-data. I also attended workshops in which the central information infrastructure was explained and discussed, and hosted a focus group with the key users of the central program planning system, which later was supposed to become central for the creation of the meta-data production within the organization.

Online communication was, as already mentioned, an important element in the coordination of the project team, although everyone was physically in the same room or at least in the same building. Therefore, one of the first tasks after I joined the project was to get access to these different communication channels, i.e., Slack, a Wiki, and the GitHub repository. The most important one was thereby the Slack instance of the development project. In the Slack instance, communication with the whole group took place, namely, in thematically separated channels. Especially important for my work was the *#machinelearning* channel, as information about the recommender system was shared and discussed there. In these channels information that was interesting to everyone was shared, like dates for upcoming meetings, bug reports, concept descriptions, reports from specialized meetings. Even team conflicts were – to a certain extent – discussed in this format. Thus, Slack was a documentation of the ongoing communication in the team and a space to save all the relevant information. But it also served as a more focused form of communication between only a few members, through private messages. I would often discuss things with Alice, Bob, and the others directly, and keep contact to the different team members of the project. Especially the conversations in which Alice introduced me to the techniques of machine learning powered recommender systems were done via private messages, as we assumed that my learning process was not that interesting to the other team members. Thus, Slack became an important source for my research in two different ways.

First, it was a documentation of the ongoing communication that I could analyze without interfering in the situation by a recording device. The recording of all this communication was part of the natural setting of my field. And secondly, the Slack instance became a starting point for me to follow the actors, as it would show the relevant sites, situations, and actors that I should investigate, like articles, written concepts, but also meetings or conferences. In addition to Slack, the project hosted its own Wiki site on which results of meetings, descriptions of features, and timelines and deadlines were documented. The project facilitators uploaded short minutes of the held meetings but also wrote down subsequent steps or necessary features that would be implemented. As such, these Wiki sites would provide me with information about meetings I could not attend but at the same time show me the project team's self-description of the experienced meetings. Thus, they hinted at what was important for the team in the discussion, what was potentially a conflict, but also what was not mentioned there. The third and last online resource I want to mention here was the GitHub repository. It contained the code base for the video-on-demand system, including parts of the recommender system. However, it was not as important as the other elements, as the discussion and practices mostly referred to techniques or iPyhton Notebooks that were applied to test code snippets for rapid prototyping. However, it was a relevant actor and medium in the project, but only one actor amongst many others in the process of enacting the algorithm.

The enactment of the algorithm then also took place in many different meetings. In contrast to the silent and focused atmosphere of the offices, the meetings were the place for discussions and heavy debating. The development project was structured according to the agile paradigm of SCRUM, which included daily and weekly meetings. In these meetings, the team decided on the goals for the next development sprint and discussed smaller problems and how to approach them. Often, these daily and weekly meetings resulted in an additional meeting that was focused on thematic issues, such as meta-data production, design question of the website, or the system architecture of the backend system of the service, to name just a few. Further, I was able to attend regular meetings between the developers and the online editorial team in which general and non-technical issues and strategies were discussed. It is important to keep in mind that I attended these meetings not as an observer but as a project member. Thus, I was also directly addressed, especially when questions regarding the recommender system came up. As a result, I did not record these meetings, as suggested by Knoblauch (2005). Instead, I had several notebooks in which I documented the debates and conversations held in the meetings. Additionally, a colleague of mine from my research group at the university was also present most of the time, and we shared and compared our notes afterwards.

Aside of these more or less mandatory meetings I applied the "follow the actors" approach described by Latour (2005). In the process of observing the use of technological artifacts, or recognizing dropped names or narrated actors in conversations, I started to ask – first myself, then others – why something became important, and subsequently followed the actor-network to different sites, situations, and departments of the organization. This approach is also well known in interactionist semiotics, where Goodwin (2000, 1508) argues that "what we have to investigate emerges from the way in which the participants themselves display a particular field to be consequential and relevant through the orientation of their bodies and the organization of their action". As a result, I ended up in the video archive, raising questions about the practices of data production, found myself in a workshop discussing the infrastructural ecology of the broadcaster or did interviews with the newly formed online editorial team. These encounters were different in character, depending on the role I took at the moment. Meetings in which I was a project member were normally not recorded, such as the meeting with the colleagues from the archive, or two workshops in which the organizational media infrastructure was explained to us, i.e., to the project team. On other occasions, however, I recorded interviews with developers, editors, or focus groups with the meta-data research team and the users of the planning system WhatsOn.

Other actors were made relevant directly in the discussions relating to the recommender system. Alice handed me many different papers and resources where to look and learn. An important reference point was e.g. the recommender systems handbook (Ricci et al., 2011), which was an essential resource for becoming part of the field through learning the techniques but also for further analysis of the ideas and values inscribed into the recommender. These documents and artifacts were part of the ethnographic document analysis, thus never detached, but always in the context of the practices that referred to them as important references.

All of these actors, documents, textbooks, colleagues from the archive or the online editorial team, were made important as part of the ongoing development process. And all of these occasions became observations that ended up in my fieldnotes, were translated into interview transcripts, or became part of an interested reading (Loukissas 2017; B. Rieder 2017) which later were analyzed through the methodological perspective of post-ANT and ethnomethodology. However, the position that I had was not one of the sole observer. Instead, I became part of the project team, thus my data collection is based on interventions and participation. I did not only sit in the corner but also proposed solutions, ideas where to go, and sometimes asked potentially stupid questions. This created the need for some methodological reflection, as such an approach creates opportunities but also has its pitfalls and problems. Thus, a quite difficile game of closeness and distance, going native and coming home, and being a colleague and researcher accompanied throughout the process of doing my fieldwork – and beyond. In the end, I had to find a way to be more than one, and to coordinate these different subjectivities of mine.

On being More than One

Quite at the beginning of the project there was some sort of uncertainty as to what my specific role in the project was. Sociology is not a natural ally for this kind of software development projects. Of course, being a sociologist interested in the genealogy of algorithmic solutions and their normativity, the role was clear to *me*. I came there to see how the traits and features of the algorithm were negotiated and implemented – and how explicit normative references were tackled and able to be tackled by the development project. However, it was not so clear to the other team members. Especially when being aligned with the development of the recommender, this created some confusion. What does social science have to offer for a technological endeavor? I was not identified as one of the "technology crowd" but rather as someone who could go and talk to people and research the organizational conditions, which I also did later. However, I also wanted to see how the developers address the algorithm, how they talk about it, how they reason about its designed qualities. For this, I had to become one of the technology crowd.

Thankfully, there was a rather straightforward way to achieve this. In the discussion of the issue of filter bubbles, the question came up whether the website as it was until then did produce certain filter bubbles or not. Finding an answer to that question was not that straightforward and Alice did not have time to tackle the issue. Therefore, I tried to find a solution. As part of the evaluation of the old website of the broadcaster we had access to user tracking data. The data comprised the videos individual users watched, and how long they did so. This is called implicit feedback. The longer a video has been watched, we assumed, the higher the users would rate this video. My task was then to deduce from the recorded user-video relations the formation of one or different clusters that would suggest that this kind of recommendation produced filter bubbles. After researching some methods, I came up with an idea that included three different steps: first, normalize the ratings. That is, if a rating was below a threshold, assign it a zero, if it is above, assign it a one. Second, calculate a transposed version of the matrix. And third, multiply the original matrix with the transposed one. This resulted in a matrix that described the relations of a user to other users, depending on whether they watched the same videos. The more common videos were watched, the stronger the relation between those two users. In a last step, I then produced network visualization from the calculated data. It was not strict science, it was rather a lot of playing around and experimenting with different parameters of my R script. However, when I presented the idea and the results to Alice, she looked at me and replied that this is a good idea. The main goal of the calculation was not to show if and what clusters there are, and the visualizations did not have any further impact on the course of the project. Instead, it helped me to prove that I was not only a sociologist, but that I was also capable of understanding what they were talking about. Instead of being a bystander I became one of them. Yet, I was not only a network analyst or that person who can do calculations in R. I still was the sociologist too. I was more than one, and sometimes this being more than one interfered in my repertoires of used accounts. This points at the core of an issue that has often been identified as the dangers of going native. And it is an even bigger issue in research that does not only observe but is embedded and interventive in nature. As Latour and Woolgar (1986) argue:

> For us, the dangers of "going native" outweigh the possible advantages of ease of access and rapid establishment of rapport with participants (Latour and Woolgar 1986, 29).

The danger, according to Latour and Woolgar, is that ascribing the actors in the field, in their case scientists, a somewhat privileged status makes the methods through which they produce sociality, scientific facts, or – as in our case – algorithms, invisible and opaque. Not instead, but because we understand them on a level that we take them for granted. Being a stranger, not acquainted with the meanings and the methods of meaning making of the field is an advantage, as we are not even able to mistake important interactions as *normal*.

However, this creates some serious problems if we take the subjective perspective of involved actors seriously. Especially, as Latour later argued that "ANT was simply another way of being faithful to the insights of ethnomethodology: actors know what they do and we have to learn from them not only what they do, but how and why they do it" (Latour 1999b, 19). This localized and situated understanding, however, requires some sort of interpretation of empirically observable practices and accounts – the Schütz'ian legacy of the program of ethnomethodology (Garfinkel 2006). In producing accounts, the subjective meaning of actions and words is made observable to others. Of course, these accounts can never comprehend everything the account giver is doing – as this also includes the internal reasoning and thinking about the accounts (Schütz [1932] 1993). In order to communicate, the account giver must always reason: if the other person connects the meanings to these signs or actions that I connect to them, then she would react in the way anticipated by me. Thus, according to Schütz, in our interpretations of a situation, we always take the (assumed) perspective of the other person. This creates an immense coordination problem with an infinite regress of interpretation and re-interpretation. Garfinkel approached this problem with the notion of the ethnomethods and normalization. Ethnomethods are for Garfinkel simply the methods that competent members of an already ordered social configuration utilized in order to produce accounts – and interpret them at the same time. Through the identification of production and interpretation routines, the communication process can be resolved to an ongoing and functional interaction setting. Deviations from the anticipated reactions to my accounts, or from anticipated accounts from others provoke itself a reaction of the interpretant, trying to bring the chain of accounts back to a situation that is known and well-defined according to the interpretant (Garfinkel 1984) – this mechanism has been repeatedly demonstrated by Garfinkel and his students in the so-called breaching experiments.

This, however, has some serious implications on how we approach our empirical field. Just observing from a detached perspective, I would be able to record how these competent members of the social group interact. However, the description of these accounts would rely on an evaluation external to the situation – which might result in (possibly misunderstood) misunderstandings. Instead of learning something about the setting at hand, I would make the reader learn more about me and my reasoning. The researcher is simply not a competent member of the social group studied. This is also one of the reasons why ethnomethodology was focusing on well-known everyday interactions. It could be assumed that the researcher is already a competent member of the situations and groups she studied.[1] This is best demonstrated in the definition of Garfinkel's documentary method:

> The method consists of treating an actual appearance as 'the document of', as 'pointing to,' as 'standing on behalf of' a presupposed underlying pattern. Not only is the underlying pattern derived from this individual documentary evidences, but the individual documentary evidences, in their turn, are interpreted on the basis of 'what is known' about the underlying pattern. Each is used to elaborate the other (Garfinkel 1984, 78).

1   Of course, this is a solution that is not dissimilar to the solution of Parsons, who establishes shared norms as an objective means to produce intersubjective interpretability, or Luhmann, who just switches the perspective from the competent members to a form of communication that is oriented and constituted based on the communication systems' shared code. However, Garfinkel complicates the picture, as he binds the methods of meaning making and interpretation to a fluid situation.

The observed account is assumed to relate to a shared understanding, a common pattern of interpretation. Thus, the aim of the researcher is to make these connections visible and available for scrutiny and analysis. The assumption then, of course, is that the researcher has the capability to make and reconstruct these connections via common ethnomethods. The competent observer must not only be able to report on the accounts but must also be able to take part in the reproduction of social order (Garfinkel and Wieder 1992). The expectation of the ethnographic researcher therefore is, according to Amann & Hirschauer, twofold: "for one, the expectation that every field has a socio-logic, a cultural orderliness, and further the expectation that by a step-by-step positioning and 'calibration' of the ethnographer in the field this socio-logic is becoming practicable and can be mobilized as empirical knowledge" (Amann & Hirschauer, 1997, p. 20 my translation). Thus, we as researchers must learn, step-by-step, to understand and interpret the actions and accounts of the studied field's members. A task that has to be accomplished in all phases of the ethnographic research and which is never finished or done, or as Knoblauch and Vollmer (2019, 603) put it: "Understanding others, their actions and their objectifications remains a task throughout the research process, so that even the research question depends on this understanding" (my translation). However, this understanding is grounded in two very different research styles, heavily impacting the role of the researcher in the field. Amann and Hirschauer (1997) argue that the researcher should make everyday practices and reasoning of a familiar setting visible by continuously practicing the 'bestrangement" of the field, i.e., keep one's distance and difference to the empirical field – an approach also advocated by Hammersley and Atkinson (2019). Others argue for an immersive approach. Especially contemporary life-world analysis, which heavily draws from Schütz' theories, argues for becoming a member of a social setting in order to obtain "information about how and what one really experiences in such worlds" (Pfadenhauer 2005, 8). We, as social scientists entering these foreign domains, never know exactly if our interpretations of accounts in the field are the right ones but must become a competent member of a social group, and learn to interact and participate within the field (Honer and Hitzler 2015). Instead of fearing to go native, going native is a central element in empirically grounding our analysis.[2] If we want to be able to empirically ground our report on how sociality in a given situation is achieved, we need to become what we are studying. This enables us, as Knoblauch (2005) argues, to

---

2   The analysis of Howard S. Becker (1997) is very instructive in this matter, showing how *becoming someone* can be understood. There is, however, a certain boundary of becoming a competent member, especially in fields that are on the margins (see e.g., Girtler, 2003, 2004) and which would require certain interactions the researcher is not willing or able to commit (Humphreys, 1976).

start an attempt to take the point of view of the people we study.[3] Turning this to an ethnomethodological perspective, this also enables us to learn and apply the relevant ethnomethods and therefore give and interpret accounts that are typical for the studied setting. This results also in a second methodological consideration. Being part of a situation and learning its practical rules also changes the very setting we are studying – especially when we intervene and sometimes produce a crisis to see how the situation gets normalized again. But as Mol wrote: "The point of stressing this is not to say observers should not interfere. They always do" (Mol 2002, 157). As researchers who are becoming part of a situation, a community, or an organization, we change the setting, we provoke different accounts, different forms of ordering. Thus, the way how we are being addressed changes the way how accounts are presented to us. This issue has also been discussed earlier within sociology by Schwartz and Schwartz (1955), where they called it the "observer effect" (Schwartz and Schwartz 1955, 346). The moment we do observations, we provoke different reactions. However, what Schwartz and Schwartz (1955) – amongst others – see as an issue of observation could also become a chance to change our way of investigation. It makes a difference if we are addressed as an expert or an outsider, as a sociologist or a member of the "technology crowd". In each of the occasions, the accounts can tell us something about the social order achieved but from different perspectives, from different angles. Each occasion can tell us how the social system, or the practically achieved ordering, reacts to our stimulus.[4] In short, if we cannot not interfere with the situation, we should at least be aware in what way we are doing so and what this tells us about the social order achieved. Law (2002), referencing Haraway (1988), argues that knowledge production – and therefore also the perspective of the ethnographer – always rests on a partial perspective. Historically, we just named one of them objective.[5] Thus, both perspectives, the one of the sociologists, the other of that person who can do calculations in R, are valuable. They just tell us something different about the object of inquiry and the surrounding practices. Law (2002) even argues that our vision becomes fractal, that is, different versions of the same phenomenon exist. This is an ontological turn of the earlier formulated argument by Clifford (1986) that ethnography always produces a partial truth. This influence and impact of the researcher's presence is then not only a necessity to observe and record the situated and

---

3   It is, however, important to mention here that Knoblauch (2005) puts this argument forward for an ethnographic conception of alterity, where shared knowledge by the researcher and the studied field is reflexively contrasted in an ongoing search for differences in settings, perspectives, attitudes, etc. Such an attitude is in my opinion the most promising in studying settings that become more familiar to the researcher over the course of her personal development and career.

4   This sounds rather positivist but aims at an interactionist perspective of social order.

5   On a very informative discussion on the historical shift of objectivity as a notion, see Daston & Galison (2010).

public accounts in a given situation (Geertz 1973). Instead, it becomes an instrument in making certain accounts observable in the first place. Taking different positions, creating different situations provides different means to probe the social structures enacted by the empirical field.

Every You, Every Me

The argumentation of Garfinkel, however convincing, hinges on the issue of inter-subjectivity of knowledge reservoirs to identify patterns and connect them with accounts. While Garfinkel was not interested in metaphysical assumptions of experiences, as he called it (Garfinkel 2006), the program of ethnomethodology still assumes a shared repertoire of interpretation, which is expressed in the notion of ethnomethods and which are essential pre-requisites for the analysis of situated and locally achieved empirical observations. This led to the formulation of the *unique adequacy criterion* (Garfinkel 2002) which would require the researcher to already be a competent member of the group in order to produce adequate descriptions about social interactions. Such a perspective of being a competent member or to experience the situation the same way as the people studied, resulted in researchers doing a second degree in math or in the case of Wacqant (2004) becoming a boxer. This has been critiqued, amongst others, by Amann and Hirschauer (1997) as an excessive demand. The proponents of a radical immersive approach argue that without being a competent member, it is impossible to give accounts that are true to the field, simply because we do not know what exactly is going on. But then again, none of the participants knows that exactly, simply because we have no access to the minds of the others. This insight was already formulated by Schütz as the general thesis of the other as an alien I, in which interaction is only possible as I assume that the structure of my alter ego's experience is comparable to mine (Schütz [1932] 1993). The exchange of accounts goes on *as if they were interpreted in the right way*. Thus, becoming a competent member of a group and reproduce the experiences of that field is an ideal that we have to look for, but which we can never be sure to achieve. When describing an empirical reality, we have to assume that our interpretations are faithful to the recorded practices and test them continuously in our empirical field. Reflecting on multiplicity, Mol therefore argues that knowledge "does not draw its worth from living up to reality. What we should seek, instead, are worthwhile ways of living with the real" (Mol 2002, 158). This is also true for our accounts of social ordering. The described orderings are still real, they still provoke resistance and stability if probed. The descriptions of the field therefore are an enactment that tries to be as faithful to the local and situated forms of knowing and ordering as possible. For this, immersing us in the field, learning the language, the techniques, simply becoming a competent member of the field we are studying is an ideal we might never reach and which in its exclusivity might also not be worthwhile. Yet, this still is an approach that offers a unique and important perspective on the empirical phenomenon in specialized domains. Instead of fulfilling a unique adequacy criterion, it might be more productive to strive for analytical adequacy (Knorr-Cetina et al. 2019).

This perspective, however, has to be recontextualized and brought back to our own disciplines and forms of reasoning. As social scientists, we are part of another ordering system (or rather many of them). We do not only describe what we observed, but we translate it into accounts that are understandable and valued by our colleagues. We become spokespersons (Callon 1987) of our empirical field, but we speak to a very specific audience. Reproducing the accounts of the settings by our acquired knowledge creates frictions. The different enacted selves have to be coordinated – here the project partner, who is able to do network visualizations in R; there the sociologist who will tell us something analytical about the socio-technical system she is studying.

Speaking Sociologically

After giving a conference talk, describing my findings of how the algorithm became an organizational actor, a colleague raised her hand and asked: "Maybe I have missed it, but what exactly is sociological about that?" My answer included terms of interaction order, contingency, and situated problem definition, but I was not able to formulate my findings, which I learned in the language of the field, in a way that would have been understood as *sociological*. And yet, that is what sociologists do – speaking sociologically, giving specialized accounts to a specific and competent group with their very own ethnomethods, their own reality. Callon and Latour (1981) urge us to apply all that has been said so far also to our own disciplines, to what we call science.

> Every time they write sociologists grow or shrink, become macro-actors – or do not – expand, like Lazarsfeld, to the scale of multinational, or shrink to a restricted sector of the market. What makes them grow or shrink? The other actors whose interests, desires and forces they translate more or less successfully, and with whom they ally or quarrel. Depending on the period, the strategies, the institutions and the demands, the sociologist's work can expand until it becomes what everyone is saying about the Leviathan, or shrink to what three PhD students think about themselves in some British university. The sociologists' language has no privileged relationship with the Leviathan. They act upon it. Suppose they state that the Leviathan is unique and systematic, suppose they create cybernetic, hierarchically integrated sub-systems: either this will be accepted, or not, will spread, or not, will be used as resources by others – or will not.

> The success of this definition of the Leviathan proves nothing about the latter's own nature (Callon and Latour 1981, 298–99).

In the quote, Callon and Latour suggest that the sociologist language does not prove anything about the nature of the object of inquiry. I disagree. It constructs the phenomenon differently, translates the field enactment into *another scientific* enactment. Just as the jungle soil in Latour's writings (1999a), the empirical field is being referenced and enacted by social scientific methods. Yet, these different enactments that are confronted with different orderings, using different accounts, must be coordinated. If this coordination fails, we fall for either empiricism with no analytical value, or empty theorizing with no connection to an empirical reality.[6] Sociological reasoning in ethnographic work, as I have conducted it, is therefore always the coordination of different forms of giving accounts. And in each moment, you portrait and construct your object of study differently. According to Law "representation is always a simplification and a deletion" (Law 1994, 165). Describing and representing what I have observed can only use so many words, and these words will never transport all of the experience, all of my observations. This book that you are reading right now is a representation of the practices, the rationalities, and the problems I encountered in the field – in this strange socio-technical world of the public broadcaster. And as such, it operates with simplifications and deletions, but it does so with an empirical basis. The story that could have been told is more than one – but certainly it is also less than many. The project of bringing across an observation and an argument is in itself the endeavor of negotiating different enactments and different modes of ordering that frame this document. Staying true to the empirical phenomenon observed (and by that also co-constructing it) and the conditions of possibility to speak to a disciplinary (and disciplined) community co-determines the shape of this report. None of my colleagues at the public broadcaster was talking about semiotics, ethnomethods, or modes of ordering. In their world these notions do not exist – as long as I do not bring them up. These things are analytically and "*usefully* imputed to the patterns of the social for certain purposes" (Law 1994, 84, emphasis in the original). I use this vocabulary to enact the broadcaster, the development project, and the algorithm in a different form. Instead of 'just' reporting what the algorithm is, I add another enactment of it to the equation. This is what social science often calls reflexivity – being aware of one's own position in the field – but at the same time forgets that we are part of another system of orderings. There is simply no outside, there is no view from above (Haraway 1988; Law 2002), there are (only) multiple enactments that need to be coordinated with each other. Therefore, my own description of the phenomenon described in this book is the result of the negotiation of different versions of myself. This coordination

6   This is, of course, a paraphrase of Kant's critique ([1781] 2008).

effort, however, is also a corrective to the issues of going native. In order to be a sociologist, I have to be able to talk to other sociologists and produce accounts that make it more probable that I can build relations to my discipline. As Amann and Hirschauer (1997) argue, every *going native* has to be coupled with a *coming home,* in which we gain the analytical distance necessary to see more in our recordings than (to us) obvious facts and phenomena. In doing so, we make the familiar setting alien to us, and the familiar phenomenon is treated "as if it is alien. [...] It is being put at distance to the observer" (Amann and Hirschauer 1997, 12, my translation).

And here we close the circle of the seemingly conflict between Amann & Hirschauer and Garfinkel. It is not either or, becoming a competent member of the group or constantly alienate us from our field. It is, in the end, always both. A disciplinary description and enactment of the issues at hand require the social scientists to make their observations relatable to their own institutional settings. Reflexivity as a necessary counter-point to going native, as Law (2004) demands it from us, is therefore also a collective achievement. In being not only the researcher at a site but also the scientist in a wider scientific system makes it a necessity for us to be reflexive in a way to re-interpret our observations and connect them to other patterns of interpretation. Just as Latour (2013) argues that objectivity is a collective achievement, so is reflexivity. Returning to the question of what is sociological about this book, about my work? Nothing. And everything. It depends on what repertoire of producing accounts is being used and to whom I speak.

Debating Algorithms as Powerful Actors

Algorithms and machine learning have not only become a constant point of reference within the broader societal discussion but also widely discussed phenomena within the social sciences and the humanities. The literature on the power of algorithms has vastly grown in the last few years, even creating its own field named *critical algorithm studies*, which itself is a successor of *software studies* or *critical code studies*. The contributions thereby utilize a wide range of different theories and concepts in dealing with the phenomenon of algorithms, which are sometimes compatible or comparable and sometimes unique and incommensurable (e.g., Willson 2014). The figure of the algorithm thereby seems to act as a boundary object – to borrow a concept from infrastructure studies (Star and Griesemer 1989) – which enables very different theoretical and disciplinary perspectives to come into conversation with each other. At the same time, this can create confusion, as different conceptions of algorithmic power are being discussed as seemingly one phenomenon, often leaving us with the question of what we are actually talking about when we refer to algorithmic power (Ziewitz 2016).

In the following, I therefore discuss the manifold and rich literature in terms of power and social order of algorithms to present an overview of the different approaches and the respective theories behind them. Such a review is, of course, never complete and the ordering it represents is to a certain degree contingent. The aim of the following section is therefore not to provide a complete and all-encompassing overview of the literature but to carve out dominant theoretical approaches and narratives when it comes to algorithms and machine learning and social order. This approach then reflects also the intensity in which different approaches are being used within the discussion of algorithms. While Marxist critiques and cybernetic approaches are important voices in the discussion, it is fair to say that Foucault's theorizing became a major perspective adopted within the academic discussion. At the same time, caution is necessary when formulating critique on a theoretical level, as most contributions make valid points by using different ideas and theories as *sensitizing concepts* (Blumer 1954). The theoretical perspectives presented always have a certain problem in mind, which different approaches formulate and also solve differently. As a result, exploring these approaches should not necessarily formulate critique from an outside position. Instead, it is the aim to appreciate the presented perspectives and explore their productivity and performativity from the perspective of their own theoretical paradigms. Even if critique is formulated, this happens in the mindset of the necessary modesty, which wants to explore the theoretical dimension and their productivity for my own observations (which will be discussed in the following chapters in more detail) and what these theories are able to highlight, and what aspects are made invisible by them.

In the following, I will first discuss different issues that have been identified in the scholarly discussion when it comes to algorithms, e.g., opacity. These parts are not so focused on theorizing the phenomenon of algorithms but to open up a critical perspective on important problems that the ongoing algorithmization of our societies poses. Subsequently, I will explore three different perspectives: a Foucauldian approach to algorithmic power, algorithms as actors in a capitalist regime, and a cybernetic approach to algorithms. The section of Foucault is thereby the most extensive, as many scholars in the discussion utilize the rich conceptual repertoire of Foucault's thinking to problematize algorithms. In the end, I will identify some possible contributions that a perspective of social ordering might offer to the debate based on the discussion of these approaches. I therefore propose a different perspective that mediates between the individual level of algorithms as powerful actors, and structural effects that sees algorithms as an epiphenomenon.

Issues With and Of Algorithms

When revisiting the questions and problems addressed in terms of algorithmic power and agency, the discussion does not always follow a clearly demarcated theoretical perspective but tries to highlight specific issues and problems of algorithmic systems. The main lines of inquiry are thereby the production of seemingly objective knowledge, the problem of black boxes and transparency, and the issue of algorithmic bias. In the following, I will discuss these different issues. In this discussion, the question whether algorithms are seen as solid actors, or structural effects is only touched – if at all – implicitly, which provoked some critique (e.g., Hoffmann 2019).

Knowledge Production and Objectivity

Artificial intelligence, in the earlier instances of expert systems and more contemporary forms of machine learning are always confronted with the problem of knowledge acquisition. I.e., the question how knowledge about the world is collected, represented and applied to the task of the artificial intelligence system at hand. Especially expert systems were confronted with the problem how to extract knowledge for their explicit rule-based knowledge representation (Forsythe 1993). Thus, early versions of artificial intelligence were trying to formalize knowledge of human experts and transfer it into a form that is understandable for computers. A problem with which actual machine learning systems are also confronted – now often formulated as the need for domain knowledge (Ribes et al. 2019). Expert systems are based on an explicit theoretical approach, which is backed up by philosophical or fundamental anthropological ideas. Berry (2011) contrasts this with knowledge produced through machine learning and big data, which is a computational one. This leaves according to Berry (2011) other forms of rationalizing behind. Boyd and Crawford (2012) further argue that, with the emergence of (so-called) big data applications paired with machine learning, the definition of knowledge changed from a rule-based system or expert accounts towards a data-driven formulation of correlations and patterns. Yet, theory and assumptions are not being discarded, but the form of rationalizing changed. What form of data is being fed into the algorithm, and how the translation between observation and codification is done represents the new theorizing within data-driven societies (Bowker 2006). These contingencies of data interpretation thereby often disguise themselves with the myth of objectiveness, and therefore perform the applied modes of interpretation as a powerful rationality. This performed objectivity based on the trust in numbers creates legitimacy for societal institutions and endeavors (G. Rieder and Simon 2016) and is a phenomenon that is not exclusively found in algorithmic applications (e.g., Porter 1995). Beer (2017) argues that the notion of the algorithm itself therefore is an important element in a more general discourse that conveys this trust in numbers and "carries a persuasive weight" (Beer 2017, 8). The power of algorithms rests on the potential to produce knowledge about society but also on a more general discourse that accepts and constitutes algorithms as powerful, objective and neutral entities. In this function, algorithmic calculations can turn uncertain observations into credible and actionable knowledge (Amoore 2009).

Black Boxing and Transparency

On the other end of the spectrum of knowledge production and control ranges the critique of software in general and algorithms specifically. In this discussion, software has become "a layer that permeates all areas of contemporary societies. Therefore, if we want to understand contemporary techniques of control [...] our analysis cannot be complete until we consider this software layer" (Manovich 2013b, 15). Algorithms and software act in this perspective as a method of restricting and controlling possible forms of (inter-)action by enforcing a certain protocol (Galloway 2004) or to enforce an implicit law which is formulated in computer code (Lessig 2006). Code is thereby conceptualized as more than just a few lines of code but represents our contemporary societies' "terms of cultural, moral, ethical and legal codes of conduct" (A. Mackenzie and Vurdubakis 2011, 4). In this perspective, the formation of society and the glue that holds it together are defined within code fragments, becoming a central medium[1] of our society. Some scholars even describe a dystopia in which centralized institutions and corporations create a top-down form of technocracy diminishing the self-organizing potential of our contemporary societies (Helbing 2015) – which leads these scholars to the conclusion that algorithmic systems eventually might threaten established democracies (Helbing et al. 2017). According to this dominant discussion, algorithmic decision systems have two important and defining elements: missing transparency and automation (Zarsky 2016).

They refer to the fact that more often than not, the algorithm constitutes an opaque actor, which acts based on rules or rationalities that are not known to the public or, at least, the subjects of its action. Thus, the algorithm as a powerful actor is withdrawn from the critical scrutiny of public discourse, and a *black box society* (Pasquale 2015) is installed. This creates issues in the governance of algorithms. Leese (2014) shows how black boxed algorithmic knowledge production poses fundamental challenges to anti-discriminatory safeguards. Some scholars therefore called for inspection routines and code reviews for algorithms (Koliska and Diakopoulos 2018; O'Neil 2016). Yet, the

---

1   The notion of medium that is being used does not refer to mass media such as TV but identifies a mechanism that lies between individual actors of society and binds them together. For Simmel ([1900] 2004), money was such a medium.

discussion on black box algorithms is built on different positions and often diverting conceptions of what constitutes a black box. Burrel (2016) discussed three different forms of algorithmic black boxes, where we either a) are not able to understand machine learning rationality, e.g., 'reading' a neural network, b) lack the technical expertise to understand computer code or c) are simply not being granted access to the code in question, based on Intellectual Property Rights (IPRs) or state secrets. In any case, the black boxing of algorithms poses serious problems for holding these systems accountable, as some scholars fear (e.g., Tufekci 2014).

The notion of transparency, however, has also been contested by scholars in critical algorithm studies (Ananny and Crawford 2018). In problematizing algorithms as a black box, all the issues of algorithmic power and agency are located inside the algorithm and its (specific) code. Bucher (2016) therefore urges us to take a broader perspective on algorithms and apply the sensibilities of an ethnographer to reconstruct the power and effects of algorithms. For Bucher (2016), the algorithm is "neither black nor box." Instead, the figure of the algorithm is just one additional element of daily interactions that are not fully transparent. By drawing on insights from cybernetics and ANT, she argues that we should instead account for the information that is accessible about these systems as part of daily interactions. In reference to Latour (2005), she argues that "objects have to enter into accounts in order to be accounted for" (Bucher 2016, 87). This perspective has been taken up by others, arguing for a situated understanding of algorithms (Geiger 2017) or even understanding algorithms as culture (Seaver 2017), i.e., reconstructing the meanings attributed to the notion of the algorithm by social collectives. Thus, transparency of algorithms is not only about opening the black box in terms of code reviews but also includes the communication of certain design decisions (Diakopoulos and Koliska 2017) and modes of ex-post evaluation (Desai and Kroll 2017). This debate then gained a new momentum in the discussion of *algorithmic explainability* (Mittelstadt, Russell, and Wachter 2019) and *algorithmic interpretability* (Gilpin et al. 2018). Yet, even the latter categories are critically discussed, as real explainability might be hard to achieve, and in turn, create a "transparency fallacy" (Edwards and Veale 2018, 50). Scholars therefore started to argue for a counter-factual mode of explanation (Poechhacker and Kacianka 2021; Wachter, Mittelstadt, and Russel 2017). These discussions are also reflected in the differentiation between formal transparency and practical transparency, proposed by Paßmann and Boersma (2017). The former reflects what we (formally) know about the workings of the algorithm, while practical transparency describes the collection and assemblage of resources that are needed to make sense of the algorithm without knowing exactly the internal workings of it.

Discrimination and Bias

Another often discussed issue with algorithms as agents of social order is being debated in terms of classification and inequality. Algorithmic forms of social sorting (Lyon 2003), such as dynamic pricing or access to insurance services, emerging inequalities in societies, or inequalities being sustained and solidified. Graham (2005) argued relatively early that algorithms and software are becoming central actors in a new neoliberal service economy that creates infrastructures to manage access to resources. Social sorting, i.e., the alignment of subjects according to relevant attributes, becomes software sorting. By placing them in central positions, such as Google's search engine (Noble 2018), societal issues, like racism and discrimination become stabilized by selectively granting access to information or reinforcing stereotypes in the search results. The result is a society that is segregated by digital and seemingly objective means (Danna and Gandy 2002). The notion of the detached and objective algorithm then also provides the means to stabilize and shield forms of discrimination from (legal) intervention, as the discrimination is a systemic one and not produced intentionally[2] (Barocas and Selbst 2016). Of course, one could turn this argument around and state that this is a troubling sign of systemic discrimination. Eubanks (2018) gives an impressive account of how automated decision-making reifies and deepens economic inequality by targeting the poor population. From the description of many similar case studies, O'Neil (2016) draws the conclusion that algorithms and machine learning are *weapons of math destruction*, as they foster social inequalities (e.g., insurances), racial bias (e.g., policing software) or become instruments of worker surveillance and control – amongst many other examples. This results in the demand that companies and developers should be held accountable for the negative impact of the developed algorithms (Martin 2019) and the search for anti-discriminatory machine learning procedures (e.g., Custers et al. 2013). This brings the algorithm as an actor and material medium back in the discussion. The algorithm – in its narrow definition – should be scrutinized to locate and govern potential biases (Sandvig et al. 2016). It is not the algorithm as a detached element that acts racist or is biased in other ways, it is a tool that can be shaped accordingly. The algorithm and its social qualities and consequences should be seen in connection with societal forms of knowledge that are being mobilized by the developers. Drawing from classification theory, Bechmann and Bowker (2019) argue that not even unsupervised forms of machine learning are detached from these societal knowledge reservoirs. In their study, Bechmann and Bowker (2019) illustrate how unsupervised forms of machine learning are dependent on many decisions,

2   *It is important to note here that this can, of course, not be an argument to justify discrimination but highlights the discourses around algorithms and shows the legal problems derived from that. The concept of intentional action regularly produces problems on the intersection of technology and law.*

such as data cleaning or ex-post evaluation of the statistical model utilized by the algorithm – and thus can reproduce societal bias.

There is some critique, arguing that this perspective favors the algorithm as an actor over systemic perspectives (e.g., Hoffmann 2019). Thus, algorithmic fairness and accountability should consider organizational and institutional contexts (Veale and Binns 2017). This then complicates the perspective of algorithmic power of digital infrastructures and classification, as it opens up the question of what form of fairness should be implemented in the algorithm and which normative ideas are being exemplified by machine learning algorithms. Thus, the issue of algorithmic fairness is not a technical one, or one that can be solved by developers, but needs a political discussion (Wong 2020). Especially, since the question of what constitutes fairness sometimes leads to multiple mathematical formulations that are sound in themselves but incommensurable to each other by definition (e.g., Kleinberg, Mullainathan, and Raghavan 2016). Burdening the decisions on the developers alone there-fore creates an issue (who decides) and an illusion of singular accountability and responsibility. Instead, some scholars argue that we should research pos-sible ways to define due processes for developing sensitive systems (Draude et al. 2019; Zarsky 2016). This perspective becomes even more plausible if – as Bozdag (2013) argues – these effects are not only the result of design processes but potentially emerge out of interactions after the implementation phase.

A Foucauldian Perspective

One of the most prominent approaches and "an almost instinctive point of entry" (Rouvroy 2011, 121) to algorithms and algorithmic power is fueled by the thinking of Michel Foucault and his theories about the genealogy of knowledge and power. Foucault's work has been highly influential in Sociology and Critical Theory, such as Critical Security Studies, examining the power of technology in general, illuminating how different modes of being are regulated and mon-itored by state authorities, but also how power as a difficile force is seamlessly integrated into the fabric of the social.

Foucault's work represents different phases and moments of thinking about power, the state, and the individual. In the following, the contributions to algorithmic power from a Foucauldian perspective are grouped around prominent concepts in Foucault's work like biopolitics, governmentality, dis-cipline or subjectivation. However, everyone familiar with the work of Foucault recognizes that such a separation seems artificial as Foucault's theoretical concepts are often interdependent and fluid over the epochs of his work. As Foucault noted in his lectures on the history of governmentality, none of these mechanisms of power replaces the other one, nor are they to be seen in isolation as they complement each other (Foucault 1979, [1978] 2009). Thus, the following classification reflects how the different contributions applied, selected and used concepts from the Foucauldian theory-building.

Discourse and Subjectivation

Coming from the French school of structuralism, earlier works of Michel Foucault emphasize the power of *the society* or central institutional actors limiting the freedom of the individual. Governing thereby is not a function of these institutions, but recurring patterns throughout different societies unfold their power through these institutions. This was most prominently discussed in his inaugural lecture when Michel Foucault (1971) was dissecting discursive order as patterns of statements and classifications that re-occur regularly and order the world. Discourse thereby is not produced by an individual but reproduces itself based on the structures of society. In this conception of society and the way it is ordered, the structuralist heritage in the work of Foucault is most visible, compared to other works by him.

It is then this part of Foucault's work that has been discussed by Beer (2017) in terms of algorithmic power. In his now well-known piece on the social power of algorithms, Beer argues that algorithmic power should also be seen in the light of the production of truth. Drawing from Foucault's idea that the mechanisms and relations of power('s microphysics) cannot be understood if separated from discourses and their capacity to produce truth, Beer (2017) describes two fundamental elements of algorithmic production of truth. First, algorithms produce truth through their calculations and outputs in the form of risk scores and classifications which gain the quality of an objective truth. Coming back to Foucault's *Order of Discourse*, algorithmic agents select, limit and produce statements, including and excluding speakers, facts and perspectives (Foucault 1971). Thus, the production of a socially accepted and distributed truth[3] is tightly entangled with the formation and re-production of power and its structures (Foucault 2016). The second dimension of algorithmic production of truth, however, is less concerned with the material interventions and calculations of an algorithm but asks how the notion of the algorithm is mobilized and used – that is, not how algorithms actively shape the discourse through selection mechanisms but how algorithms themselves are (part of) discourse. The question then is how the notion of the algorithm travels in different social arenas, connects practices and words, includes and

---

3   It is important to note here that the notion of truth – which is an evergreen battleground of philosophical and scientific discussion – is here not understood as an objective truth about reality, life and everything, but describes the shared beliefs and assumptions produced and distributed in a social system via the system's own operations. Thus, this concept does not contest a given reality that can be described but focuses on the social mechanisms of describing reality and negotiating these descriptions.

excludes other meanings and orders social relations. Beer (2017) argues that algorithms in that sense can be separated from the material and technological form of the algorithm as engineers and computer scientists know them. The notion of the algorithm becomes – as discourse – something else and very often conveys notions of precision, neutrality and objectivity (G. Rieder and Simon 2016). Aside from the traditional narrative of trust in numbers (Porter 1995), the notion of the algorithm managed to raise several fields of academic research, without them necessarily sharing a common definition or understanding of the term algorithm (Ziewitz 2016). Thus, the notion of the algorithm a) orders social relations and phenomena as discourse and b) legitimates the material and calculative interventions of the algorithm by framing them as objective truth.

Discourses do not only produce truths about the outside world but also create the very subjects they address (Foucault 1971). Thus, the person you are, including categorizations like gender, professional identity, etc. in a specific situation is determined by the dominant discourse (Foucault 1979). Algorithmic processes of subjectivation, i.e., ascribing an identity to individuals based on collected data and inferred categories, are an important element in the new modes of digital governance. According to Cheney-Lippold (2017), these processes of subjectivation include individuals into sub-populations defined by the algorithm. This definition, however, does not follow pre-defined ideas of individual qualities, such as religious groups, or nationality, but is derived dynamically from the collected data. This dynamic and data-driven subjectivation, however, does not represent our authentic self for Cheney-Lippold (2017). Thus, it follows the Foucauldian idea that processes of subjectivation, i.e., the assignment of a (temporal) subjectivity, represent an act of violence. Who we really are, our embodied identity (Cheney-Lippold 2017), is being reduced to the classification set and perception of the algorithm. This can range from everyday interactions, e.g., what advertisement is shown to me, to life-changing events like being classified as a (potential) terrorist. In reference to security programs of the NSA, Cheney-Lippold (2016) argues that subjectivation by security algorithms grants or revokes rights from the individual. This mixture of control and subjectivation threatens the fundaments of modernity, namely, the possibility of self-assertion.

In contrast to other authors, Rosalind Cooper (2020) connects algorithmic forms of control with pastoral power, which works through the mechanism of confession. This algorithmic form of control does not just harm the true self of individuals but looks into their inner being. In analyzing the emotional contagion study with Facebook users and the Cambridge Analytica scandal, Stark (2018) argues that the aim of Facebook and similar social media sites is "tracking, measuring and manipulating the moods of its users" (Stark 2018, 206). Thus, algorithmic power aims not at violating our self in the process of quantification but to mold and shape it. The confession, in the form of produced data traces, allows to produce psychometric profiles, making it possible for the *shepherd* to look after us. This new way of forming and molding the self (and with it entire communities and publics) based on algorithms and data is underlined by a new 'algorithmic episteme' (Fisher and Mehozay 2019). Bucher (2012) also turned the logic of the concept of disciplinary panopticon upside down, arguing that the threat of contemporary digital societies is no longer to be visible to the authorities but to become invisible within the world of social media (see also Gillespie 2017).

Extending on the paradigm that code is law (Lessig 2006), this argument puts the material interventions and knowledge production of algorithms in direct contact with state executive institutions – thus putting it into a wider context. And it is exactly that context that we should not ignore when it comes to subjectivation, as Prey (2018) argues. Instead of assuming a true self or authentic individuality, Prey puts forward Simondon's idea of individuation, where the individual always is the product of situated interactions. Lury and Day (2019) argue further that algorithmic individuation "is refracted in multiple partial orderings that allow for specific forms of comparison and competition" (Lury and Day 2019, 31). The *self*, as it is being proclaimed by other scholars, becomes a contextual attribution of communication and interaction.[4] Thus, violating the true self asks always already the question how this true self is perceived and determined – and what ethical and normative meaning the users give the categories and attributions of algorithms (Magalhães 2018). Subjectivation cannot be discussed without the context and the negotiations of meaning in interactions between algorithms and humans.

From Biopolitics to Governmentality

Amoore (2009) draws on the Foucauldian power conceptions of governmentality and biopolitics to apply them to algorithms. Taking up the idea of political power as a form of silent war to "reinscribe that relationship of force, and to reinscribe it in institutions, economic inequalities, language, and even the bodies of individuals" (Foucault [1976] 2003, 16), she argues that we experience algorithms as a means of political power and state security. Through mining associations of people, places, and events, a model of social interaction is built which allows it to recognize deviant behavior based on a

---

4   There are also interesting connections to different conceptualizations of the subject in other theories, such as concepts of systems theory of the subject as the product of system-specific communication, narratology, which found its way into ANT, where the individual gets narrated by the actants involved, or new materialism, where the individual is the product of an agential cut, let alone role theory ala Goffman. Thus, the idea of an authentic self is not as prominent in contemporary social theory, as this discussion might suggest.

statistical construction of normality. This deviates from the idea of disciplinary regimes. In disciplinary societies the norm is – by its definition – a given that serves to distinguish between the normal and the abnormal. Whoever is able to fit into the definition of the norm is considered as norm-al. Discipline then is a mode to transform individuals in a way that they fit the idea represented by the formulated norm – by disciplining the body, the behavior, etc. Disciplinary power aims at a moment in time, for "the stable point of normality to be reached" (Aradau and Blanke 2017, 377). Statistical means, to the contrary, do not assume a pre-given norm but represent a self-reflexive form of deriving norms from a given population via means of statistics. Normality precedes the norm and the latter is derived from a calculated and observed normality: "The norm is an interplay of differential normalities. The normal comes first and the norm is deduced from it, or the norm is fixed and plays its operational role on the basis of this study of normalities" (Foucault [1978] 2009, 63). Foucault notes that this resembles more a process of normalization than normality. Instead of positively setting a norm to adapt reality to it, statistical methods construct the norm from the observed reality. Without referring to Foucault, Gerlitz and Lury (2014) describe processes of calculative (re-)evaluation of individuals based on their dynamic and changing position in a digital population. This also demarcates different conceptualizations of control in the digital realm (Cheney-Lippold 2011). While the idea of Lessig (2006) where code is law resembles the explicit norm setting through material boundaries – described in the control society by Deleuze (1992) – machine learning and statistical approaches dynamically calculate a model of normality.

These statistical methods thereby not only calculate probabilities but also apply models of associations or react to certain signals towards an algorithmically recognizable regime of "politics of possibility" (Amoore 2013). In this understanding, the term algorithmic also deviates from common understandings of calculating correlations or producing models through machine learning. Instead, the idea of algorithmic security as it is presented by Amoore's idea of associations works in two ways: the first is the described outlier detection. Singular events that are not part of a calculated normality are marked as suspicious and deviant. There might not be any proof or correlation between actual deviant behavior and observed actions, but the deviance from a general societal trend alone labels subjects. The second form works more theory-driven, as given signals are being used to determine the classification as potential deviant individuals. Association rules mark potential threats and make the observed individual object of further inquiry.

Within the scholarly discussion the term of algorithmic governmentality has been coined, describing "the use of algorithm[s] that governmental agencies and institutions wield over users and through which we seek to assemble the present structures, practices and processes from 'governing of others' to 'governing the self'" (Janssen and Kuk 2016, 375). Algorithms in this line of discussion are described as crucial elements of a new form of government that manages the agreement of the liberal subject with the governance regime (Foucault [1979] 2008). Most prominently formulated by Annette Rouvroy (2011), she argues that algorithmization of contemporary societies marks a shift towards post-modern forms of governance, in which causality and transparency are being replaced by inscrutable and calculative forms of managing societies. Thus, connecting to the biopolitics already described in an earlier section, most famous by Amoore's writings, and processes of subjectivation, thus establishing new forms of knowledge/discipline configurations. Through these forms of subjectivation and disciplining the individual, the population is not so much managed in forms of productivity and scientific rationality. Instead, a form of reducing contingency of human nature is introduced by algorithmic forms of governmentality, making predictions – an often-observed application of algorithms – possible. Introna (2016) argues in a similar way that algorithmic governance cannot be seen outside the performative effects the algorithms themselves produce – or in other words, algorithms produce the subject of intervention with the intervention together. This performativity of effects and the production of predictability is directly connected with each other (Sheehey 2019). Thus, the future and the past become important sites of governance for applications like predictive policing. The past is being performed through modeling and data collection and subsequently projected into the future – but both are governed through algorithms. Interestingly enough, the same phenomenon is argued to be a method for the production of space (Thrift and French 2002). In a later contribution, Rouvroy (2013) coined the term 'data behaviorism' to describe this shift from causality to manageability, emphasizing the shift from intentionally created governmental statistics, to manage populations towards ubiquitous processes of data collection (see also Roberts 2019). However, in the process of producing predictable populations, these government techniques violate according to Rouvroy (2013) who we are and therefore our individuality. This violation is the result of a) ignoring certain aspects of ourselves and b) installing mechanisms that make the predicted behavior – and thus the prediction – more likely. That is, through selectively disciplining and assigning subjectivity, the predicted system is re-produced in a reflexive way.[5]

This classification work is connected with an externalized form of control which is understood as *governing at a distance* (Rose 2012). Algorithmic power here is the connection between shifting and dynamic classifications in a regime where algorithms act as "guiding mechanisms that opens and closes particular conditions of possibility that users can encounter" (Cheney-Lippold

---

5   Reflexive is here used in a way that describes becoming self-aware or self-referential, thus in a meaning similar to cybernetics of a second order.

2011, 175). Thus, the management of a population is now governed through dynamically allocated subjectivities and risks which guide material interventions of algorithms in a dynamic process or produce social order through limiting potential actions. Algorithmic calculations therefore are no longer rooted in a disciplinary society, which would control and govern individuals through mechanisms of the panopticon (Foucault [1975] 1995), but "sorting individual bodies into flows through events of in- and exclusion" (Erwin 2015). Power does no longer operate with "the art of watching" (Beer 2015, 3) and the subsequent internalized feeling of being watched. This critique aims at the often-applied notion of the panopticon from Foucault's work, describing the disciplinary power of surveillance and straightens the way of connecting biopolitics and governmentality to the control society of Deleuze (1992).

From Biopolitics to Control Society

Starting from the perspective of biopolitics, Cheney-Lippold (2011) expands the notion of bio-politics and bio-power from Foucault and builds a bridge to the notion of the control society (Deleuze 1992). In the Foucauldian theory-building, biopower came up as its own concept to describe the historic shift from a disciplinary regime, aiming at individual bodies and subjects, to the construction of entire populations. According to Cheney-Lippold (2011), however, algorithmic agents introduce a new mode of governance to contemporary societies that the author called soft biopolitics. While Foucault's thinking was based on observations of (relatively) static categories in statistical measurements – such as male, female, etc. – algorithms work in another way. Categorization is no longer based on a fixed signifier-signified relationship but creates modulated and therefore highly dynamic classifications. If a person is classified as male – the example that Chenney-Lippold uses throughout the text – depends not only on the bodily features of the person but is derived from other features and observed behavior *in relation to other individuals*. Yet, since it is dynamically generated, it can also change at any given moment – or differ in different situations.

Algorithmic classification is less a tool of traditional biopolitics but resembles more what Deleuze (1992) has described as the process of modulation. Instead of producing (undividable) individuals, the process of algorithmic subjectivation produced dividuals. Identity has become a highly fluid statistical representation that does not represent a stable identity over different settings but acts according to a specific and situated function fulfilled by the algorithm in a process of "automated integration and disintegration" (Terranova 2004, 34). For Galloway, such an algorithmic production of dividuals has "no reason to know the name of a particular user [...]. The clustering of descriptive information around a specific user becomes sufficient to explain the identity of that user" (Galloway 2004, 69). Thus, the biopolitical impetus of the governing bodies to become self-descriptive in terms of the entire population breaks up the former solidified and manageable population in many different subpopulations that are very dynamic in their constitution – a development which Rogers (2009) called post-demographics.

Applying the term soft biopolitics to the algorithmic mediation of communication shifts the focus of governance away from the state, where it traditionally belonged, and locates the power to govern in platforms like Facebook or Google. Through capturing huge amounts of user data and designing platforms and algorithms according to norms, the algorithms manage our everyday interactions and the resulting social capital available to us (Schwarz 2019). In this perspective, the aim of biopolitical governance is no longer to strengthen the state and its means (of production) but to create surplus value for the Internet platform. An argument that has also been brought forward in other theoretical constellations and more or less implicitly by Morozov (2014) and Mayer-Schönberger and Ramge (2018).

Taken together, the approaches discussed on algorithmic power connect the control society by Deleuze (1992) with a new, non-state and fluid form of biopolitics. The body of a state's subject is no longer the aim of intervention, nor is the internalization of the powerful gaze 'from above' the method of choice to govern. Taking the approach of dynamic and fluid micro-management of soft biopolitics seriously, this also seems no longer a possible modus operandi, since the individual does not know the norms she should adhere to, as they are dynamically derived from no-longer pre-defined populations. Instead, different and ever new emerging populations are calculated, dynamically addressed and in- or excluded from possible paths of (inter) action. Thus, algorithmic governance defines what we can and cannot do in the current situation in a spectrum of control which is defined by mostly invisible actors that rather define what we cannot[6] do than what we can do (Sadowski and Pasquale 2015). The notion of control societies then has been taken up in surveillance studies, where the sorting aspect has been emphasized and was actively positioned against the dominant metaphor of the panopticon (e.g., Bogard 2006; Haggerty and Ericson 2000; Lyon 2003). This shift has lately been criticized (de Laat 2019), arguing that predictive modeling still enforces changes in behavior through adoption to social norms as we directly feel the consequences of a norm violation.[7] Earlier, however, Amoore

---

6   Here we can already see an interesting connection to the idea of social control and social order that was formulated by Latour (2005) and other ANT scholars, and which will be discussed in later chapters.

7   This argument misses two important points about disciplinary power. First, the very important notion that disciplinary power even works without intervention and, second, that it is not enough to know that there might be consequences, but also the norms that we violate (see e.g., Curchod et al. 2020). In terms of algorithmic governance and machine learning, however, we very often do not know them in terms of problematic

(2011) argued that the data derivatives produced by algorithmic risk calculation – through association – is defined by the decision to reduce the manifold input to one score or label, not transparent according to the association rules (see also Leese 2014). If they are not transparent, however, then the disciplining effect cannot surface. Additionally, prediction is a biopolitical instrument to manage the consequences of an event, not to stop it from happening (Aradau and Blanke 2017, 377) – as a disciplinary logic would suggest. This difference is important, as derivative norms – calculated from the referenced population – can only come into existence after the observation of events. Normality and abnormality cannot be pre-defined – different from modes of disciplining the individual. What the norm and the abnormal is, is thus defined by finding outliers of a fluid calculated norm (Roberts 2019). The orientation according to a given norm is no longer possible. Especially, if the norm not only changes over time but is also different in different contexts, as Cheney-Lippold (2011) suggests. This does, however, not mean that disciplinary power disappears, as also Amoore (2011) stresses. For example, in the case of eBay, forms of power are in place that resemble characteristics of the panopticon as well as soft bio-politics (Curchod et al. 2020). However, the emergence of an algorithmic control society poses problems not only in understanding but also in regulating these calculated norms (e.g., Lenglet 2019).

The perspective Foucauldian scholars offer us here is interesting indeed, as especially the idea of the control society seems to explain many aspects of the phenomenon that we call algorithmic power. In the control society, the biopolitical aspect of managing the population multiplies, and the question which rationality drives the governmental interventions immediately comes up. This, however, is not always a biopolitical imperative described by Foucault ([1979] 2008). Further, the idea of centralized institutions supporting the government in governing the general population falls apart. The central institutions of power are now multiplied and replaced by the algorithm as a knowledge production device, and breaching the borders of state institutions (Harkens 2018; Müller and Pöchhacker 2019). This decentralization of power raises questions how to locate the power of algorithms, and how these multiple enactments of algorithmic power intersect. Decentering the object of inquiry might provide a way of exploring these difficile interactions and relations. As Introna (2016) argues: understanding algorithms' agency in terms of socio-material networks and situated action might provide us more basis to describe the governmental rationalities of algorithmic societies. However, this does not only include the performative effects of algorithms, as Introna describes, but also the question

behavior. A problem that became well known as the black box problem. In addition, it also ignores the chilling effect that has been observed with surveillance systems, raising further doubt about the panoptic power of algorithms. However, whether algorithmic governance has a disciplinary effect is a question that is better addressed by empirical research.

of how algorithms *become* actors of a network of power and agency. Introna refers to a quote by Miller (2008) which states that "it is through technologies that programmes of government are made operable" (Miller 2008, 57). Following this thought then raises two important questions: what is the government program? And what governmental rationalities come together in the actor of the algorithm?

Cybernetics and Algocracy

A perspective which is only discussed by some scholars, but with a large impact on the discussion, and which again focuses more on the algorithm, is being debated under the term of *Algocracy* or *Algorithmic Governance*. In line with insight that technological decisions have an effect on the constitution of societies, the *algocracy thesis* (Aneesh 2009, 349) states that algorithms and software act as a form of governance. Through code, structure and privileges of (global) organizations and societies are encoded into the system. Aneesh (2009) even goes so far as to argue that code is a new generalized medium, comparable to money, and thus a constitutional element of contemporary societies, which are characterized by the *rule of the algorithm* (Aneesh 2009, 350). The algorithmization of social processes is thereby distinguished from bureaucratic forms of governance (Weber [1922] 1978), as it does not require legitimacy and socialization (Aneesh 2009). Code and algorithms constitute the new laws of contemporary societies, however, without being legally binding nor being formulated by a legislative institution, but through instantiating new forms of behavior regulation. A phenomenon that led Lessig to equate code with law (Lessig 1999, 2006) and which is often identified by the acronym ADM – automated decision-making. The algorithm ultimately selects the options of further actions for you and therefore exerts power by regulating possible forms of interaction. In arguing this way, the algocracy thesis is very similar to the notion of the control society (as discussed earlier), without explicitly referring to it. This notion of an algorithmic form of rule has also been called *Technology Paternalism* (Spiekermann and Pallas 2006) that threatens to take over control and make human intervention unlikely. This form of governance therefore can regulate the production of space (Kitchin 2014), the rhythms of interactions, i.e., a governance of temporal structures (Coletta and Kitchin 2017), and the governance within companies (Raffetseder, Schaupp, and Staab 2017).

For Yeung (2017), algorithmic forms of regulation therefore constitute a regulatory regime of nudging, i.e., influencing the decisions of individuals. It should be noted that the notion of nudging already introduces some nuance, which does not degrade the individual to a mindless receiver of control instructions. However, with the appearance of big internet platforms, such as Google or Facebook, this becomes an even bigger problem, as it does not regulate by force but suggestions, and not only addresses singular individuals but entire populations. Seaver (2019) even introduces the metaphor of algorithms as traps. Based on his observations of the development of a recommender system, he shows how the developers design the algorithmic system in a way that tries to keep the users on their website – not by using some sort of regulatory force but by applying behavioral and psychological principles in the design of the system. This nuance differentiates the relatively forceful idea of the control society with a subtler form of governance, which is in the end not less effective – but might produce less resistance. The perspective of power of algorithms as nudging devices therefore also speak to conceptions of social order and power as a reflexive endeavor, in which the ordering regime depends also on the cooperation of the governed subject (Giddens 1984). Nudging therefore marks an interesting line between the differentiation of power and governance brought forward by Max Weber ([1922] 1978). As a result, the legitimacy of these techniques is brought back into the discussion by Yeung (2017).

A second way in which the notion of the control society is differentiated from the *algocracy thesis* is how it refers back to cybernetic forms of regulation or social theories that are derived from cybernetic ideas (Aneesh 2009). Similar to the accounts of a new biopolitical regime (Amoore 2011; Cheney-Lippold 2011), the cybernetic approach complicates the idea of governance. Instead of deriving the norm from the collected inputs, a cybernetic approach derives the necessary actions to achieve a system state that reflects the previously defined normality. Thus, not the normative setting is dynamically calculated but the regulatory interventions are (Yeung 2018). This requires the system to collect data all the time in order to adapt its interventions into the social system.[8]

Aside from the question whether algocratic forms of governance are legitimate in itself, Danaher (2016) warns us that an increasing reliance on algorithmic agents in public domains could undermine legitimacy of democratic institutions. For Danaher (2016), the threat of algocracy therefore is characterized by "a situation in which algorithm-based systems structure and constrain the opportunities for human participation in, and comprehension of, public decision-making" (Danaher 2016, 246). Thus, public and democratic processes might be undermined by algorithmic decision systems. The issue here is therefore not so much the control aspect but the construction principles of deliberative democracies and its forms of discourse.

Approaches to algorithmic governance or *algocracy* are insightful, as they provide nuance in their conceptualization of the governed, i.e., the individuals

---

8   This argument resembles the one discussed in the part on Foucauldian power conceptions. Thus, through different theoretical perspectives, a convergence of arguments can be observed.

and populations, and create some interesting links to cybernetics (Yeung 2018) or sociological systems theories (Aneesh 2009). Thus, these approaches walk the thin line of taking the algorithm as a medium of control seriously without focusing only on this actor. Instead, the algorithm is decentered within a specific governance regime. However, the conceptualizations of algorithms as cybernetic systems create some conceptual and empirical issues that need to be addressed. For one, the notion of an algorithm as a black box (in a cybernetic meaning) raises the question of how the black box got there in the first place and how the different qualities of the black box are negotiated. Or in other words, the ways how the black box is held stable have to be explained in a systemic perspective. Especially in the very instructive taxonomy of Yeung (2018), it becomes clear that the algorithm is not an independent technical actor but a socio-technical collective that acts *as if* it were a black box. And where algocracy does not argue with a cybernetics approach (e.g., Lessig 1999, 2006; Spiekermann and Pallas 2006), it becomes vague what the relations to broader sets of social order are. However, the algocracy thesis is instructive as it gives nuance to the notion of the control society and hints towards systemic ways to think about algorithms.

Algorithms in Digital Capitalism

Capitalist critique of digitized societies and digital transformations has mostly been discussed on the examples of social media or platform capitalism – focusing on new modes of labor, worker surveillance, and the blurring distinction between producers and consumers. In comparison, the role of algorithms plays only a minor role in these theoretical perspectives and approaches. However, algorithms and accompanying phenomena have also been discussed in terms of capitalist modes of production (Fuchs 2020) or markets (Beer 2015). These discussions range from arguments that market interests are a driving force in the shaping of algorithms (Mager 2012) to algorithms as market devices that perform economics (Callon and Muniesa 2005; D. MacKenzie 2006) to the reinforcement of market power through prediction and digital infrastructures (Beverungen, Beyes, and Conrad 2019; Poechhacker and Nyckel 2020). These observations led scholars like Zuboff (2019) to form the notion of "surveillance capitalism." Although there are different conceptualizations of capitalism, e.g., Weber's idea of capitalism as rationalization, the dominant perspective on digital capitalism is rooted in a Marxist understanding of the phenomenon (e.g., Fuchs 2019; Srnicek 2016).

Central elements taken up within these discussions are thereby motives of surplus value theory, exploitation, and estrangement of work forces. Capitalism and algorithmic systems thereby extend classical Marxist critique on the modes of production. For Vioulac (2009), the increasing utilization of information technologies is a continuation of *human alienation* in industrial capitalism. For Marx, alienation was the process of detaching the worker from her true self by mechanistically following the goals and instructions of the bourgeoisie. The estrangement ("Entfremdung") therefore is twofold, from oneself, separating the subject of the worker from the individual, and from the product, as it no longer represents what one would have produced and done by oneself. A free worker would therefore realize oneself in the product and also in the actual practice of producing it. For free workers "[o]ur products would be so many mirrors in which we saw reflected our essential nature" (Marx 1844 cited in Torrance 1995, 55). Through the production processes in which the capitalists – i.e., the individuals who own the production means – define what has to be produced, and also how the work processes have to be carried out, the true and essential self is violated. Taking up this perspective, Nygren and Gidlund (2015) argue further that the process of alienation in the digital realm not only affects the production of (industrial) goods but impacts us in a more fundamental way, as our digital selves become the commodity. What we are online reflects the visions and imaginaries of the online industry (Nygren and Gidlund 2015).[9] In the omnipresent digital realm of self-marketing, we are not only alienated from our product, but our digital selves become the products we are alienated from. Since we have to manage ourselves as something that is appealing to others in multiple ways, e.g., on Instagram, we orient our self-presentation on the emerging market logic of digital plat-forms. This speaks to the previously discussed new logic of visibility within algorithmically sorted communities (Bishop 2019; Bucher 2012) – even if the authors did not take up a Marxist perspective.

Another aspect of worker alienation and control is taken up by Rosenblat (2018) who describes the complicated and algorithmically mediated relation-ship between Uber and its drivers. By providing a communication platform powered by different algorithms, Uber in its self-description provides a plat-form for independent entrepreneurs, i.e., the drivers, while at the same time controlling them and their practices through the services provided. Again, the driver becomes the product of the platform, and the data points produced on it are constantly used for further experimentation and value extraction (see also Lee et al. 2015). While the classical Marxist idea of value extraction was developed with industrial societies in mind, it has been translated into the digital condition of contemporary societies by some scholars (e.g., Staab 2019). The surplus value thesis of Marx ([1867] 1990) thereby is based on a simple but powerful insight into the process of valuation of industrially produced goods. Marx states that the added value that a product represents cannot stem from the used resources, as their value is simply a given. Thus, what adds value to the processes or produced product is the work that goes into it – realizing

9   Nygren and Gidlund (2015) not only discuss Marx's theory but also connect them with the concept of pastoral power of Foucault. For the sake of simplicity, however, the relation of the concepts is not discussed here.

the value of any given product as the simple addition of the worth of used materials plus the added work. The work, however, is not performed by the capitalists but by the workers, who receive compensation for their work force. This creates the problem that capitalists, on the one hand, need to produce profit but, on the other hand, add nothing to the value of the product. The solution – in Marx' terms – is to lower the compensation of the workers, thus paying them less than the added value. The margin is the profit for the capitalist class – and value is produced by exploiting the work force. In algorithmic conditions, the application of this principle to analyze capitalist societies, however, was adapted a bit. Analyzing Google's Page Rank algorithm, Pasquinelli (2009) argues that Google creates surplus value not (only) by exploiting their work force but by using the work of every single website owner. Since the page rank algorithm analyzes the link structure of websites and monetizes the results with their advertisement business, the page rank algorithm utilized the free work that was performed by the website owners as a collective. However, companies like Google do not only rely on weblinks that are being set by website owners but also on an extensive apparatus of tracking users in the internet – producing surplus value from human relationships and practices (Couldry and Mejias 2019). Zuboff (2019) even argues that we are living in the age of surveillance capitalism, in which profit is produced from *"behavioral surplus, [which is] fed into advanced manufacturing processes […] and fabricated into prediction products that anticipate what you will do now, soon, and later"* (Zuboff 2019, 8, emphasis in the original). Bringing these arguments together, Staab (2019) argues that surveillance and prediction technologies, combined with the insight that platforms create surplus value out of their users, create a new and unique control regime. Control – as thought by Marx – utilizes a topdown hegemonic form of order. But actually, as Staab argues drawing from Giddens, it requires the cooperation between the hegemon and the subject of the ordering regime, as the reflexive adaptation of control creates a time lag. Between the observation of deviant behavior and the correction through forceful means, the subject – or in the Marxist terminology, the worker – enjoys freedom of being able to act differently. Through modes of surveillance and algorithmic automation, this time lag is being closed – constructing a swift and ever adapting control regime. Examining the history of AI and the automation of work, Upchurch and Moore (2018) highlight that this development was foreseen by Marx in his writings:

> Marx refers specifically to the potential of mechanization to dominate the production process. The machine appears as an all-powerful force, both in fragmenting the input of the individual worker and engendering a subservient relationship to technology through the division of labor (Upchurch and Moore 2018, 54).

This process of extraction and commodification of relational data can thereby be put into the context of processes of colonization, introducing a regime of exploitation via means of digital platforms and the colonization of the self. Drawing from Habermas, Gilbert (2018) argues that algorithms colonize our lifeworld, as they change, influence and steer the ways to see, experience, and interpret the world, which is the resource of our knowing and acting. Gilbert refers thereby to the idea of Habermas that the world is *always already* constituted by meaning and semantics, a communicative system in which we are socialized and that is reproduced through communicative (inter-)action. Through algorithmic systems, these life-worlds can be (overly) shaped by other logics, such as market or state rationalities, leading to a less free, less meaningful, and less democratic society (Gilbert, 2018). Especially in the field of information selection on the internet, and thus co-constructing the shared social reality, a dominance of private companies exerting algorithmic forms of governance has been identified (Just and Latzer 2017). Through tracking and algorithmic classification, individual humans are made available to each other for exploitation, undermining the potential to recognize and develop ourselves over time. This process thereby can be understood as a new form of colonization tendencies, in which classical divides of *the north* and *the south* or *the west* and *the rest* are being transcended (Segura and Waisbord 2019). Instead, the colonization is now furthered through multinational companies, such as Facebook or Amazon, and state-corporate alliances on an infrastructural and epistemological level – realizing a "transnational informational capitalism" (Fuchs 2012b, 128). These new formations within contemporary capitalism reflect also the diagnosis that the state as formerly central player within capitalism – an idea found within Marx's writings – becomes less influential (e.g., Bauman 2000). Data production and analysis represents a new form of knowledge on which colonization is based (Ricaurte 2019) and thus needs new forms of thinking about a new phenomenon of data exploitation (Segura and Waisbord 2019). Thus, initiatives to theorize big data from the south emerged as a contra-point to this development (e.g., Milan and Treré 2019).

Both arguments rest on the assumption that algorithms operate in an environment that uses them in order to either extract value or furthers a process of colonization. Both perspectives are valuable as such, but again the power of the algorithm is not so much explained but assumed as a given. This follows to some degree Marx's understanding of technology as a means to enable new forms of exploitation and surplus value production, where technology is a means to increase productivity (and therefore exploitation) and reinforces class divides. Christian Fuchs (2012a) argues that:

> Transnational information capitalism is the result of the dialectic of continuity and discontinuity that shapes capitalist development. Surplus

value, exchange value, capital, commodities and competition are basic aspects of capitalism, how such forms are exactly produced, objectified, accumulated, and circulated is contingent and historical. They manifest themselves differently in different capitalist modes of development. In the informational mode of development surplus value production and capital accumulation manifest themselves increasingly in symbolic, 'immaterial', informational commodities and cognitive, communicative, and co-operative labour. Digital media mediates the accumulation of capital, power, and definition capacities on a transnational scale (Fuchs 2012a, 419).

The algorithm is thereby a techno-determinist element of historical materialism in which the way of one's own being determines the consciousness (expressed in the catchy German phrase *"Das Sein bestimmt das Bewusstsein"*). However, reducing algorithms to moments of (post-)industrial production might miss important points, where the socio-technical system of the algorithm might not only follow an economic rationality, e.g., when Facebook not only tries to produce value from the data gathered but also installs regimes of evaluating content and users in terms of fraudulent behavior or problematic accounts. While the predominant aim of Facebook might still be the collection of profit, other normative ideologies and imaginaries are mixed together and negotiated in the algorithmic system. The value extraction argument sees algorithms as mere extensions of capitalist modes of production, raising the question what it is that the algorithm adds to the equation and how the interaction system can be understood in terms of algorithmic power and agency. The colonization thesis argues that one domain (forcefully) enters another one in a hegemonial way. The demarcation lines of colonization are north/south, corporate/private, or state/citizen. Yet, the multiplicity of colonization processes makes it hard to pinpoint the actual power the algorithm exerts but at the same time hints at the complexity of the phenomenon. In both instances, the power of the algorithm – or better, the power through the algorithm is a given.

This has also provoked some remarks, e.g., from Astrid Mager (2014, 30): "However, all these contributions cannot explain why search engines have become powerful actors in the first place and how they – and the algorithmic ideology – are stabilized in contemporary society." In a way, the Hegelian heritance of Marxist conceptions become visible in these critiques. Algorithmic modes of ordering are implicitly seen as historic-materialist processes of accumulation and distribution of (production) goods. Instead, Mager (2014) argues, algorithms are a part of a hegemonic ideology that is not only defined by the capitalist class of the bourgeoisie but is (re-)produced by a wide variety of actors. The social power of algorithms is, as she argued in an earlier paper, thereby an emergent quality of different perspectives, needs, and issues

(Mager 2012). Interestingly, some scholars started to bring Marx' surplus value theory in conversation with Foucauldian concepts of power (Nygren and Gidlund 2015).[10] There is some interesting scholarship emerging that might be worth following in the future.

The Power of What?

The discussed theories about algorithms are manifold and approach the phenomenon from different perspectives – each one valuable in itself. However, there is a common ground in all of the applied theories that the algorithm itself is an actor through which power is exerted or that exerts power itself. While most Foucauldian perspectives emphasize the calculative power of algorithms, the algorithm and an algorithmic logic become a central element in a dispositive, where power is not effective because of the algorithm but *through* the algorithm. A similar construction can be found in (post-) Marxist perspectives where the material setup of the algorithm is a mere expression of the social dynamic of class struggle. Other approaches take a comparable perspective when the algorithm becomes a focal point of a post-hegemonic power structure (Lash 2007) or when *algocratic* forms of govern-ance are installed. The same is true when we conceptualize algorithms as black boxes or inherently biased agents. In all of these analyses, however, the algorithm as an actor takes a central role and its *object-ivity*, i.e., the algorithm as a stable object, is not in question. This results in a productive but also a somewhat puzzling paradox. The algorithm itself is discussed and presented as a powerful actor. At the same time, however, it is a mere expression of a power apparatus – provoking the question of how the algorithm became this powerful actor and if there is only one rationality at work in which it is embedded. It is not my intention here to devalue these different approaches, as each of them offers an interesting, productive, and valuable perspective on the phenomenon of algorithmic power and social order. Instead, I want to present this (seemingly) paradox situation, which others would describe as dialectical, as a starting point, exploring an alternative perspective. Starting from empirical observations from the development of a specific algorithm, I am interested in how this actant became a powerful actor and how it is integrated in a wider system of interaction and normativity. Other scholars have argued the same, claiming that we should understand algorithms as networked information systems (Ananny 2016), take a design perspective

---

10   This is especially interesting, as it brings us back to the roots and origins of Foucault's thinking and philosophical socialization, reflecting the complicated and ambivalent relationship of Foucault with the French communist party. At some point Foucault even described himself as a Nietzsch'ian Marxist, which creates fascinating and potentially productive tensions in the understanding of history / genealogy (see e.g., J. S. Johnson and Thiele 1991)

(Crawford 2016) or see algorithms as the results of organized and organizing practices (Neyland 2015).

Drawing from these questions, the algorithm appears to be neither a powerful actor in itself, nor is it just an amorph instrument of an already powerful system – but an important element in the constitution of social order with its own issues, challenges, and obduracies. Following the observation of Adrian Mackenzie (2013), the analysis of algorithms, data structures and protocols can therefore be a productive counterpoint to very general descriptions and conclusions – but without neglecting the broader systemic processes entangled with these elements. Instead, the instantiation of an algorithm as an actor of social order marks the production of something new, changing interaction orders and power relations (Campbell-Verduyn, Goguen, and Porter 2017). Algorithms are elements of social order that are being applied to (social) situations as a form of normative delegation (Willson 2017), in which they become an element in the practical and situational achievement of social order and algorithmic power.

Algorithms and societies are co-evolving and co-dependent, as the former are increasingly essential institutions of the latter (Just and Latzer 2017). Through putting emphasis on how the algorithms are being produced and taking a closer look at the algorithmic principles itself, we can read these as "the signature of predicting practice" (A. Mackenzie 2013, 393) and thus reconstruct the rationality and materiality of social ordering of algorithms. By doing so, the algorithm is not seen as the stable and powerful actor that exerts power over a given society but understands the algorithm as a practical achievement, shifting the perspective to study socio(-technical) order *from within* (Garfinkel 1984, viii; A. W. Rawls 2009). This raises two different questions: first, how is the social structure organized that instantiates an algorithm as a *successful* tool of power delegation, and second, how are the attributes of such a delegate negotiated between different interest groups and actors. The latter also opens up the discussion for the inquiry as to what the algorithm as an actor adds to the equation, without fully attributing the governing power to it. Answering these questions possibly leads to new ways of not only understanding how social and institutional order is organized in digital democracies and how democratic visions and values are impacted by it, but also what forms of governance would be possible. I will therefore explore such a perspective of the algorithm as a socio-technical achievement in the following chapters.

3

Algorithmic Discipline

We reject: kings, presidents, and voting. We believe in: rough consensus and running code. – Dave Clark (1992).

When taking a computer science class, one develops an intuitive understanding of what an algorithm is. We are able to write them down in pseudo code,[1] implement them in different programming languages, like Java or C, analyze their complexity and compare their performance to other algorithms. We learn terms like *Quick Sort* and *Traveler Salesman Problem*. And yet, the figure of the algorithm has sparked some discussion when trying to account for the social power of these constructs, culminating in the question of "what actually is an algorithm?" (Ziewitz 2016, 4).[2] Several scholars have found an answer to this question, sometimes more, sometimes less connected to definitions and understandings of computer science discourses. Algorithms are powerful entities regulating our daily lives (Beer 2009), an "interpretative key of modern rationality" (Totaro and Ninno 2014), a replacement of "self-critical judgement" (Daston 2010), an instrument for classification (Bechmann and Bowker 2019) or the material implementation of otherwise "abstract 'effective procedures' (finite sets of exact, 'mechanical' instructions) of mathematics or computer science" (D. MacKenzie 2019, 41), to name just a few. Given the

---

1   We will come back to the difference of pseudo code and code later.
2   One can observe an interesting convergence between critical algorithm studies and software studies in terms of ontological uncertainty of the phenomenon in question. In 2008, Wendy Chun raised the question "What is software"? (Chun 2008, 2).

diverse perspectives on the phenomenon of algorithms, it is easy to get the impression that these different scholars, while in each account refereeing to algorithms, are talking about fundamentally different things (see also Burke 2019). They do not necessarily share a common definition of algorithms, yet according to them, there is something about algorithms to be found in general, may it be rationality, agency, or classification. This, of course, does not help to answer the question of what an algorithm is, nor how the social power of algorithms can be explained. Yet, it demonstrates that algorithms and their effects became a matter of concern.

As Seaver (2017) argues, there is no "proper" definition of algorithms. Relying on anthropological sensitivities, and drawing from post-ANT conceptions, Seaver argues that we should account for the different enactments of *the algorithm*. With this, an algorithm and its qualities are no longer an essence to be found, or a generic principle. A general statement about algorithms can no longer be made, as it depends on in which social arena one asks the question of what an algorithm is. Thus, Seaver (2017) urges us to not answer the question of what *the algorithm* is, or what is special about it. Instead, we will find the answer to this question in the field studied. By taking into account the multiplicity of algorithms, the question of what an algorithm is has been complicated even further. The perspective of *algorithms as enactments* has also profound impact on how to research these actors. Since enactments of algorithms are different in the way they operate and how one can access them, the mode of inquiry must change. All of them point towards *the algorithm*, albeit in different ways and from different perspectives. Algorithms can be opaque actors producing inequality (Noble 2018), they can also be a video surveillance procedure that needs to be explained to an ethics board (Neyland 2016), they can be a discursive narrative (Beer 2017) or they can be a concrete set of instructions that are implemented (Dourish 2016). Thus, when talking about algorithms, *at least* three different versions of *the algorithm* are mixed together when discussing these actants. First, the general principle of an algorithm is a set of instructions to solve a given problem within a finite amount of time. That is also the textbook definition of an algorithm, and one that is often found in the domain of computer science and engineering. Secondly, the multiple forms of unstable and uncoordinated assemblages, where everything is open for discussion, decisions are to be made, code is to be written, requirements have to be engineered, etc. This includes the initial implementation of algorithms into code but also the ongoing development and adoption of algorithmic systems to a changing set of demands. I call this here *the algorithm in the making*, which is also represented in studies similar to classical laboratory studies in STS – and therefore my own work presented here. And third, the implemented and materialized algorithm *in the wild*, deciding on whom to give a job, where to send the police, or whom to present which information. The latter is a stabilized, institutionalized form of an algorithm, located somewhere within organizations, behind APIs and as an indeed powerful actor, hiding all the mess, the multiplicity, the diagrams, charts, etc. in a black box. In any case, algorithms are a product of manifold interactions, associations, and translations. The question then is, where to start, where to look and where to go. These different perspectives, while each in itself valuable, created a discussion as to what we are actually studying when we say algorithms. Positions thereby rank from the situational enactment, i.e., narration, of algorithms, asking how the term 'algorithm' is being laden with meaning to observations in media theory that media artifacts, such as a concrete sorting algorithm, have very manifest effects. The former makes an argument for the researcher as social scientist, who should not blindly follow disciplinary and technical definitions (Seaver 2017), i.e., not become an engineer, but to trust social science and humanities methodologies to carve out the qualities of an algorithm. The latter, however, presents a counterpoint to this position. Manovich (2013a)[3], amongst others, argues that one should be able to program one-self to fully grasp the ordering effects of technology. To be able to understand what an algorithm is and how it orders the world, we must start from the technical qualities of that actor, i.e., start from and with technical expertise. Somewhat in between ranges the idea that we should follow the emic terms of the field we are studying (Dourish 2016), i.e., use the computer science definition of algorithms. This argument is then taken up by Burke (2019) who shows that the term algorithm remains an important one for computer science – in spite of its problems in finding a common definition. In this chapter, I therefore want to explore this argumentative tension, starting from the assumption and observation that algorithms are something that is (also) done in software development projects, and to follow the material and discursive elements necessary to deal with these actors that are so difficult to grasp. I start with the discussion about the ontological status of algorithms and software as discussed by media theory scholars and complicate the issue by asking how the algorithm gets enacted through practices of software developers implementing different techniques, using software libraries, setting up developer environments such as iPyhton notebooks, to name just a few examples. Thus, to understand the ordering effects of algorithms, we also need to turn to computer science as one of these many enactments for our analysis. Based on my experiences as part of the development project of the recommender algorithm, I argue that, in the end, the two perspectives are not in opposition to each other but instead represent distinct elements of the same phenomenon: the manifest and durable algorithm is a product of a collective and situated enactment. In the following, I will reconstruct a media

3   The text was originally published in the year 2011 via the website of Manovich as a preview for the book 'Software Takes Command', but became soon a central writing. It therefore can also be found here: *http://manovich.net/content/04-projects/066-there-is-only-software/63-article-2011.pdf*

theory perspective on algorithms and argue that the making of algorithms relies on two different forms of collective enactments. In the process of implementing the recommender algorithm, the project relied a) on a working order of always already given tools from a community, and b) on structures of discourse and knowledge distribution from which techniques are being mobilized. The algorithm that Manovich (2013a) or Dourish (2016) talk about are already enactments – but specific ones. And, as we will see in the discussions on algorithmic institutions and politics, they are not the only ones.

Doing Computer Science

Latour (1999b) once said society emerges out of sociology and culture emerges out of anthropology. The production of such terms makes them meaningful only in relation with regimes of knowledge production. Consequently, it seems legitimate to formulate the working hypothesis that algorithms emerge out of computer science. One aim of the inquiry at hand therefore is to understand the term of the algorithm "as term of art within a particular professional culture – that of computer scientists, software designers, and machine learning practitioners" (Dourish 2016, 2).[4] Otherwise, as Dourish (2016) argues, we would not be able to find adequate forms for intervention or critique. This position is also one to be found in the earlier proclaimed software studies:

> To understand the logic of new media we need to turn to computer science. It is there that we may expect to find the new terms, categories and operations that characterize media that became programmable. From media studies, we move to something that can be called software studies, from media theory to software theory (Manovich 2001, 48).

This idea has its foundations in earlier discussions, partly originated in the field of Media Theory – especially the *Berlin School* of Media Theory – where Kittler (1999) argued for a deep understanding of technology in order to grasp their cultural and societal impact, as "media determine our situation" (Kittler 1999, XXXIX). In this context, only a thorough confrontation with the technologies surrounding us can create the necessary perspective for critique, analysis, and emancipation. The promise of such a perspective is that turning to a theory of software or algorithms, social research and cultural studies will be able to talk about this phenomenon in novel and – more importantly to the advocates of such approach – apt terms. For scholars in software studies and critical code studies, this meant turning to the actual code that makes the software in order to understand how the social and cultural realm are being influenced and determined in the new digitized condition. In his famous formulation, Lessig (1999, 2006) equated code with law, or technological code

4   This understanding of algorithm as an emic term (Dourish 2016, 2) has later been contested by Seaver (2017).

with legal codes. Instead of being subject to regulation, code and software increasingly became a regulatory force itself. In real space, we recognize how laws regulate – through constitutions, statutes, and other legal codes. In cyberspace we must understand how a different "code" regulates – how the software and hardware (i.e., the "code" of cyberspace) that make cyberspace what it is also regulate cyberspace as it is (Lessig 2006).

Code – here in the makeup of cyberspace – is a powerful regulator deciding who can access digital objects or services, what forms of communication are possible and where the information is being gathered. Taking up on the same phenomenon, Galloway (2004) describes the Internet as a place that has never been about freedom but about control. An important mechanism to exert control is to this author the implementation of protocols – a form of control that allows exerting power in de-centralized structures like the Internet. Galloway (2004) means that quite literary, as he identifies communication protocols like TCP, DNS, or HTTP, to name just a few, as political technologies. These protocols regulate the way we act and live within the Internet the same way as a speed bump regulates our driving behavior through a "physical system of organization" (Galloway 2004, 241).

Montfort et al. illustrated this attitude by analyzing the cultural, historical and social meanings of just one line of computer code, arguing that "in order to fully understand the way that redlining [...] functions, it might be necessary to consider the specific code of a bank's system to approve mortgages" (Montfort et al. 2012, 10). One line of code can make a difference. Thus, understanding the digitization of society,[5] accessing the concrete lines of code becomes important for critical inquiry – also for seemingly opaque applications like machine learning. Adrian Mackenzie notes "whatever the levels of abstraction associated with machine learning, the code is hardly ever hermetically opaque. As statements, everything lies on the surface" (A. Mackenzie 2017, 26). Studying algorithms and machine learning therefore means studying code from a new perspective. The challenge identified by these scholars then is: what form of cyberspace do we build? Which regulatory – Lessig even compares them with constitutional – regimes are we willing to implement? The ability to formulate – however incomplete – answers to these questions requires us to read, write, and discuss the code and the algorithms of our digital societies. Consequently, Manovich (2013a) argued that in order to escape the prison of software, we need to learn to write our own code.

---

5   This formulation could be read in two different ways, first hinting at a systems theory approach, arguing that digitization can only be understood as a product of a (auto-poetic) society. Following Luhmann's (1997) ideas, this would be in line with titles such as "the politics of society," "law of society" or even "the society of society." Another way to read these three words would hint at an ANT perspective, arguing that digitization should be understood as a building block of society, as it constitutes an element of producing collectives through rhizomatic chains of translation.

Thus, we must mobilize practices and paradigms from computer science and software development to formulate our critique. Doing software, code, and algorithms from a different perspective, namely, a critical one, turned also into a form of political inquiry.

Algorithmic Media and its Materiality

Computer science, however, is a wide field. Where should we locate algorithms? How is the effect, the difference it makes, actually being created? From the arguments provided so far, this level would be computer code written in programming languages. Open up these .java files, look where the incriminating statement is, and we are close to finding the social impact of this technology. And yet, this position has not been uncontested. Dourish (2017) notes that we should acknowledge that the realization of an algorithm, which also includes the actual code, requires more than the abstract procedure. Algorithms are concrete and material actors in our world. They are "identifiable, concrete media artifacts, and they are easier to identify when seen as part of a larger machine" (Burke 2019, 4). According to Hayles (1999), information or digital societies live in a condition of virtuality in which cultural perception creates differentiations between materiality of information and code and information as abstract entities. But this virtuality is only an achievement in making central characteristics of information, i.e., the medium on which it is stored and potentially executed as a computer program, invisible through our perception. Information without material information is non-existent, as it is always dependent on a material manifestation on a medium. Abstracting code or information (at least in the von Neumann architecture this distinction is rendered moot) away from their material base is, according to Hayles (1999, 13), an imaginary. And in order to fully understand how software and algorithms work – and how they produce ordering effects – we should also consider the material world of computing, i.e., the CPU, the mainboard design, the data storage technology used, etc. Without it, the perspective on code is incomplete. A similar insight led Kittler (1995) earlier to the statement that "there is no software." This statement also reflects the deep involvement and interest of Kittler in hardware as the central element of technological mediation. To him, this signifies a "descent from software to hardware, from higher to lower levels of observation" (Kittler 1995, 150). In this context, neither software nor an algorithm exists as such but only as a perspective abstracting away interactions of hardware elements. Instead of a theory about software, there was a need for "hard(ware) theory" (Parikka 2012, 64). In contrast to this position, Manovich (2013a) stated that *there is only software*. Not referring, at least explicitly, to Kittler, Manovich argues that the term Digital Media is misleading, as the translation of digital content, such as image files, differs tremendously given the used software. Manovich (2013a,

138) writes: "Depending on which software you use to access it, what you can do with the same digital file can change dramatically". Software is to Manovich the defining element of the digital, as it transforms and presents digital data in different ways. The level of software is the relevant one if we want to understand the construction of the digitized world, as it introduces the logic to our mediated interactions. Thus, not the materiality of information is what we should take into consideration but the different logics introduced through computer code. Computer hardware is a generalized machine, but software orders our world. Rossiter (2016) formulated this argument in a similar way in reference to digital infrastructures and code. In his work, Rossiter (2016) describes software as the coordinating force of our modern worlds.

While Manovich does not deny the argument brought forward by Kittler, the relevant level of inquiry is, to him, a different one. He focuses on the level of code for interventions. Yet, the two statements – there is only software and there is no software – brings up the question of what the relation between these different levels is. As Lessig (2006) argued, cyberspace is built from software *and* hardware. If we follow Kittler's argument, then software does not add anything to the situation, it has no quality in itself. Everything is reducible to hardware interactions. There may be software, but even if it is, it does not matter. But what exactly then is the relevance of the ontological status of software, hardware and maybe even runtime?[6]

Computer Language

It is exactly this problem of inquiry that puzzled scholars of software studies. If there is no software, how can we intervene in the construction of a digital society? Galloway (2006) combined these perspectives, arguing that they are not different levels of inquiry – each with their own rationalities – but that they are logically equivalent.

> One should never understand this "higher" symbolic machine as anything empirically different from the "lower" symbolic interactions of voltages through logic gates. They are complex aggregates yes, but it is foolish to think that writing an "if/then" control structure in eight lines of assembly code is any more or less machinic than doing it in one line of C, just as the same quadratic equation may swell with any number of multipliers and still remain balanced. The relationship between the two is technical (Galloway 2006, 321).

There is an interesting chain of translation at work here. Software, like the BIOS, the operating system, or the word processor that is being used to write this text, are abstractions of the computer system, but abstractions that

---

6   This formulation is borrowed from Passoth (2019).

work together through different levels of translations (Hayles 1999). Each level of abstraction is a signifier of the level beneath but also signified by the level above. Machine code is signified on the level of compiler language, which must be translated into it. But then again, machine code signifies the logical operations within the processing unit (ALU). And they not just work together but are logically equivalent. The effect produced by the IT system is the same, no matter where we enter. No level of translation adds or takes away anything, as the different levels of translations only act as an intermediary, not changing the quality of the statements but representing the same logic structure. Following this argument would mean that the level of inquiry becomes irrelevant, as we can enter the chain of translation wherever we want. No matter where we enter, we find (just) another element in a chain of significations. This explains then a direct mapping between statements written in a programming language, such as C++, and the observable effect. Statements written in these programming languages are performative. By writing certain lines of code, the engineer can exert power, define situations, as Kittler argued, and create realities in a direct way. A simple *if … then* statement can change the way software influences the social (and technical) situation (Neyland and Möllers 2017). In short, code is performative through the formulation of written expressions, comparable to language. Bernhard Rieder (2017, 102) argues that "[c]ode […] is the medium to express [these] techniques in terms a computer can understand." Algorithms are the logic structure, code a language to express them. In reference to Kittler's (1990) early work, Parikka writes: "[L]anguage in the age of technical media is not just natural language: it is the new technological and physical regimes introduced by media, such as the typewriter, and later computer software languages, which should methodologically be seen in a similar way" (Parikka 2012, 70). The issue of hardware vs. software is being resolved in this perspective by understanding programming languages as a form to communicate with a computer to mechanically translate the meaning of the statements into (computer) action. In other words, there is just hardware, but we need software to communicate.

The idea of understanding code as a form of language, with its own effects, has been around in Critical Code Studies (CCS) for some time. Cox & McLean (2012) argue that code can and should be understood as such in terms of a speech act as described by Austin (1975). In acting through speech, Austin argued that we can actually produce realities, i.e., act with consequence, when speaking. Austin argued that with performative speech acts, we are "doing things with words." An example to illustrate this form of speech acts: imagine a priest saying the words: *I hereby declare you husband and wife.* Just by saying these words, a fact has not just been invoked but created. The priest acted only by using her voice. In a similar way, code has been read within CCS as such an act of speech. Just by writing down some code, one can construct realities, be it through decisions in software architecture or by letting the computer act according to the formulated script. Analyzing code therefore reveals an act of language which "is active in the world and has a lived body" (Cox and McLean 2012, 110).

By following this argument, we can treat code as language, but it poses a special form of language, as it is executable (Galloway 2004, 165). This creates a distinction between the forms of language Austin had in mind and the way CCS and Software Studies think about code as language. Code, in this perspective, is regarded as more powerful than simple speech, as it performs actions in the world through the execution at runtime level. This has led Hayles (2005) to the distinction between *linguistic performance* and *machinic performance*. And the argument is compelling at first: linguistic performance first and foremost exists in human minds, which then has to be translated into behavior, i.e., there is a process of (subjective) interpretation mediating between input and output. In comparison, the performativity of software is much more direct, as the execution of code happens directly and without mediation (Hayles 2005, 50) or variation (Galloway 2004, 165). Thus, the problem of software vs. no software is resolved, as the different signifiers let you traverse easily from one level to another, without explaining the addition or subtraction of effects. Code is performative, as it can directly be mapped to a considered outcome. However, consequently following the approach of semiotics leads us away from such an understanding. Technology not only signifies different levels of technology but also different collectives that hold this relation stable.

Speech Act and its Collectives

In the argumentation described so far, two important elements are brought together justifying a focused analysis of code. First, the level of inquiry of code or algorithms does not matter insofar as one enters a chain of significations and translations. The code is a representation or abstraction of the levels of execution. Secondly, the translations are deterministic, i.e., the different abstractions are logically equivalent to each other. This allows us ultimately to understand code as a special form of language that is performative in a model in which we can move back and forth between cause and effect without any problems. The relation between coded speech acts and performative effect is machinic. In the perspective of Kittler or Galloway, the translation between code, software and hardware is logically equivalent and therefore lasts the same effects. The translation of abstract algorithmic principles into code and software, however, is contingent. But once implemented in a concrete sequence of code that can be translated into a running program, an algorithm stays stable. This then is the ultimate argument for critical code studies or software studies. If we want to study algorithms, we have to study the concrete code, not some pseudo code representations or principles, nor the actual practices of developers.

However, this conception of machinic performativity and the translation of action into different – empirically equivalent – levels run into some argumentative shortcomings. Adrian Mackenzie (2005) shows in the example of Linux[7] that code could be understood as speech act, performatively producing effects in the social world, without just producing effects in the translation into direct action but by defining the situation. It is worth reflecting on the kind of speech act we are facing here. Normally, Austin is invoked when referring to speech acts that are ends in themselves. Like, "I promise you …". Here the goal of the act is fulfilled as soon the words are spoken. These speech acts are – in the language of Austin – illocutionary. They require no further action to be performative. Perlocutionary speech acts, however, create an effect in a causal link. Here the speech act has the aim of making someone do something based on the spoken words. In terms of code as a speech act, we are dealing (most of the time) with a perlocutionary speech act. The simple statement *print "This text is produced by an perlocutionary speech act";* would print the formulated string on your computer screen – and therefore be perlocutionary. If we, however, see software structure (A. Mackenzie 2005) as a speech act, the effect is already realized in writing the code, ipso facto it is illocutionary. This example illustrates one problem of the argumentation of Galloway (2006). If we understand the different levels as empirically equal, we ignore that – as also argued by Manovich (2013a) – hardware acts as a more generic medium, whereas software re-defines the situation by changing the conditions for subsequent software packages or interactions. At the same time, the structure of a software package or an operating system defines the parameters for developers working with them. Therefore, writing software for Linux works differently than developing software for Windows. This is also true for hardware: it permits certain operations but prohibits others. We may be able to traverse down, but "the whole is always smaller than its parts" (Latour et al. 2012). We can understand the performativity of the code in question only if we take into account each element that is brought into relation with each other.[8]

Thus, conceptualizing code as a speech act raises the question of the sociotechnical context of enunciations that allows it to become performative. That requires us to read Austin's work a bit differently. Instead of focusing on the generative operation of a phrase, such as: "I declare you husband and

---

7   Linux is a prominent operating system, which came out of the FOSS (Free and Open Source Software) movement as a competitor and alternative to proprietary operating systems.

8   There is a wonderful historical example for such a dependency, where Intel Pentium Processors used to calculate float numbers in a different way than AMD processors – which led to many different checking routines on the software side.

wife," one could also ask under what circumstances such a statement becomes true. In other approaches, such as pragmatism and its practice-oriented definition of truth, this question has been addressed more extensively than Austin did. Famously, the Thomas theorem states that "[i]f men define situations as true, they are true in their consequences" (Thomas and Thomas 1928, 572). This formulation addresses an important connection that also Austin already saw: in order to become performative, or "operative" as Austin formulated it, the conditions to have it to have consequences are important. Or in other words: performing such a fact works only if others take up the definition for it to have consequences. Speech acts are not isolated events but the effect of community interactions and shared practice. Thus, speech acts must be made performative in an inter-subjective process of meaning-making (Berger and Luckmann 1967). In her discussion of Austin's theory, Butler (1997) argued that speech acts are the result of a conduct.

> For instance, I may well utter a speech act, indeed, one that is illocutionary in Austin's sense, when I say, "I condemn you," but if I am not in a position to have my words considered as binding, then I may well have uttered a speech act, but the act is, in Austin's sense, unhappy or infelicitous: you escape unscathed. Thus, many such speech acts are "conduct" in a narrow sense, but not all of them have the power to produce the effects or initiate a set of consequences (Butler 1997, 16).

This argument has even been taken a step further by Latour (2009), extending it to the material world that makes speech acts possible. The setup for speaking, taking the spoken up, realizing it, etc. unfolds in a collective of human and non-human actors. Introna (2016) takes up this point to critique the differentiation between machinic and linguistic performativity. He claims that "it is possible to argue that all forms of code must be "executable"— otherwise it would not translate into any form of agency. Legal code, to translate the agency of the legislative body, also needs to be executable. The difference between these various types of "executability" is the nature of the *necessary constitutive conditions* for such execution" (Introna 2016, 26, emphasis in the original). Thus, the reality and executability of every statement, including speech-acts and code fragments, is inherent to an actor-network and not external to it (Latour 1990).

In the following, I will therefore argue, based on my empirical observations, that the stability of algorithms is an achievement of at least two different forms of collective endeavors. First, the entire ecosystem of tools is in itself an element and achievement of a broader community making the implementation and realization of algorithms possible. The performativity of software and code is a result of the interplay of mobilized technological actors, such as compilers or libraries, that enable and limit potential actions of algorithms – or transport already implemented algorithmic techniques themselves. And secondly, algorithms themselves do not come from nowhere but are techniques and discourse elements being mobilized from a whole disciplinary community, e.g., in the form of text books or best practice examples. Thus, algorithmic techniques are a knowledge resource taken up, appropriated, adapted, and fed back into the community. Both forms of community achievements make algorithms matter in actual development projects. And both forms of referencing a community have to be taken into account if we look for the disciplinary enactment of an algorithm.

Instability of stable translations: the always already ordered world

As Passoth (2019) argues, there are at least three different materialities involved when we talk about the digital – hardware, software, and runtime. And they are not logically equivalent. Following Chun (2008), the assumption of stable translations down to the level of transistors is in itself an effect and cannot be taken for granted.[9] Detaching code from the manifold interactions just described renders the conditions of possibility of translating the code into concrete action invisible. She calls such an attitude "the logic of sourcery" (Chun 2008, 9). Without the right CPU, the interpretation of the machine code, stored on a disk, would not work, and without the right compiler, a translation of high-level code into machine code would not work either. But to question the givenness of these actors, and opening the associations that put them in the place, means to find a wide network of other human and non-human actors involved in stabilizing such a trivial thing like the compiler we use to translate the source code of any program into an actual runnable binary file. To do so, we relied on quite many resources that have not been questioned but assumed to be givens. The compiler alone is a tool that has assembled many different actors behind it. The developer community, descriptions of machine code of the processor, many books describing techniques on how to parse, optimize and then translate code expressions.

Or in other words, the assumed stability of translation between algorithms, software, hardware and even electrotechnical signals is an effect and not a given. Instead of seeing source code or algorithms as an essence, we should understand them as a "re-source" (Chun 2008, 9). In the case of the recommender system, the enunciations of the algorithms were based on the Spark Hadoop environment and the iPython notebooks, the server farm with all its soft- and hardware behind it. Without it, the code would not have any effect, and the specific form of it determines the outcome. The stability of these elements is the result of the negotiations of an entire community.

---

9   For everyone who was searching for a bug in her code, just to realize many hours later that the optimization routine of the compiler messed things up, will intuitively understand the argument.

Assembling the recommender system included these systems, which became assembled themselves and were provided "as-is" black boxes.[10]

Algorithmic Infrastructures

As part of the project, Bob, the project leader, and Alice were part of an international working group, experimenting with different forms of recommender algorithms and sharing their algorithms.

> There will be an international working group, which wants to develop an inter-institutional framework for user tracking and experimental development of algorithms. They will utilize iPython notebooks to run it against their system of hadoop and spark. This system allows to upload one's data and algorithms to test it. If it works quite well, it will be possible to define an API endpoint for that setup. Bob explains to us further that it is possible to copy and share these iPython notebooks with others, to let them see what you have done (Fieldnote).

During my field work, I not only learned algorithmic principles people were working with – such as collaborative filtering with explicit and implicit rating, content-based filtering based on stemmed description text, tags and categories, etc. In addition, I also got to know that the algorithm was shared amongst a larger group of researchers and developers, testing implementations on Spark and Hadoop setups, where the code was typed into iPython notebooks. Figure 1 shows one such tool that allowed development within the predefined framework of the European Broadcasting Union (EBU) and that also shows where some of the iPython notebooks are listed. Instead of just learning algorithmic principles, I also had to learn existing and emerging frameworks and infrastructures for machine learning and data-intensive applications.

What happened? I was introduced to a world of already made up tools and setups that were seemingly needed to develop an algorithm and to enable collaboration within the team and beyond. Spark, a programming language often utilized in data heavy projects, was used, not least because of its MLib library. In this library, many machine learning algorithms and utilities are implemented, ready to use and to experiment with. In addition, Hadoop is a software framework used for data-intensive and distributed computing solutions. Both are developed and provided by the Apache Software Foundation. And both were accessed via the iPython notebooks, creating an interface to implement, test, and share possible variations of the recommender

---

10   All of the mentioned software packages are, however, open source. Therefore, the term Black Box does not refer to the technical or legal impossibility (for a further distinction, see Burrel 2016) to look into the technology but indicates that the software comes as a working entity that needs no(t much) more work to be used.

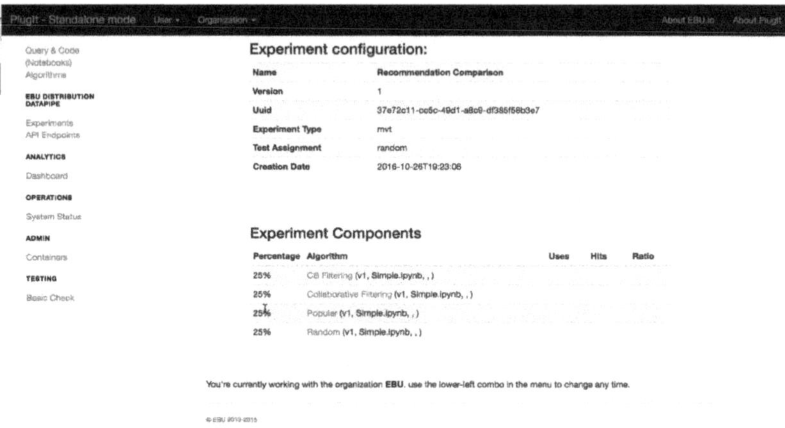

[Figure 1] A screenshot of the development tool to test different recommender algorithms.

algorithm. The development of the recommender system rested not on general tools but utilized specialized development environments to base the project on. These are developed by a specialized expert community in a collaborative way, down to a standard implementation of a recommender technique called collaborative filtering.[11] Thus, the development project started by mobilizing all these different actors into the actual project and to set up an environment in which the recommender system could be developed, tested, shared and discussed. As part of my inquiry I started to setup my own iPython notebooks on a virtual machine to understand what they were doing, and to be able to test things out myself. With every installation process I made sure that the relevant libraries were installed, that I got the right version of the software – or that it was actually compatible with the Linux distribution I was running. This process of mobilization was far from trivial, but it was quintessential to further possible code developments. As Adrian Mackenzie states in relation to software: "Left alone, it tends to fall apart" (A. Mackenzie 2006, 12). Without these steps of making the environment, the recommender system would not be thinkable. Burke (2019) also shares his observation that the computer science community increasingly relies on the (re-)use of shared software libraries or services. Burke (2019) describes that in the realm of machine learning, Tenser Flow has become a well-known and often used framework to realize one's machine learning applications. As a result of the distributed nature of actual algorithmic applications, there is a seeming impossibility to nail down the actual algorithm in an ongoing chain of translation between principles, software, protocols, hardware, electrotechnical representations of bits as volt levels. That is, *the algorithm* in its entirety is not one of these items but all of them. Take away one of these elements, and *the*

---

11   https://spark.apache.org/docs/1.1.0/mllib-guide.html, accessed 25.02.2020

algorithm as an actor ceases to exist. On each step of translation, we find more productive and ordering black boxes in the form of tools, libraries or services.

Software and algorithms do not (only) depend on a top-down ordering but also on an environment that makes the stable translations possible, which delegates power to a protocol or an algorithm in order to achieve an ordering effect. As Latour (2004) in reference to Heidegger argued: it is more productive to move from matters of fact to matters of concern, seeing everything not as an essence in itself but as an achievement of manifold associations. To give an example, the set of different instructions on a machine language level only works because many different entities could be assembled to keep it together, from standardization papers to needs of programmers, hardware characteristics of the processor, encoding methods, down to production sites, etc. Each of them in itself a stabilized and organized black box with its own associations, complexities and arrangements, enrolling "a mass of silent others from which it draws its strength and credibility" (Callon 1987, 96). The stable translation assumes that all of these elements are in place, usable and work in an expected way. Only in a given set of (an always already[12] given) order is the meaningful translation and implementation of algorithms possible. The levels of abstraction are no longer a hierarchy but different black boxes of their own on the same level. Thus, moving between the different moments of translations also means to take into consideration what has been mobilized to stabilize the signified as a black box – and what does this mean for the process of translation in which the chain of signification has been made – and remade over time. This relation between signifiers, mobilization, and stabilization then constructs *the algorithm*. By enrolling different actors in the (action) program of the (technical) program, the characteristic of the final actor is defined a bit more, stabilized and equipped with agency. Understanding now an algorithm as an effect of all these elements leads us to another conclusion. The performativity of an algorithm refers back and builds on the delegated black boxes of a collective. Thus, the mobilization of these productive actors makes the development team within the broadcaster much bigger. By association, not only Alice, Bob, and I were working on the algorithm, but many more people involved in the management, debugging, patching and further development of the used tools and frameworks. As a result, the way the recommender system was realized has also been shaped by these actors. The development of the system had to be embedded in an already existing (and very productive)

---

12   Habermas (1989) uses this expression to show that our way to see, experience, and act
      in the world is a result of a given modus of being in it. Through socialization we acquire
      the knowledge that guides our experiencing and acting of and in the world. I extend the
      notion here toward the material world or world of tools as an always already ordered
      world that dis- and enables certain forms of (inter-)action.

socio-technical order.[13] In this section, I reconstructed the algorithm as a collective enactment based on the technological setup found in the development situation. However, to fully grasp the phenomenon we also need to look at the discursive enactments of algorithms. Therefore, in the next section, I will discuss algorithms as narrated actors.

Algorithmic Discourses: Narrating Algorithmic Techniques

Latour argues that Austin's distinction of declarative and performative speech acts is only based on grammar and short-term interactions, but is not "following the whole regime of enunciation" (Latour 2009, 225) to make the difference between the two visible. As already discussed, the production of a performativity hinges on a certain order that is maintained and in which the enunciation takes place. A fact is not created just by saying something. Instead, the act of speaking must be taken up by other actors in order to believe, contest, or act according to the just provided offer of a fact. Speech acts are inherently inter-subjective. In terms of code, this can be observed in the wide-going order and assemblage of actors, including soft- and hardware components, other developer communities, etc. However, there is a second dimension in which the enunciation must be embedded. If the performativity is only effective in an always already ordered world, and needs interpretation, how do the recipients of performative statements understand these? And how does an individual come across the idea of speaking these words in the first place? Austin also acknowledges that it connects to a wider system of social norms, beliefs and knowledge (Austin 1975, 14), and calls these forms of knowledge "conventions" and "rituals" which are well known within a given society. As such, in order to know about the possibility of a performative effect within a certain ordering, one ought first to have learned that such words relate to the position of the speaker and the range of possible formulations. The performativity of a speech act, as Austin (1975) imagined it, refers to a shared knowledge that makes the effect of the spoken word possible.[14]

What does this mean for an understanding of code as speech acts? While the performativity of code still has to be taken into account, the agency of

13   It is important to note here that social order in terms of ANT is based on the critique of macro-structural social theories and situated interactionist theories alike. While drawing heavily from Ethnomethodologists ideas of a practically achieved social order, delegation of non-human actors is conceptualized as a possibility to establish trans-situational order(ings) (Latour 1994).

14   Of course, as Butler (1997) remarks in her comparison between Austin and Althusser, the person addressed by speech act does not necessarily need to understand or agree with the speech act. However, as long as someone takes up the speech act, it still has an effect. Thus, the individual producing an effect and the addressed subject are not necessarily the same entity.

code always refers to a social and material context, as "computer code never actually exists or operates apart from a prior set of practices which allows it to do things" (A. Mackenzie 2005, 76). Part of that assemblage of making speech acts effective, or even probable to happen, is the embeddedness of ideas, code fragments, etc. within social communities, in which these stable acts of doing things with words become stabilized through repetition. As Butler argues:

> If a performative provisionally succeeds (and I will suggest that "success" is always and only provisional), then it is not because an intention successfully governs the action of speech, but only because that action echoes prior actions, and accumulates the force of authority through the repetition or citation of a prior and authoritative set of practices. It is not simply that the speech act takes place within a practice, but that the act is itself a ritualized practice (Butler 1997, 51).

As such, the constant repetition and circulation stabilizes code as speech acts and makes them (disciplinary) discourses. In accordance with this observation, Wendy Chun argues that software is always embedded in structures of knowledge-power (Chun 2008, 4). This is also true for algorithms as abstract procedures. While an algorithm lasts effects, a sole focus on code and the run-time materiality or *the algorithm* itself would therefore obscure the fact that algorithms are also an effect of an interplay of diverse other actors, epistemic positions and discourses. As Mackenzie puts it:

> Materially, code is only one element in the diagram of machine learning. It displays, with greater or lesser degrees of visibility, relations among a variety of forces (infrastructures, scientific knowledges, mathematical formulations, etc.). It is aligned by and exposes multiple institutional, infrastructural, epistemic, and economic positions (A. Mackenzie 2017, 22).

As I argued at the beginning of the chapter, when taking a computer science class on algorithms, we get an intuitive understanding about what an algorithm is, how we can use them and in which terms to think about them. As such, code and code fragments are hardly ever a simple speech act without repetition or circulation. A whole discipline with study programs, conferences, journals, standardization committees, etc. is connected with the algorithms that we normally talk about. A simple example for an insertion sort, taken from Cormen et al. (2013, 18), is shown in figure 2.

When we look at this representation of an algorithm, many things are implicitly assumed. For example, the expression *A.length* is a signifier to the size of the set that is to be ordered, assuming that we do know the size of the given set. A, the set to order, is not defined, but it is assumed that it is given. Other formulations refer to known elements in programming practice, such as the *while* statement. If you have any experience in programming, you know

```
INSERTION-SORT(A)
1   for j = 2 to A.length
2       key = A[j]
3       // Insert A[j] into the sorted sequence A[1 .. j − 1].
4       i = j − 1
5       while i > 0 and A[i] > key
6           A[i + 1] = A[i]
7           i = i − 1
8       A[i + 1] = key
```

[Figure 2] Insertion Sort taken from Cormen et al. (2013, 18)

that this refers to the formulation of an execution loop. Other than you might have learned in your math classes, the equals sign here is not an expression that two terms are equal, but instead it is an operator copying the result of the right term into the variable that is named on the left side. In other words, the formulation of an algorithm refers to disciplinary knowledge that makes it possible to understand the expressions used to describe a specific algorithm. Without ever having taken a computer science class or an introduction to programming paradigms, the formulation at hand could hardly be deciphered.

At the same time, the representation is a form of discursive element insofar as it shows the students of computer science classes how a prototypical *insertion sort* looks like.[15] This example has not been chosen randomly but because it is part of a prominent text book on algorithms and data structures. If you are uncertain how a specific algorithm works (or should work), you can always turn to these textbooks. They will show you how sorting algorithms are put together. Distributing these forms of representations as disciplinary knowledge gives these techniques durability and also legitimacy of implementations. When someone doubts your implementation of an algorithm, you can always mobilize these text books, best practices, scripts from your university studies, etc. as allies to back up your program. And while this example is simple in its nature, the principle is important to the computer sciences. *Programming patterns*, way more complex than insertion sort, are being thought and distributed in programmer communities as solutions and structuring elements to your code.[16] As such, when turning to computer code, it is important to understand how developers "do things with words" (Austin 1975), but evenly important is the context behind the code fragment that explains why these lines of code have been mobilized and not others, why this machine learning technique, and not another one, and what difference

---

15   There is an interesting overlap in the ideas how social collectives stabilize in discourse theory and Tarde's conception of society being the result of imitation. Looking at algorithms as discourse elements could then even open the way to a theory of digital isomorphism.

16   I will not go into detail here, as it might become too technical, but if you are interested, search for singleton pattern, which is a good start.

it makes. An algorithm is not only determined by the lonely programmer. Instead, the principles and logics of algorithms are distributed and stabilized by different means, such as text books, libraries, and scientific communities. The implementation of algorithms "draws on rich reservoirs of knowledge made available by disciplines such as computer science and software engineering" (B. Rieder 2017, 101). Algorithmic applications emerge always out of a coding culture with common approaches, methods and paradigms. In the project, I experienced this many times when I was confronted with standard text books on recommender systems and machine learning. Whenever I was asking for *the algorithm*, I was confronted with another textbook, yet another paper, explaining the algorithmic approach. I was told about contributions on the ACM RecSys conference. *The algorithm*, in that sense, consisted of many different discursive devices that have been mobilized within the development process.

Looking for the Algorithm

When I started my inquiry into *the democratic recommender algorithm* in early 2016, I was too – unknowingly – undecided as to what kind of algorithm I was searching for. Having experience in implementing and analyzing algorithms myself, I wanted to look at code, play with development environments and APIs. But I was supposed to find something else. There I was, sitting in a room full of software developers and computer scientists. I got my own desk, my own key card and had been introduced as the project's own sociologist. Where should I go now? Where would I be able to find that algorithm? I wanted to understand the inner workings of the procedure and – like in the old days, when I used to work in IT – read the code, drink lots of Club Mate, and reconstruct the meaning of hundreds or thousands of lines of code. I even had access to the documentation repository of the project. I started to look into it. What I found was not the expected algorithm but descriptions, diagrams and references to literature.

The things referring to *the algorithm* that I was searching for were mere representations of what I had in mind. Figure 3 shows an early conceptual idea of the system's architecture. As can be seen, the recommender system was envisioned as quite central. At least, now I knew how it was conceptually embedded into the whole system. But still, I wanted the crunch dimension of the recommender – how could I get there? Luckily, my position in the project was primarily aligned with the developer of the recommender system: Alice. Alice was responsible for developing the algorithm and to integrate it into the overall product structure of the video-on-demand platform. I asked her how the algorithm works and where I could find it. As a result, I received links to slides, chapters, and articles. I received the following lines after some weeks

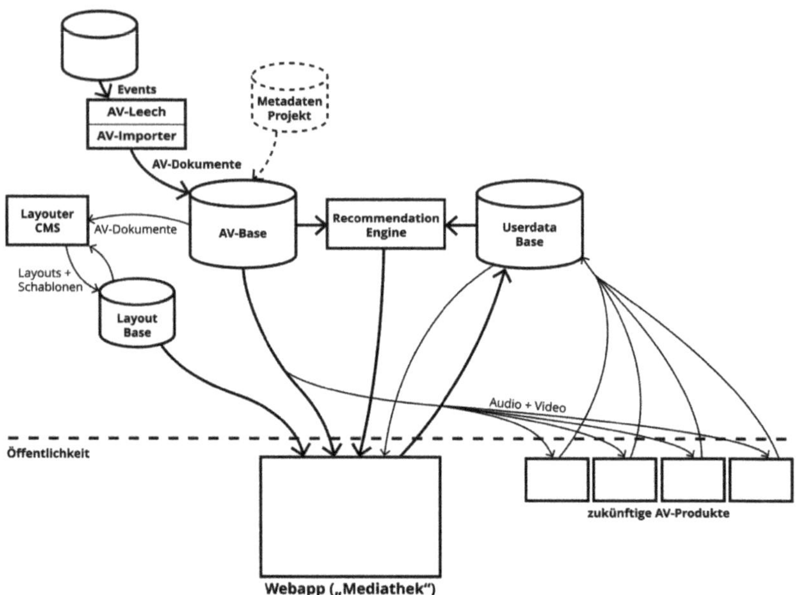

[Figure 3] Reconstruction of an early conceptual description of the project

into the project from Alice, providing me with a paper on collaborative filtering with implicit feedback:

> Hi! After you have read this article you understand what collaborative filtering with explicit feedback is. But: we are actually dealing with implicit feedback (users don't rate videos directly) and so we have to use different approaches :simple_smile: This article explains how to do collaborative filtering with implicit feedback and why it is different. If you feel like it is useful now, you can read it. But probably what you are doing now with clusters is more important - I didn't get around to trying it myself yet. See you on Friday!

> PDF
> CollaborativeFilteringWithImplicitFeedback.pdf
> 288 kB PDF — Click to view

Not only Alice and I were working on that problem. Instead, we were in a room filled with computer scientists, mathematicians, and engineers, transported to us via immutable mobiles of an entire community of academics and practitioners. The algorithm that I was searching for consisted of code lines, waiting to be deconstructed by me. However, what I dealt with in my time as a discipline was an accumulation of visualizations of vector spaces, optimization formulas, and network diagrams.

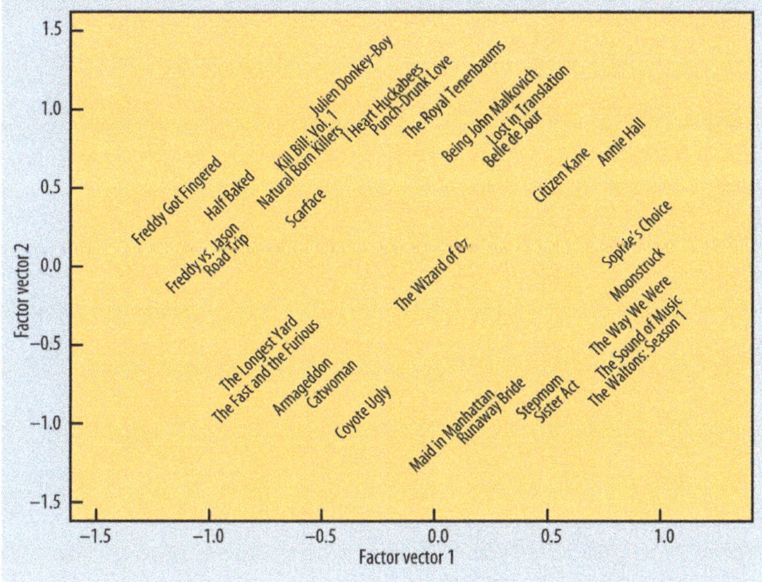

[Figure 4] Snippet from a paper provided to me (Koren, Bell, & Volinsky, 2009)

Figure 4 shows a short snippet from a paper I was provided by Alice to understand a recommender technique, how it works, where the problems are and what we need would we decide to implement the technique. The context of the paper was the Netflix Prize. The fact that it was given to me by the developers as a reference for the algorithm shows its relevance for the project. In my time as a discipline I was provided even more literature and references to slides from academic and educational presentations. These references included the chapter on recommender systems from "Mining of Massive Datasets"[17], a text book for the Stanford Computer Science program.[18] I also got slides from conferences discussing and explaining these techniques and their problems.[19]

What happened? Instead of providing me with the actual code base for the recommender, I was given material with no direct relation to the algorithm to be developed. And yet it was an important step on my way to understand the project, the actual challenge we were facing. Without that, I would not have been able to grasp what the recommender – in the terms of the developers – is or is about. Instead of finding files filled with source code, I was finding myself surrounded by literature and slides from computer science, inhabited by

17   *http://infolab.stanford.edu/~ullman/mmds/ch9.pdf*, accessed: 24.01.2020
18   The book can be downloaded for free from the website of www.mmds.org and states on the home page: "The book is based on Stanford Computer Science course CS246: Mining Massive Datasets (and CS345A: Data Mining)." (www.mmds.org, accessed: 24.01.2020).
19   E.g., *http://ijcai13.org/files/tutorial_slides/td3.pdf*, accessed: 25.01.2020

mathematical formulations, matrices and pseudo code. But according to Alice, this all was quintessential to understand what the recommender algorithm does and is. I felt like I was put back in my time at the university, where you first learn to code a Hello World program – a piece of code which has no practical application, and whose existence is purely educational. However, something else can be learned from that interaction and my personal transformation. I was not let loose on the code, but Alice mobilized many other resources from outside the organization or her office. Concepts, ideas, and techniques from the Recommender System Handbook and articles from developers of Netflix were taken up, made relevant for the project at hand and even for my inquiries as a social scientist. Alice and the other developers mobilized many different resources from universities, conferences (such as the ACM RecSys Conference) and text books to give *the algorithm* an initial and provisional shape. By doing so, the recommender systems became concrete in a sense that the techniques applied became durable. The assemblage, or actor-network, that was imported into our offices defined the features of the to-be-implemented algorithm. This was a first important step in defining what the algorithmic system will look like in the end and to make it tangible to the involved persons. However, with giving the technique of the recommender durability and concreteness, it also got a certain resist-ability, which made a whole class of further translations and transformations unlikely. By defining certain features of the recommender algorithm, also an environment of tools, infrastructures, and interactions was assumed (a detailed description will be given in the next chapter). The algorithm went from fiction to contingency. By standing on the shoulder of giants, the algorithm was still more than one but certainly less than many.

Disciplinary discourse plays an important role in the enactment of *the algorithm*. Through taking up the techniques and knowledges created and delegated by a community, algorithms gain form and – to a certain extent – durability. Thus, discourse – different from structuralist ideas of Foucault (1991), where discourse is omnipresent and self-sustaining – here is selectively taken up, treated as resource, and comes in materialized form – via text books, articles, conference papers.[20] Thus, it is the practice of mobilizing discourse that connects accounts, e.g., texts, to a situated order (Lynch 2000, 34) and defines relevant actors, as they are "assigned a 'role' to speak or be spoken for" (Passoth and Rowland 2010, 892). By doing so, the algorithm – as the enacted actor – is being narrated in the development project together with the whole community the developers are turning to. In the end, it is not us who has to turn to computer science, but the field actors do so themselves. We merely follow the actors.

20   For an ANT-driven critique on Foucault's discourse concept, see also Law (1994, 106). This critique is also oddly in line with the arguments Sartre brought forward against Foucault in an interview (Pingaud 1966).

The algorithm was not only a local enactment but constituted by different actors that were mobilized (by Alice) but also delegated (by all the other invisible people in the room). And although we did not apply an *a priori* definition of the algorithm as an abstract principle taken from computer science or software engineering, somehow, we are back at exactly this place. Mackenzie invites us to go beyond the local setup, shifting the focus on what is being mobilized beyond the concrete situation, when we follow the code "as it moves across the terrain where the different forces, formations, dynamisms, knowledges, bodily habits, [...] and things associated with code are situated" (A. Mackenzie 2006, 10). What *the algorithm* is and does depends on the situated enactment and the mobilized delegations outside the actual situation, thus determining also the chosen level of concreteness of the algorithm in question and its durability. Through the enactment of *the algorithm* it subsequently gains concreteness – it becomes a thing.

Putting Algorithms into Context

Coming back to our question at the beginning, asking "what actually *is* an algorithm?" (Ziewitz 2016, 4, emphasis in original), we – it seems – do not come to a satisfying conclusion. There is a seeming impossibility to talk about algorithms in an adequate way. Should we move away from computer science and software development altogether? Instead of abandoning the term of *the algorithm*, it might make sense to rephrase the question: "Just what is it that we have in view when we focus on 'algorithms' as the central object of analytic attention?" (Dourish 2016, 2). What an algorithm is cannot be decided with an essentialist perspective, as it keeps slipping through our fingers. As Gillespie (2014) argues, we should resist putting algorithms in the driver seat. Instead, it might be more productive to understand an algorithm as an achievement, as an entity of social materiality – as an enactment. The question then is no longer what an algorithm is or where do we – as social scientists – locate it, but in which situations do the actors in the field open which black boxes to tinker with the otherwise stabilized and ordered chains of translation to achieve an effect. What is made relevant in the interaction? What became a matter of concern when dealing with algorithms?

This might be a good moment – or maybe as good as anyone – to reflect on what the notion of enactment is doing here for us. In this chapter, I was much concerned with showing that *the algorithm* is an object of a whole collective, from which techniques, scripts, and other resources are being mobilized. Treating algorithms as narratives, and extending semiotic and linguistic ideas, implicitly brought us close to the notion of performativity. And yes: algorithms and algorithmic techniques can be understood as performative effects of a socio-technical system. However, the notion of enactment occurred repeatedly – not only but also following Seaver who urges us to "understand algorithms as enacted by the practices used to engage with them" (Seaver 2017, 5). In this, he follows Mol's (2002) account of the enactment of ontology – of reality itself. Mol thereby moves beyond the notion of construction, as to her this idea of construction implies the idea of stability once the object in question has been constructed. Instead, enactment argues that the identity of an object is always contingent, depending on how localized practices engage with it. Instead of just producing different perspectives on the same object, the object itself multiplies. This also reflects a long and ongoing discussion between radical versions of social constructivism and realism, raising issues about the epistemological question whether our sensations of the world can be taken for granted in order to build a coherent and appropriate vision of the world. Mol, resolves the issue at hand in the formulation that objects are "more than one – but less than many" (Mol 2002, 55). Contingency is included in the enactment – but not an arbitrary attribution of meaning. Materiality – or more philosophically: ontology – limits the possibilities of enactments. Ontology is not just the result of one-directional practices but subject(s)-object(s) interactions. All of them are real, all of them are enacted. And this is why Mol revokes the term of performativity, as it implies for her that there is a back-stage where we can find the real thing.

As discussed earlier, however, the interaction with the object – here an algorithmic technique – alone does not delimit the ways of enactments but also the whole socio-technical structure around it. As Latour (1994) argues, there is hardly a situation in which we do not encounter delegated actors to influence, shape, restrict, or enrich our possibilities of action. The same is true for its development. We are constantly confronted with all kinds of tools, such as compilers, development environments, databases, etc. And each of them is a socio-technical black-box, consisting itself of many human and non-human actors. These black boxes are productive, they enable the development and realization of the project, but at the same time, they also restrict the possibilities. This is especially true for software libraries, where ready implemented routines and algorithms are provided to include them in one's own software project. As Latour once wrote: "the whole is always smaller than its parts" (Latour et al. 2012, 591). Thus, an algorithm has to be embedded in a given ordering of tools and infrastructures that make the performativity of code possible in the first place. As such, the development project is not only a situated enactment but mobilized many different actors – as black boxes. Algorithms only work on specific constellations of these actors. Shor's algorithm (Shor 1994), for example, is specifically designed for quantum computers, where it assumes a given configuration of other actors. It assumes a specific order.

Further, the algorithm is a discourse device, referencing to an entire community of developers. The local enactment of the algorithm is connected to and part of the ordering practices of a whole discipline. Through textbooks, scientific articles, conference proceedings and slides, even techniques provided by developers at Netflix, algorithms are also elements of a professional culture of interaction and mobilization of resources. These disciplinary discourses give them a shape, and provide the developers with a point of departure for the realization of such an algorithm. These algorithmic techniques thereby come as abstract solutions to abstract problems. And to apply them, to create a productive solution that has indeed an effect, specific disciplinary knowledge is assumed to read, understand, and realize these techniques.

Looking at actual development practices thereby is an important starting point to understand one enactment of an algorithm as an ordering effect. Algorithms do not come from nowhere, but they are also no objects of pure technology. There is a whole discipline and collective that makes very practical efforts to produce environments and disciplinary discourse to make algorithms possible. And as such, we return to our starting point. In order to understand the emergence of algorithms as (techno-)social actors, we must mobilize computer science and software development – but in a different way. We end up in a situation where we do not look for *the algorithm* as an essence but start our inquiries in how *doing algorithms* works. As Dourish argued, we then start to understand algorithms "as objects of professional practice for computer scientists, software engineers, and system developers" (Dourish 2016, 9). Following the practices of the development team then led us to look beyond the current situation, the current organization. The development project was deeply embedded in the community of IT developers and the discipline of computer science. Instead of developing the product on their own, a whole collective of present and (seemingly) absent actors were working alongside us.

Developing an algorithm is to mobilize different actors and relate them to each other, bringing them in order to each other. In tinkering with the set of delegated actors, including tools, knowledges, and techniques, the developers re-align and re-order these actors in order to produce an effect. Where do we locate *the algorithm* then? Everywhere. The algorithm is not just the technique, nor is it the actual code, nor is it to be found in the tools. Only when all of them come together does an algorithm emerge as an *actor with agency*. The question what an algorithm is therefore shifts to the question how these different elements are (re-)assembled. As the developers tinker on the different levels which are important to them in order to enact an algorithm and its effects. To find *the algorithm*, we do not look in a pre-defined place, we do not open just source code files, nor do we just read the algorithmic techniques. Instead, we trust the knowledge of the developers in place. What becomes relevant for an algorithm then means following the actors, namely, those that are given a status of an actor through practice, discourse, and ordering. An algorithm may be a material artifact that is locatable (Dourish 2016), but it is also much more. It is the enactment of an entire discipline. Instead of doing computer science, we follow the associations of the algorithm into the communities of computer science and software development. The materiality of an algorithm is then defined as what matters as and for the algorithm. However, what I have discussed so far is only one possible enactment of an algorithm. And as we will see in the next chapters, it cannot define the characteristics of a stabilized algorithm in isolation. Instead, it is one enactment that requires coordination with other enactments, other forms of doing the algorithm. In what follows, I will therefore describe two more enactments and how they relate to each other.

4

Algorithmic Institutions

Sir, I think I speak for everyone when I say: To hell with our orders. – Data, Star Trek: First Contact

An important aspect of every development project that incorporates any kind of machine learning or data-intensive application is the – often pressing – question, where the data that is being processed should come from. The same happened unsurprisingly in the development project of the recommender system. In order to produce recommendations, we needed data sets to calculate the machine learning models. Within the academic discussion, Dourish (2016) takes up the notion from Wirth (1975) that *Programs = Algorithms + Data Structures* to make us aware that data structures are "relations that give them [i.e. algorithms] meaning and animate them" (Dourish 2016, 2). This animation of algorithms as actors is contingent and relies on the data that is being utilized in order to build software programs as materialized forms of algorithms. However, the mobilization and construction of data is thereby a difficult and challenging endeavor in itself. In addition, the chosen algorithms must be brought into alignment with the available or selected data structures. Taking a material-semiotic perspective, I will therefore argue that each element – the data structures and the algorithms – anticipates and references specific social orderings that have to be brought into accordance via *algorithmic reflexivity*. I will discuss the problems that the mobilized algorithmic techniques encountered and what implicit social (and semiotic) order these actants were assuming. For this I will be looking at these entities through the notion of inscription (Akrich 1992) and reflexivity (Lynch 2000).

The concept of inscription allows us to understand algorithmic techniques as artifacts that transport assumptions of a specific social order, materialized in the formulated problem to be solved and the available data to solve it. I will illustrate this point in revisiting the two recommender techniques, collaborative filtering and content-based filtering, and reconstruct the assumptions carried by these algorithmic techniques. The notion of reflexivity, as used in ethnomethodology, complements this picture by referring to processes in which available data has to be re-interpreted or normalized according to the language of the algorithm (Ziewitz 2017). I will then discuss three vignettes in which we tried to produce data for the different recommender algorithms. These cases thereby illustrate that the socio-technical structures of the public broadcaster already in place referred to specific forms of social ordering that were not compatible with the ordering processes assumed by the algorithmic technique mobilized in the project's context. We started our inquiry into the depths of the organizational and technical structures of the public broadcaster equipped with different algorithmic techniques and the assumption that there will be plenty of data. However, the journey was more cumbersome than we anticipated in the beginning. Data was available, yet, for some reason, the socio-technical structure that enabled the production of large archives of video and meta-data collections seemed to hinder us in realizing the recommender system. This eventually led to the construction of new organizational structures that allowed us to produce data that was enabling the algorithmic system. In the end, it became an issue of how we, as the development project, tried to integrate the algorithm into the organizational and institutionalized structure of the public broadcaster by matching these algorithmic scripts with the socio-technical order of the institution. The socio-technical structure that the public broadcaster as an organization *explicitly* realized and the socio-technical structure that the algorithmic technique *implicitly* assumed were not translatable out of the box. As a result, we had to negotiate terms, explain problems, and adapt the organization as well as the algorithm in order to be able to realize the algorithmic system. In short, the algorithm had to become an institutionalized actor which had to be integrated into the social order of the organization.

Exploring Algorithmic Scripts

Before discussing the difficile entanglements and interactions of different orderings, it is important to understand how different algorithmic techniques operate – and what assumptions are built into these solutions. Algorithmic techniques are not only technological actors who are neutral or detached but artifacts that are being designed and stabilized via a heterogeneous community of developers and computer scientists. The design of these algorithms is thereby open and must be actualized with other elements, such as data structures (Dourish 2016). However, the algorithmic techniques do carry specific assumptions about the social world in which they will operate. In a first step, it is therefore necessary to reconstruct the assumptions of the algorithmic techniques that were used within the software development project. To do so, I will refer to ANT and the theoretical concept of scripts and inscriptions, as described by Akrich (1992) and Latour (1992), as these allow us to conceptualize further the inscribed assumptions found in the algorithmic techniques.

A central premise of Actor-Network-Theory is that non-human entities do have agency within interaction processes and can produce regulatory effects and enable actions within social situations (Latour 1994). Thus, the durability and resistibility of non-human actors itself has effects on possible interactions. These effects, however, are not random or given by nature but are produced by the makers of material artifacts and inscribed in them. Latour names this the *action program* of an artifact (Latour 1994). The design of an artifact reflects the ideas and expectations of the developers of how an interaction will and should play out. Thus, the material artifact incorporates an action program that represents an imaginary of social order(ing). Latour describes these effects in many different examples. An automatic door closer (J. Johnson 1988)[1], which forces the users of the door to adjust their pace and timing if they want to pass the door unharmed. Speed bumps that regulate driving speed, without relying on legal operations (Latour 1994). And heavy hotel keys constantly reminding the hotel guest to drop them off at the reception (Latour 1990). What is common to all these examples is that a) the material actors have been delegated a task to fulfill a regulatory effect in a given situation, and b) they incorporate assumptions about the situation at hand, e.g., the hotel keys hold the assumption that it is too cumbersome for guests to carry the keys along. By inscribing ideas of potential interactions, the developers also inscribe in the artifact their ideas about the situation in which these material actors are being used and interacted with. The developers become social scientists themselves, as they imagine the interaction structure of and with their products (Callon 1987). In these writings of ANT, artifacts produce social order through their materiality and their interactions with other actors.

Other contributions complicated this picture. Akrich (1992) distinguishes between processes of inscriptions from processes of de-inscriptions and pre-scriptions. Inscriptions describe the process of incorporating scripts and action programs into the artifacts as described earlier. De-Inscriptions conceptualize the process of actually using the artifact and interacting with

---

1   It might be worth mentioning here that Jim Johnson, the author of the Door Closer article, actually is a synonym that Bruno Latour used to publish the article. In fact, the article became quite a central writing for ANT scholars, which makes this an entertaining as well as interesting point of reference.

it – which can deviate from the ideas of the artifact's designers. This breaks with the assumption that social order is the product of non-human materiality but takes artifacts and their scripts as one (important) element of ordering processes (see also Law 1992). In the process of de-inscription, the artifact itself gets actualized and the meaning and functionality ascribed changes based on the situated uses. This prepared also the basis for later post-ant conceptions of enactment and multiplicity (Mol 2002). The ontology of an object – and therefore also its regulatory force – gets enacted in situated practices (see also Law 2002).[2] As Akrich (1992) argues further, – and shows in her discussion of the expansion of an electrical network – technological scripts do not come unequipped or alone. They are accompanied by documents, explanations, contextualizations, advice, and often also formal procedures. Akrich (1992) called that pre-scriptions.[3] Thus, pre-scriptions transport knowledge about the normative ideas of the developers and can be grasped best as discursive elements. As a result, the assumptions of the developers that inscribe their image of the situation in which the technological artefact or technique is being applied are made explicit and are transported to the situation in which the technology is being used. The artifact does not occur alone but with many allies already. This embeddedness of the artifact has later been conceptualized further by Law (1994), who argues that social ordering is the complex interrelation between discourse, problems, and networks of materiality. All of these come together already in the notion of scripts.

Algorithms, in their complexity, can also be analyzed with this notion of scripts. As discussed in the previous chapter, the implementation of algorithms relies on the disciplinary enactment of algorithmic techniques – which also includes pre-given scripts, pseudo code and ready-made libraries that are part of this enactment. Algorithmic techniques do incorporate specific scripts with assumptions about the available data, its meaning, and how data and algorithmic technique can be put in relation with each other (B. Rieder 2017). A sorting algorithm assumes that we have some sort of (at least) ordinal values, with an identifiable index for their position. Otherwise traversing over n elements, comparing element i with element $i+1$ (as long $i<n$) would not be possible. The algorithmic techniques do not only assume a given set of datafied descriptions of a world, on which they should and could be applied to, but these assumptions also formulate the very problem in the first place. The sorting algorithm also assumes that we want *to sort* the (at least) ordinal values. The problem definition and the assumed data available cannot be separated. Recommender algorithms act on similar assumptions, solving

2   A certain proximity to the semiotics of Peirce ([1900] 2010) cannot be denied here, although ANT traditionally is based on other semiotic traditions, esp. Greimas (1983).

3   That is not to mix up with prescriptions, which are the (imagined) actions that are allowed or denied by the artifact's script, or pre-inscriptions, which are the assumed competences of the artifact's users. For a summary, see Akrich and Latour (1992).

the problem of finding and recommending similar items for a user in a given data-universe – based on some form of comparability – which can be seen as relevant for a given user. However, different recommender techniques come with their own ideas of comparability and relevance – and therefore require different forms of de-inscription.

The assumptions inscribed into algorithmic techniques are thereby much more abstract but are nonetheless consequential for the subsequent process of implementation. Yet, algorithmic scripts differ in two important aspects from the scripts discussed by Akrich (1992). First, they are much more easily available, as algorithms are expressible in code fragments of pseudo-code. Thus, reconstructing the scripts very often means *reading* the (code) scripts (see also A. Mackenzie 2017). They are also very often accompanied by pre-scriptions, like text books or articles, explaining the principles behind them that are not just artifact-specific but have the status of standard references. In the project, the Recommender System Handbook was such a stable and standardized reference, which Alice handed me to learn about the topic. But she also referred to it regularly in our conversations. Secondly, however, algorithms are actualized when combined with data. For example, the same algorithmic technique of *near repeat patterns* is used to predict earthquakes or burglaries (see Pöchhacker 2016). The technique is in both cases the same, but the results in terms of power, social ordering and meaning differ tremendously. This creates a situation in which the selection of data sources requires further interpretation and production of data by the developers and the socio-technical system of which the algorithm will become a part of. As Dourish (2016) and Gillespie (2014) argue: in order to understand the power of algorithms and code, we must see the intersections of these elements with data and databases. I argue that combining algorithmic techniques with data is a further process of inscription – through data production and application. By combining an algorithmic technique with specific data structures alters the scripts of an algorithm, as it changes the way the implemented artifact interacts with the world. As a result, understanding algorithmic agency means reading algorithmic scripts but also observing the moments (and problems) of combining them with data. The de-inscription of the algorithmic technique thereby becomes an inscription process in the making of the algorithmic system – without going back to the original designers of the algorithmic techniques.[4] This results in a situation in which reading the code as a form on inscription alone does not suffice. Instead, we also have to refer to the actual practices of combining the algorithmic scripts with plenty of other things

---

4   While this seems to be very specific for the case of algorithms, this can also be formu-
      lated as a general principle. Every engineering practice is based on always-already avail-
      able tools, which are in themselves artifacts that carry inscriptions. Thus, in the practice
      of producing technological artifacts, we adapt and combine the different scripts of our
      tools, resulting in an – often black-boxed – actor with its own script.

that go into running code. It is important to note here, however, that the combination of algorithmic techniques with other elements, especially data structures, is not arbitrary but contingent. Thus, we can combine algorithmic techniques with some different forms of data structures but not with all of them.

The actual characteristic of the algorithmic system thereby depends (also) on localized re-interpretation of data, which is not always straightforward. Bringing together algorithmic techniques with data requires the coordination of different interpretation practices in the implementation of an algorithm. Ziewitz (2017) explored the notion of the algorithm from an ethnomethodological perspective. In giving a group of people, including himself, the task to navigate the city of Oxford by the instructions of an algorithm, the problems in applying the algorithmic techniques became available for (critical) scrutiny. Ziewitz describes the process of defining the algorithm as the following:

> We start by listing a number of ideas: take every third on the left, take right turns only, turn in the opposite direction if you see a yellow backpack, or take the street that starts with the letter closest to "A" in the alphabet. All these seem useful in that they define events that trigger our algorithm to produce directions. However, they also appear to be somewhat arbitrary. After some discussion, we settle on the following procedure: [...] At any junction, take the least familiar road. Take turns in assessing familiarity. If all roads are equally familiar, go straight (Ziewitz 2017, 4, my emphasis).

The formulation of the instructions on how to choose a path through the city seemed clear enough. However, when applying it, he encountered manifold problems. What makes a road a road, how do we define a junction, how do we handle Y-junctions, where going straight is not possible? In the course of executing this path-finding algorithm, its interpreter[5] came into many ambiguous situations that needed clarification to make them applicable for the algorithm. They required interpretation.

> As we had to parse our observations in a constant struggle to re-specify the situation in the image of the self-imposed constraint, the walk was not so much a case of recognizing patterns but an exercise in explicating observations in the language of the algorithm while figuring out whether and to what extent they could facilitate the job at hand – a determination

---

5   There is an entertaining convergence of terminology, as in computer science an interpreter actually is a piece of software that interprets a given set of instructions and immediately executes them. Classical examples are the BASIC language, or shell scripting environments like CSH or BASH.

that itself was subject to the contingencies of real-time navigation (Ziewitz 2017, 10).

Data that we feed into any algorithm is understood here as "explicating observations in the language of the algorithm" (Ziewitz 2017, 10). In order to make the algorithm work, data was re-interpreted and the meaning of the assumed data, as provided by the algorithmic script, got updated in the situation. Instead of *just* making the analog reality readable to the algorithm, the act of doing so includes a translation of the observations and experiences of the involved translator into the categories used by the algorithm. While we may not be able to pin *the algorithm* down, we can understand what the affordances and inscriptions of an algorithmic technique are in order to work in a specific setting. For a successful interaction with algorithms, we must be able to speak in their language. And in the process of doing so, the script and agency of the algorithm is updated at the same time. The struggles observed in translating the city and its structure into something that is understandable to the algorithm but also useful to the users – in this case the researchers – meant a continuous process of repairing a situation that was on the brink of collapse. This translation of observations into an algorithmic logic was one major problem for the software development team – one that is normally discussed under the term of *good data*. A concern that can be found in all data-driven endeavors (e.g., Mützel, Saner, and Unternährer 2018). The interpretation of available data and the suggestion of what even counts as data is therefore inherently important for algorithmic systems – but depending on the mobilized techniques, it is so in radically different ways.

Situating Recommender Techniques

Algorithmic systems are contingent products of the combination of algorithmic techniques and data structures. However, the possible combinations are not arbitrary but must be able to translate the assumptions of the algorithmic technique's scripts with the available data structures. As a result, it is important to reconstruct the inscriptions of the utilized recommender algorithms. Doing so will allow us to understand the issues the project faced when trying to get corresponding data for the recommender system. Quite early in the project it became clear that two ideal-types of recommender techniques are being used. In the meetings and in our conversations, Alice and Bob mentioned collaborative filtering and content-based filtering and provided me material to study these approaches.[6] Both techniques follow completely different ideas of recommendations. Collaborative filtering draws from the idea that the patterns of usage between

---

6   The distinction between the two approaches is not exclusive to recommender systems but has a long history (B. Rieder 2017, 106).

different users are able to inform the predictions about relevant new videos. Content-based filtering, on the other hand, does not compare usage patterns for different users but tries to predict the user's taste based on her individual viewing history. These different approaches of producing relevant recommendations then are also reflected in the way the algorithmic scripts – i.e., the assumptions about the interactions inbuilt into these techniques – played out differently. They were assuming different forms of data provided but also different forms of actor-constellations to which they are connected via data.

Item-based Collaborative Filtering

A technique that is widely used when it comes to recommender systems is the one of collaborative filtering. Even though its origins can be traced back at least to the early 1990s, collaborative filtering has been heavily popularized by Netflix (Amatriain and Basilico 2011) and other commercial actors like Amazon (e.g., Smith and Linden 2017). The idea behind collaborative filtering could be summarized as: *similar users like similar things*, and is often applied under the headline of *users who liked the item you just looked at also like this.* This raises the question of how the similarities between users and items are identified algorithmically.

Collaborative filtering systems calculate these similarities on the basis of user feedback, which is interpreted as a rating. These ratings are then used to make items and users comparable to each other by finding patterns in the collected data sets (Koren, Bell, and Volinsky 2009). The approach does thereby calculate so-called latent features of the user-item relations in order to describe the users as well as the items in an abstract vector-space. User feedback can be explicit or implicit. Explicit user feedback thereby often ranges from zero to five stars, where users actively rate the items that they watched (Liu et al. 2010). The system is by now very well-known from sites like Amazon or IMDB. This can, however, produce a problem for collaborative filtering, as the technique assumes a rather densely tracking of interactions. If this assumption is not met, the calculation gets less precise, as the algorithm would have to assign non-ratings either a value of zero or needs to estimate the values based on the recorded ones. Less values therefore means less statistical certainty that the model derived fits the real behavior of the users. In the context of a public service broadcaster, however, it was expected that the users did not provide much explicit feedback. This was also one of the reasons why the project team also implemented collaborative filtering with *implicit feedback*. With implicit feedback the tracking does not only record if an interaction between user and video has occurred but also the intensity of it (Hu, Koren, and Volinsky 2008). This is being measured by the percentage of the video the user watched. E.g., let's assume we watch a documentary about software development, which has a total length of 60 minutes. If we close the video after 20 minutes, this would result in a rating of ⅓ or 0.33. If we stop after 30 minutes, the rating is 0.5. The longer we watch, so the assumption, the higher the rating. This results in ratings of 0% to 100%.[7]

However, the interpretation of these signals, including explicit as well as implicit user feedback, was not as straightforward to the developers as one would assume when reading the related publications from conferences or academic journals. The developers were concerned whether these ratings give them actually the real picture of the users' intentions. Or in other words: when is a rating a rating? And what is a good rating?

> So far we have only implicit feedback of a video watched (% watched). This leaves us without any negative feedback (e.g if 30% watched, does it mean that user didn't like the video or something else?). We could introduce a "like" button or rating, but this might also give us a wrong picture: for example, if user watched a video with a politician who he hates, he would give the video 1 star, which, however does not mean that the video is irrelevant to the user (Alice via Slack in #machinelearning).

In the project meetings these issues were often discussed. In the reflection on the users' intentions of giving ratings, different layers of interpretation and situated issues were anticipated and mixed together. In the quote given, at least three different interpretations are presented. The first revolves around the relevance of a video to a user. This does not ask the question whether the user likes the video, but if it is assumed by the developers or editors that it is important to and for the user to see the video. This ambiguity is addressed by the distinction between relevance and valuation of the content provided. While the video might be relevant, what does the rating really reflect? Did she disapprove of the message, or does she disapprove of the fact that the video was shown to her? The assumption here was that direct rating might not be connected to relevance but how the user relates to the presented content. But also implicit feedback raised the question of how to interpret the percentage and if we could define a threshold where we think that the user liked or disliked the video. For the calculation itself, this interpretation process is irrelevant. You can always provide recommendations based on these implicit ratings. But the concern of the developers was that this would lead to ill-informed recommendations, with a negative impact on the recommender's performance. This sparked some discussions on how to account for user ratings, and potentially adding other forms of rating mechanisms. In addition, the assumption that the developers had enough tracking data for the calculation of collaborative filtering posed a practical problem, as this was simply not the case. Thus, for the launch of the recommender system, content-based

---

7   A short remark: although it is theoretically possible to have 0%, it is practically hard to achieve, as the user would have to start and stop the video with an incredibly low delay.

filtering was the technique that should be deployed, while collaborative filtering should be added later, when enough tracking data would be available.

Content-based Filtering

The second algorithmic technique that was mobilized within the software development project was content-based filtering. This approach does not try to look at patterns in the ratings of all users in the population but aims to identify similarities between items that in turn fit the viewing history of the individual user (Pazzani and Billsus 2007). While collaborative filtering is agnostic about the content of the items to be recommended, content-based filtering relies on a database of computer-readable descriptions of the videos that serves as the base from which items' similarity is calculated for recommendations. A common approach is the TF-IDF technique (Term Frequency–Inverse Document Frequency), in which a vector space over all used words that describe the items is built (Meteren and Someren 2000). Similarity is constructed by the relative distance between the vectors describing items derived from the available meta-data. Comparability is therefore the result of data production processes of editors, who write short texts or apply typical tags and categories to their items to make them identifiable.

In this approach, different forms of action are made relevant to each other to calculate relevance based on the produced meta-data. Instead of relating the actions of users to each other, the algorithmic mediator constructs relevance for the recommender based on relating the actions of data-producers to the media consumption of users. Thus, how behavior makes certain information relevant is different here – another script is built into this approach. This can happen through tags applied, categories, description text or titles – and many other ways to describe the videos in the database.

What became clear very soon, however, was that having such a description alone does not suffice but that the description needed to adhere to quality standards. Alice, Bob, and Dave were very concerned about the quality of the meta-data generated in the organization. As a result, several meetings and discussions were focused on the question of how to ensure high quality meta-data. In one of the very first meetings, the developers stated: "Quality of the metadata defines the quality of the product" (fieldnote). Metadata in the case of the public service broadcaster meant: data that described the videos through keywords, text descriptions, and categories. With this data, the algorithm could make sense of the video database provided by content providers within the organization. However, when we inquired about the conditions of good description data at a meeting with the online editorial team, something interesting happened:

> We were about to discuss the new category list and the general workings
> of the recommender algorithms. Alice explained the difference between
> collaborative filtering and content-based filtering and the issues that
> each one of them has. Especially collaborative filtering has the cold start
> problem, i.e., when the system goes online there is no prior tracking
> data to calculate the recommendations on. Then the editors presented
> the newly designed category list. It is now much leaner than the one
> before and seems much clearer. Trent asked if this list is one that the
> recommender can work with. Alice looked a bit around. Alice then said, as
> long as they use it in a coherent way, the list is just fine (fieldnote).

Good metadata here means that descriptions are applied in a comparable and systematic way, and that every item *has* this kind of description. In contrast to the interpretations of ratings, where the developers were discussing the meaning of the data considered, the only concern here was the systematic and comparable usage of the established category list. In the meeting it became not only clear that the descriptions have to be used in a systematic way but that the production of references is externalized. "As long as they use it in a coherent way" means, not me, not the algorithm. The interpretation of what the categories actually mean, how they reference back to an actionable world, is outsourced to the other departments of the organization.

Doing Comparability

Both techniques aim at the production of comparability. Through transforming given data into an abstract vector space, the techniques create a reference frame to make the users and items comparable to each other (see also A. Mackenzie 2015). This comparability then makes it possible to derive recommendations from the provided data. Items that are similar to you or the videos you watched *in this calculated vector space* are then recommended to you. However, the ways the techniques create comparability are fundamentally different. In the case of collaborative filtering, the algorithm calculates a vector space of latent factors to make the users and items comparable to each other based on patterns of interactions of these users with the video-items. In the other case, content-based filtering compares the description of the videos with each other to produce similarities. The mode of organizing the items, by creating relations between them, differs throughout the algorithmic techniques. This, then, also means that the assumptions about existing data production regimes are different ones.

Collaborative filtering assumes a dense tracking regime, where many data points describing the interaction between items and users are needed. Otherwise, calculating the vector space in order to compare items and users is not possible or very faulty. However, precisely this data also produced problems of interpretability and intelligibility. *Content-based filtering*, on the other hand, works under the assumption of an organized and comparable description of video items. This assumes therefore shared knowledge and practices of producing meta-data within the public broadcaster. Thus, the inscription process in an algorithmic technique constitutes specific assumption about the datafied world and the meaning of the data available. Or in other words, the algorithm resolves the meaning of data in relation to the formulated abstract problem. Mackenzie argues that while machine learning approaches "classify in very different ways, they all assume that the world is made of things or events that fit in stable and distinct categories" (A. Mackenzie 2015, 433). This production of stable and distinct categories, however, was then an issue we had to tackle by finding what I call *algorithmic forms of reflexivity*.

Producing Algorithmic Reflexivity

As discussed in the previous section, the assumptions formulated by algorithmic scripts had to be aligned somehow with the wider network of the digital infrastructure of the organization in order to obtain the needed data. However, this process of aligning with data is in itself a coordination between different practices that constitute the algorithmic system. In the following, I will therefore discuss how the production and utilization of data structures in algorithmic systems can be understood as a form of *algorithmic reflexivity*, in which the meaning of symbols has to be resolved and made sense of. For that I will draw on pragmatist and ethnomethodological accounts of semiotics and interpretation, arguing that data structures are durable references to social orderings and then discuss three different vignettes, demonstrating how we tried to produce forms of algorithmic reflexivity via different means.

Coordinating Data

As Bechmann and Bowker (2019) argue, the goal of classical machine learning approaches is to classify. In supervised learning, for example, there is a known outcome for given data configurations. Let's say we train neural networks to recognize kittens in images. To do so, however, we have a collection of images that are tagged with kitten/no-kitten, define this label as the desired outcome and then train the machine learning algorithm to learn the features, which makes it possible to recognize other pictures with kittens that are not pre-tagged. Recommender systems, as they have been applied in the project, however, represent a specific form of machine learning. Instead of classical categorization work of machine learning, such as recognizing spam, fraud detection, etc., the aim is not to search for a generalized model to extrapolate on new data but to describe available items in a common mathematical reference frame, i.e., to transform them into a vector space to make them comparable (see also A. Mackenzie 2015). This could also be seen as classification through the description of different dimensions in the shared vector-space. In both cases, collaborative filtering and content-based filtering, the developer tried to establish this form of comparability in the description of an outside world. That was problematized to create a certain order of things. This problem of resolving the references of given data was then one issue during the development of the recommender system. In both approaches – *collaborative filtering* and *content-based filtering* – there were issues regarding the quality and the interpretation of the data provided. And in each case, resolving these references and producing an algorithmic system that *made sense* in the given organizational environment was a challenge.

The way that input data is being used to generate a decision model becomes important to understand parts of the building blocks of a subsequently generated algorithmic agency. An algorithmic technique alone does not yet tell us how the algorithm will act in the end, as we still need to understand how the abstract principle is translated into an actual entity, dealing with data. Interactionist and constructionist approaches within the social sciences[8] argue that data is never raw or objectively given (Bowker 2014; Gitelman 2013). The production of data always includes interpretative work and an, often only implicit, theoretical perspective. Thus, meaning of data is always produced in a process of *meaning making*. The usage of symbols always includes an act of interpretation. Peirce ([1902] 1976, [1900] 2010) developed a pragmatist theory of semiotics, which in contrast to the structuralist account of Ferdinand de Saussure ([1916] 1998), a) includes not only language but all forms of communication, such as visual media, music, etc. and b) extends the signifier-signified relation with the act of interpretation. For Peirce, signs therefore consisted of a triadic structure: representation, object, and interpretation. The notion of symbol or sign is thereby complicated in use, as different theoreticians used the terms differently. In the pragmatist account, however, a symbol represents a cultural artifact with constructed meaning. Examples are traffic symbols or iconic representations of men or women. Symbols, as described by Mead ([1934] 1967), refer beyond the current situation, i.e., they are interpreted in a general way. A specific form of that would be significant symbols, which are interpreted by all members of a given community in the same way – and result in similar reactions. However, also in the pragmatist thought and in later developments, as in symbolic interactionism (Blumer 1986) or labeling theory (Becker 1997), the meaning of symbols is the result of interaction, i.e., the meaning of a symbol is updated within the situation in coordination practices of the involved parties. The interpretations of signs and symbols must be related with each other in the interaction, which can also

---

8   And, of course, the philosophy of technology, media theory, and in parts computer science.

result in a divergent meaning derived from that. Therefore, the meaning of a symbol is not inherent to the symbol itself but a) is learned in a socialization process and b) is updated *in situ* (Blumer 1986; Mead [1934] 1967).

The school of ethnomethodology, famously founded by Garfinkel, complicates this picture a bit more. While Garfinkel (1984) also refers to shared knowledge and competent members of a social community, he and later ethnomethodologists showed in several studies that all forms of spoken or written communication is theoretically underdetermined, i.e., we do not just interpret the signs and symbols, but we also have to relate them to a fluid situation. Every action redefines the context of communication. Thus, the situation that is being created through the interactions of participants is also the frame of reference for making the indexical notions understandable. As a result, also significant symbols vary in their meaning in relation to the context and the situation. In order to make communication happen, individuals constantly resolve possible meanings and fill the gaps – Garfinkel (1984) called this the indexicality of language and practices. That results in the observation that the meaning of the expression is only reconstructable within the interaction that constitutes communication.[9] The meaning of symbols always refers back to different formations of knowledge that must be coordinated. Interaction always unfolds in a complex process, where one's own interpretation of the situation is compared with the reaction of the present alter-ego. The involved actors reflexively resolve and update potential meanings of produced accounts.

Reflexivity has, specifically within STS and qualitative social sciences in general, gained a somewhat privileged status. Thus, several scholars argue that individuals, institutions, or entire societies should become more reflexive. But there are many different meanings invoked when the word reflexivity is being brought to the arena (Lynch 2000, 27). The reflexivity, which I am referring here to, relates to everyday-practice of *making the world*, as it has been proposed by scholars in interpretative sociology. In ethnomethodology, reflexivity is the ability to resolve the inherently indexical meaning of language. Garfinkel argues that "[t]he activities whereby members produce and manage settings of organized everyday affairs are identical with members' procedures for making those settings "accountable"" (Garfinkel 1984, 1). For Garfinkel, this ability to situate and resolve indexicality is (practical) reflexivity, and as such a property of accounts "that is furnished by

---

9   This, however, addresses also another problem of communication: namely, that meaning is never transparent to the interaction partners, as they never can be sure that the other party means the same thing as I do, i.e., the problem of double-contingency. That led other theorists, like Luhmann (1996), to the formulation that only communication but not attached semantic categories are relevant. As long as the communication goes on, the social system is stabilized.

taken-for-granted usage in recurrent circumstances" (Lynch 2000, 34).[10] Thus, social order is being produced and re-produced by the reflexive observation and production of accounts which are organized according to the concrete situation. If that form of (implicit) knowledge is not available, the production of locally ordered and recognizable accounts becomes problematic.

The so far discussed approach to everyday communication can be transposed to another set of symbols that are used to coordinate and describe our world: data. What data is referring to, in the initial reference, therefore is more of the situated negotiation of the data production. Data is the result of and therefore the reference to a given social order, where a contingent observation of reality is stabilized and delegated by "proto-semiotic practices and local interactions which signs, objects and signed-objects achieve identity and sensibility" (Lynch 2000, 34). Turning an observation into data means to coordinate the interpretation of the observed accounts with the interpretation of the available data symbols. And these meanings are – as argued in interactionist sociological approaches – not inherent to the symbols. They are open to interpretation and re-interpretation to fit them at the local interaction patterns. However, data is not only produced locally and situated but also acts as a mediator between different communities. There is a longstanding and ongoing discussion on the role of data in coordinating different communities, most prominently discussed with the notion of information infrastructures, like the International Classification of Diseases (ICD) (Bowker and Star 2000) or the social and historical meaning of numbers (Hacking 1990; Porter 1995). According to Bowker and Star (2000), classification regimes serve a given purpose and stabilize and normalize solutions. While this does not result in a common and stable frame of interpretation, it does delimit the possible ways of interaction, making cooperation of different communities possible. As Bowker and Star (2000) showed, data and classification systems are devices to coordinate practices and actions of collectives over space and time. Data structures and classification systems refer to the practices of other collectives and need to be resolved accordingly to achieve coordination. These practices thereby always include interpretation and situational production of order, which refers to shared knowledge and allows interaction. Thus, data can be understood as accounts that travel between situations and that the 'user' has to reflexively resolve their meaning.

Coming back to the development of the recommender system, in both instances of the recommender algorithm, the developers struggled with the (re-)interpretation and the availability of data. The ambiguity of the data's meaning became a major concern within the project, and some time and effort were invested to tackle these issues. However, the two areas of

10   For further work, it might be a productive endeavor to compare the different semiotic approaches of pragmatism, ANT, and ethnomethodology.

ambiguity – rating and meta-data – were tackled in fundamentally different ways. In the case of collaborative filtering, the developer team had to interpret the signals to make sense of them. The developer team thereby followed the assumption that they do not possess the power to change the situation or the social order in which the data was produced. That, then, created the problem for the developers of missing context-information to bring the signals in order. The reduction of users' intentions to a single number, without updating the meaning in the situation, meant that valuable information to actually understand what is going on was missing. The efforts and discussions in the development team therefore were trying to resolve the indexicality inherent to the data by making their methods of sense-making explicit. In the second case, however, the developers assumed that they have the power to change the social order to which the produced data is referring to. By creating the imperative of coherent application of categories, interpretation was no longer necessary at the level of the algorithm. Instead, the developers tried to mobilize many different actors to ensure the comparability of the recorded meta-data. These two different approaches show us that the production of algorithmic reflexivity specifically, and the institutionalization of algorithms in general are connected to questions of social ordering and power. In the first case, we could have tried to influence the behavior of the users, provide them with explanations, and order the situation in which they 'rated' the videos in a way that would ensure that the process of interpretation of these signals would have been easier. But the development team decided that they were not capable of doing so. The *envisioned* ordering in the described situations was stable enough to keep the developers from trying to change it. The formulation that the developers only assumed that they do not have the power to change the socio-technical structures is thereby not chosen by accident. Instead, it implicitly refers to Schütz' conception of social action in a reply to Parsons (Schütz and Parsons 1978). Thus, what are means and conditions in a given situation refers, according to Schütz, to the knowledge and experiences of the actor at the time of evaluation of the situation. In the case of content-based filtering, however, the development team evaluated the situation quite differently. With content-based filtering approaches, the changes had to be made within the organization of the public broadcaster. Something the development team was confident enough that they could foster the needed changes there. As Latour (1990, 2005) argues, opening a black box and changing durable sets of practices relies on how many allies you can mobilize on the side of the actor that wants to foster change. As such, institutionalizing algorithmic systems is not just about technical details but about the power to influence the socio-technical structure in which these technical details need to take place.

This was the part where I, the project's own sociologist, came back into the picture. I was sent out to the other departments and groups within the organization to find solutions for the problem of meta-data production. This outsourcing of meaning making for the algorithm involved interpretation of another sort. Instead of thinking about the meaning of signals, the developers, including myself, were thinking about the processes of data production and how they create problems or could solve the issue at hand. The developers themselves applied many implicit sociological and psychological theories – without me bringing them up – how the social setting was producing meaning and how it could be controlled in order to enable high-quality recommendations. Thus, the developers turned into "engineer-sociologists" (Callon 1987) who anticipated and theorized the situations relevant for the recommender system.[11] In the following, I discuss the attempts to reorganize the institutional structure to produce this stable description needed for the recommender system to work.

Scripting Algorithmic Ethnomethods

Collaborative filtering basically needs ratings provided by users in order to find patterns in their behavior. Relevant is not so much how the content is being described but rather which users did relate to the videos, and in what intensity. This intensity of relation is thereby expressed as a rating. One of the more promising approaches, implicit ratings, however, produced problems in interpretability. This was especially articulated by referring to different situations that create ratings but where the assumed intention of the users might deviate. What came up repeatedly in the meetings was the so-called lean-back mode. At the end of a video, the auto-play feature automatically starts the next video from the recommendations or the playlist. However, the concern was that the users could have fallen asleep or left the room without turning off their TV. We discussed these issues in a weekly meeting in which recommendations were especially addressed:

> There are uncertainties, how to interpret implicit and explicit feedback. What does it mean if a video has a rating below 60%? Does it mean that the video is not relevant for the user? The same for ratings beyond 60%. What if the user was on the toilet or fell asleep? (fieldnote)

The question then was, how to account for these scenarios? This would produce high ratings for videos but would not reflect the reality of the viewing habits, as the algorithm would account for it the same way as intentional viewings.[12] A similar problem was identified in relation to mobile usage when

---

11   This then is also one of the challenges for sociology in the 21st century. Data science and machine learning are becoming direct competitors in the realm of social analysis. This can also be seen by calls for integrating these techniques into the canon of sociological methods (Marres 2017; Mützel 2015).

12   Netflix seemed to have had the same issue, as – at the time of writing this book – they started asking the user if she is still watching after some time without interaction.

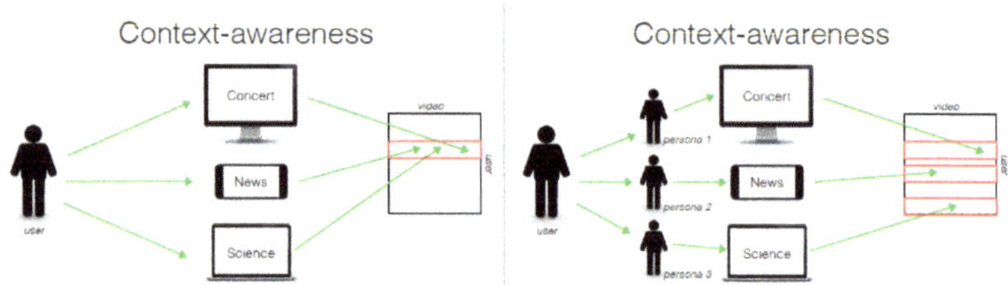

[Figure 5] An image shared by Bob on Slack illustrating the problem of context in tracking

the ratings are low. The concern of the developers was that users stop viewing videos might not do so because the video is not relevant to them, but because they are interrupted by external conditions, e.g., the train ride ends. This reflects the assumption of the developers that the viewing habits of the users on mobile devices is much more dynamic in comparison to the TV at home, where an encapsulated situation, without many external influences, is created. The second concern regarding mobile devices was connected to the digital infrastructure of the country. Simply spoken, losing connection is a realistic issue for mobile applications. However, in the tracking system this would be recorded as a low rating of the video. While the measurement of implicit feedback seemed straightforward and required no further data collection or production on the side of the organization (which became a problem, as I will discuss later), the technique produced problems in interpreting the data available.

As a result of this reasoning, different solutions were thought of. One especially focused on the issue of usage context proposed to evaluate the signals from different devices differently.

[Figure 5] An image shared by Bob on Slack illustrating the problem of context in trackingshows an image that Bob shared on Slack to describe the issue of context and posted the following explanation with it:

> Left: the user is in different contexts, but her user behavior ends up in the same profile => mixed up data, hard to find clear preferences, because they can be context-dependent. Right: each context gets its own profile ("persona") and will be tracked separately. Recommendations then will be calculated based on the actual context => context dependent preferences will be recognized and satisfied (Bob via Slack in #machinelearning).

The solution proposed by the developers here is to track not a singular user but to create personas for each device of the user to take different situations into account. This, however, also requires treating each of these personas as a different subject in the item/user pairing of the tracking database – and the subsequently calculated model. This modifies the original idea of the recommender algorithm and its assumptions. According to the developer team, the signals received did not only reference a singular preference of the user but have to be interpreted as a reference to different situations and their specific contexts, including Germany's communication infrastructure or mobility habits of users. The described uncertainties in regard to the different forms of user ratings are based on a situation, in which the software developers did not rely on their implicit and taken-for-granted knowledge about the situation. However, since there was no direct communication with the (anticipated) users, a misinterpretation on the side of the developers could not be repaired through communicative means.[13] The solution proposed by Bob then changed the way the algorithm was able to resolve the situation, creating a different meaning. Technically speaking, the model did only include additional personas in the model production. However, this also meant that the part of the data matrix did identify users not only based on tracking a singular individual but that the device that was used changed the definition of the situation – and thus how the algorithm *made sense* of it. Identifying the device worked here as a proxy to apply different understandings and methods to resolve the situation. Thus, in order to account for different contexts, the algorithmic ethnomethods had to change as well, and with it the tracking system, which made the accounts available to the algorithm. Relatively early in the project we were able to have a look at the old tracking data.

> I have something for you. In the old video-on-demand platform the user preferences have been tracked. The session_ids of the user is combined with the proportion of the item that the user saw/heard. [...] The prefs consist of user_id, item_id, pref, timestamp, play_time, play_count (Erni via Slack in #machinelearning).

As we can see from the description of the old tracking data, the used device to access the service was not included. That is, while it seemed easy to go for collaborative filtering, as no data production would have had to change, this assumption was actually not true. The organizational problems were just on another place than producing meta-data for the video items. Instead, we were facing the issue of changing the data production practices for the tracking software. Changing the tracking parameters was a possibility to resolve the issues of indexicality within the software development project in a way that seemed well enough. As a result of these changes, the technical structure, including the data storage facilities and tracking technologies, had to be adapted and institutionalized. Yet – and this is the interesting point here – these changes became necessary not because the data had to be produced or adapted from somewhere else, but because the ethnomethods of the

---

13   Interestingly, this has also been an issue for other platforms, like YouTube. There are guidelines and FAQs describing how to tinker with the recommender algorithm by changing the signals processed by it. Thus, these texts try to repair the communication by giving the users context, how YouTube interprets their signals, not the other way round, asking how YouTube should interpret the signals. *https://support.google.com/youtubemusic/thread/160722?hl=en (accessed: 6.9.2020).*

algorithm that made sense of these signals had to be adapted to a social order already in place. Changing the technical structure allowed the algorithmic script to make sense of the accounts of previously only insufficient intelligibly situations. For content-based filtering, however, this was not an option. As described before, Alice remarked that the indexicality of video metadata had to be resolved somewhere else. The next sections therefore focus on our journey to find a solution for content-based filtering.

Archive

Public broadcasters are not only organizations that air video and audio material but also need to produce structures in which this material is being managed and made available to the different editorial teams. In short, a public broadcaster is always also a large data storage institution – with specialized sub-units that manage enormous data collections. Thus, one (somehow obvious) idea that came up was using the existing archive of the organization. Every video that has been aired can be found there, and the archive provides metadata description for every item. As a result, the idea emerged of building a data interface to the archive to get the relevant data for the recommender system. However, no-one in the development team knew exactly how the archive worked, nor what the technical infrastructure to connect to the database looked like. Charlie, one of the project managers, and I therefore made an appointment with one representative of the archive to discuss possible connections and interfaces. The idea was promising on different levels. First, the videos were tagged with metadata at the archive centrally for re-use. Therefore, the data was already there and, furthermore, the data was produced centrally, which made it probable that the central affordance of stability of meaning in the references was met. As we learned later, there even exists an own training for archivists.

In this meeting, Charlie and I learned that the archive worked on two different levels.

> 1) Formal description: the formal description happens a few days after a video entered the archive. Data from the editorial teams, like planning title, title, sub-title are being entered and completed. This happens on the level of whole episodes. On this level, also a classification is done. If it is not clear how the video should be categorized, the category is not entered.

> 2) Documentation: The second level is much more precise and it can take up to several months until it happens. Entering the data happens on the level of the whole episode if it is mono-thematic, or on the level of segments if it is part of a magazine. At the same time, the categorization is being completed. Episodes are also getting an abstract describing their

> content (one sentence). Indexat: the episode is summarized in keywords. Thereby two different "philosophies" exist. For radio contributions this happens according to a norm database. Video contributions are being tagged freely (fieldnote).

The archive is a very important element in the work of the editors. It is the place where they find older video-items that they can use for future programs. One of the editors used the video clip of the moon landing in 1969, which could be used in very different shows and contexts as an example. However, the timing and the style of producing metadata is aligned with the needs of the editors. During this meeting, the archivist raised concerns for using the archive data for the recommender system. According to her, the metadata produced in the archive is pretty complicated because it has to match an inter-institutional categorization norm database. In addition, the archive was built for editorial research and the production of new shows and movies. It was part of another set of translations and functional interdependencies, which also echoed in their self-description. During the meeting, *"[t]he archivist explained to us that the used category list is built for editorial research. Episodes are opened up for such inquiries, by adding tags to different segments of the episode"* (fieldnote). This issue also concerned the developers of the recommender system themselves. In a weekly meeting, Dave argued the following:

> The colleagues from the archive could be overwhelmed by the amount of work if they have to tag all the videos centrally. In addition, their way of tagging content is way too dense for the recommender system. It produces too fine-grained data and this needs too much computational power (fieldnote).

The data that resulted as a description of the video items was part of another ordering in which the videos and their description played another role, and solved another problem. In the description of the archivists' practice, the organization and the imagined function of the archive had been invoked repeatedly. Namely, to enable editorial work of finding archived material for new episodes. The archive is a very important element in the work of the editors, as they find older video-items that they can use for future programs. In a later interview the term "pearl of the archive" (Online-Editors Interview, my translation) was mentioned. With that, the online editors hinted at the importance of the archive for finding high quality content for further productions. For them, the archive was not a place of consistent meta-data but a rich reservoir for creative engagement.

A second issue was the timing. As mentioned in the process description, the work processes were timed differently. The items were equipped with rich metadata only a few months after they were aired in the linear program of the channel. This means, however, that these items would not have been available for the recommender for a pretty long time. In addition, the videos were not taken up as they came in, but the order in which they are queued changes based on a prioritization scheme.

> In the archive meeting Charlie and I were told that "there are priority lists with three different priority levels." This means that videos are not edited in the order of arrival. This whole process can take up to three months (fieldnote).

As a result, actual content would near to never be recommended by the system. This was also mentioned by a developer at a dev-meeting: "Dave was asking: How long do the people from the archive need to complete the data? If that takes too long, new content probably will not be included – which poses a problem" (fieldnote). As a result, the archive was not a suitable place to get the needed metadata for the recommender.

Although we have not been in the archive, observing the practices of actually producing the meta-data, the colleague explaining the archive to us invoked the function of these practices, and their relation to the editorial work repeatedly. By narrating the archive's work as essential for editorial teams, the colleague did what Maynard and Clayman (1991, 407) called "reveal[ing] an orientation to institutional or other contexts". The timing and the style of producing metadata are aligned with the needs of the editors and therefore invoked and performed the archive as an essential institution for that kind of work. Based on this performativity of the institution, reducing the density of meta-data to an amount that the recommender system could handle was not an option. The performativity of the archive showed the interdependence of the organizational structure[14] – here between the archive and the editorial teams – in the orientation of the archivists' practices and narratives. Thus, institutional and organizational interdependencies could be observed in localized practices and speech.[15] While organizational and institutional rules and procedures as described in strategy documents or guidelines are not directly translatable into observable practices, they offer a resource to understand institutional rationalities, especially if they are invoked in localized practices (Maynard and Clayman 1991). As Suchman argues, interactionist perspectives on social order "propose, in sum, that it is only through their everyday enactment and reiteration that institutions are reproduced and rules of conduct realized" (Suchman 2006, 16). This locally enacted institutional conduct, however, became problematic here. Instead of building an association between the archive and the algorithm, the two ideas of producing meta-data

14   This would also allow an interesting re-interpretation of Norbert Elias' process sociology (1978), putting the focus on the coordination of multiple performed interdependencies.
15   Drew and Heritage (1992) show in their ethnomethodological approach that organizational interdependencies can be reconstructed by locally enacted orders.

became incompatible in practice, and the development project could not align the archive to its own local social order. Through not changing the modes of data production, the archive stabilized their own idea of a normality of institutional order, which they deemed important. The means of producing data was not interpretable by the algorithmic ethnomethods.

Technological Fix

Since the archive was not a viable option for getting the needed meta-data, other forms of getting or producing it needed to be thought of. As we, the development team, got a first idea of what it would take to change or adapt the organization, we started searching for other options. And so, a typical engineering solution to the problem came up: could we use a technological fix to solve the problem?

> As the question on quality of metadata came up, Edward said that we could use Voice-To-Text software. This way the audio track of the video could be used to generate meta-data. Later Charlie asked me if I could help out with this problem. I agreed. [a few days later] I met with the developer. He explained to me that they already tried it once with different videos. They set up a test server for that and it worked quite well. However, one prominent show failed. The software did not recognize the local dialect. We laughed. Then we discussed this further. This is a rather big issue, as this show is one of the most successful of the broadcaster. This way it would not show up in the recommendations. Difficult situation. I will talk to Charlie about this (fieldnote).

Speech recognition was one way to create the metadata needed for the recommender system. By deploying a speech-recognition-software, the recommender would use show-specific self-descriptions and match similar shows with each other. By doing so, the organizational structure would not be touched, but – not unlike the online service itself – an additional system would be added to the existing structure without the need to change it. The speech-recognition software would be mobilized from outside the company to create a stable relation between the video database and the recommender system. It would act as a mediator, altering the original form of the videos to something that the recommender system could work with. Further, the developer team showed proto-sociological insights. The idea behind the suggestion is from a sociological perspective (e.g., Bourdieu 1984) quite intriguing: similar productions would surely use genre-specific language and therefore create descriptions that would create a stable description regime for the videos. They did not only try to mobilize a technological tool but tried to use it as a machine of cultural comparison. The technological tool became an instrument of social inquiry.

However, there was one big problem: the most valued videos of the channel could not be recognized by the voice-to-text software, which was produced by a big North American company. The productions were using variants of the German language that the software was not able to understand. As such, the production of metadata would not include all of the videos, and it was not clear what percentage of the videos would actually be equipped with a textual description derived from their audio track. The approach was not compatible with the content that should be processed by the recommender system. Instead of creating stable translations of the videos, the distributed self-descriptions of the videos could not be translated nor coordinated at the central position of the software. Why so? Because the speech-recognition software already assumed a certain form of referencing the world. It needed a specific form of language usage and was not able to tackle the different forms of expression. Instead of coordinating different forms of self-descriptions expressed via the audio tracks of the videos through a variety of language usage, it failed to acknowledge these different forms of language. Thus, instead of making videos comparable with each other through speech-recognition, the software would have selected only a subset of the available video items. The speech-recognition software was trained with a data-representation of the world that was different from the one found in the public broadcaster. On the other hand, the way the show was produced was not changeable. It was one of the broadcaster's most successful shows, and above all, by using the local dialect, it expressed the broadcaster's local identity. Something that was highly valued.

Machine learning and pattern recognition algorithms rely to a large extent on the data that they are being trained on – and which becomes a representation of the world for them (Jaton 2017). The training data, however, (co-)produces in case of ML the algorithmic ethno-methods as *taken for granted* assumptions about the world – which is not "the natural world simpliciter but the natural world under interpretation or the world as construed by us through language" (Suchman 2006, 76). The algorithmic script that had been implemented in the speech recognition software was based on the developers' assumptions of a specific language use – realized through the data sets used to actually generate the software. However, the expressions of the local TV show were just not included into the accounts that would be able to be interpreted by the language recognition software. In order to produce a stable socio-technical order in which the recommender system could operate, this mutual understanding is a pre-requisite. Locally produced order is based on mutually understandable accounts and their reflexive interpretation. As Suchman (2006) writes: "The stability of the social world [...] is not due to an eternal structure but to situated actions that create and sustain shared understandings on specific occasions of interaction" (Suchman 2006, 83). Just as Ziewitz (2017) had to make his observations accountable in a way that the algorithm could make sense of the expressions, the speech recognition software was assuming a certain way of using and then resolving language. In order to match the expressions of the local dialect, it would have been necessary to translate them into a form of language that the speech-recognition software could resolve. However, in the example of Ziewitz (2017), many occasions of repairing the situation could be observed, reasoning about questions of what qualifies a street, or if the application of the rule would make sense here. The expressions needed for the algorithm had been re-interpreted and re-negotiated in the situation of their application. Repairing the situation here, however, would have meant to either change the language of the show, re-train the speech-recognition software, or to install a team of translators, who would have done the work of "explicating observations in the language of the algorithm" (Ziewitz 2017, 4).

The strategy of mobilizing an actor outside the actual organization to solve the problem failed because the very ecology that could not accommodate the first algorithm could also not accommodate the second one. While in the example of the archive, the problem was that the institutionalized practices within the organization did not allow the integration of the algorithm, an inter-institutional solution failed because the practices of meaning-making of these two organizations (and their delegated actants, i.e., the TV show and the speech recognition software) were simply incompatible. The two different organizations with their taken-for-granted perspective of the socio-technical world could neither produce accounts in their encounter, nor did they have the methods to make them intelligible for each other. To mediate between the video database and the recommender algorithm, the speech-recognition software would have needed a differently pre-structured, pre-normalized world that is interpretable for it. Instead of solving the problem at hand, the issue only shifted to a different moment of translation. The envisioned chain of translations ended abruptly. Neither was it possible to create an order that would make the usage of the black-boxed software possible, i.e., changing the way the actors in the show were speaking, nor was it possible to open the black-box and reorganize its inner working.

How Data Structures

All of the above described attempts to attach the recommender system to the existing organizational structure of the public broadcaster or to mobilize external actors as inter-institutional solution into the enactment of the organization failed. Therefore, the focus of attention shifted away from using existing solutions, and instead moved to the creation of our own organizational procedures and structures to realize the algorithmic system. The central system for planning the linear program, called WhatsOn, came into the focus of our attention. In a meeting, the developers asked the online editors if they could produce the metadata. This, however, would create too much workload for the rather small online-editorial team. The solution for the dev-team and the online-editors was a combination of centralizing and de-centralizing. The metadata production should be part of the thematic editorial teams, not the online-editorial team. As a member of the editorial team argued, the information infrastructure for such a process was already in place. Trent from the editorial team argued that "entering the metadata should best happen at the editorial system. No-one can avoid WhatsOn" (fieldnote). WhatsOn was the central planning system for the broadcaster's programs and was used up to that point for the linear program only. In this system, the different editorial teams noted down when which show was planned and entered relevant descriptions, such as title, short description, time of airing and length of the video. The idea to use WhatsOn and the meta-data there, however, produced two major problems that had to be tackled. The WhatsOn system provided input fields for keywords and longer texts to describe the individual videos programmed for airing. They were not used by the editorial teams in the process of registering their shows in the central system, as these fields did not have any effect till then. The meta-data the organization used so far had a purpose for the editorial teams, i.e., providing descriptions for the linear program. That means that providing data for the used field did solve a problem for the editorial team, while providing key words or extra descriptions had simply no use and therefore no value, as the keywords and categories were not important for the broadcasting of the linear program. In an interview, an informant from a meta-data team told me:

> For what do you need that? Because metadata is naturally not what you see directly, only indirectly, simply that you can then automatically control something. That you have categories. That you say, I have here the category cinematic movie or the category documentary. And, I mean, that is relatively plausible. But there are many other meta data. They are in the first moment not intuitive, why one would need them? Because they are not necessary in classical on-air distribution. (Interview Metadata Team, my translation)

This, however, posed a problem, as the metadata was too scarce for good recommendations. Something had to be done about it. As the project's own sociologist, I started a diplomatic mission. I attended meetings in which I was explained how WhatsOn was used in the organization and how it was connected to other departments. In addition, I also hosted discussion rounds with representatives of the editorial teams. They were so-called key users who would provide me with information, and in turn would instruct WhatsOn users in the other editorial teams. Thus, convincing them of the recommender system's value was essential. In order to make the recommender system possible, I had to make them the allies of the algorithm. Without their enrolment in the actor-network of the algorithm, the project would face a major problem.

Another issue with this solution was born out of the fact that over 300 editorial teams enter the information of their shows into this system. Even if the fields were used, the data producers would potentially follow 300 different ways to describe the common video universe. This problem identified by the developer team is a known condition to the recommender systems community, where it has been identified as social tagging recommender. Instead of centrally creating tags and descriptions for items, the production of meta-data has been externalized to *the crowd*, allowing users to upload content and apply tags and descriptions in an open way, i.e., not inside a given classification scheme. Interestingly, in recommender system literature this has been called an "unstructured collaborative classification scheme that is commonly known as folksonomy" (Cantador, Bellogín, and Vallet 2010, 237). The way data-production works here has shifted from the approach from common patterns of usage or centralized production of classification schemes to a crowd-sourced form of classification, decentering how similarities are being constructed. The relationship between content provider and algorithm has been complicated and multiplied. No professional editors or data-workers with a pre-given classification scheme would be included. However, the team did not trust the wisdom of the crowd when it came to producing comparable meta-data within the organization. In a dev-meeting, Gillian argued "that the people are simply entering different things" (fieldnote). And Bob said in an early interview in relation to tagging of videos: "I don't know how good they are, but what I have heard so far from other products, this is a big problem, that things are not tagged well" (Interview Bob, my translation). This ranged from team-specific ways of writing description texts to the fact that the field for keywords in the central planning software was a free text field, i.e., one could enter whatever text one would like. Therefore, the development team, including the selected editors, envisioned the installation of a central control instance.[16] The online editorial team should act as a central point of passage in which the metadata is being controlled. Incomplete or dysfunctional tags or descriptions should be played back to the thematic editorial teams for correction. When asked how they want to control the proper description of video items – amongst the selection of good pictures – the online editors told me: "We even will have a co-worker, who will wrap them over the knuckles" (Online-Editors Interview, my translation). At the same time, workshops for the thematic editorial teams were envisioned to train them on the usage of the common classification scheme. Further, a change in the possibilities of entering data in the first place

---

16   It is important to note here that at the time of doing the ethnography, this still was a plan. The full installation of this group happened later.

was envisioned. Instead of using the old category list, which was large and hard to comprehend, a new one was created, one that was much simpler, and seemed to make sense for the online editorial team. This was accompanied by the plan to provide a style guide to the different editorial teams.

> In relation to the metadata, there will be a style guide, so that the editorial boards have something they can stick to. And then we have to look how it works (Online-Editors Interview, my translation).

Through installing this common classification scheme and implementing it at the central WhatsOn System, the development project additionally implemented – or rather: updated – a common infrastructure, connecting the different groups in a common regime of data production. As a result, the project approached the issue at hand from three different directions, a) making the WhatsOn Key-users to allies of the algorithm, b) updating the category list and *hard-wiring* it in the central planning system and c) training the WhatsOn users in order to learn how to apply the new category list. In doing so, the development team tried to establish and naturalize common categorizations, i.e., build an organization-wide standard. Instead of leaving the standard without any allies, and therefore less power, they went even a step further and installed a central point of passage – the online editorial team – to ensure the quality of the produced meta-data. Thus, through installing an organization-wide standard and aligning it with guards who would support and enforce the standard, an information infrastructure to coordinate different sub-communities was put in place.

Of course, we have to be cautious when it comes to the idea of common categorizations as a naturalized form of common knowledge. While the classification system is being installed as an institutional and organizational device to produce common accounts, assuming a deterministic idea of translating observations into classifications might lead us on a slippery slope. As Suchman (2006) argues, plans (or in our case classification systems and guidelines) become a resource of orientation for localized practices, but our "ability to act according to the plan ultimately turns on the embodied skills available to you in situ" (Suchman 2006, 72). As argued before, interactionist theories assume that the meaning of a symbol is not just a given but is produced in the interaction amongst competent members of a social group. Interpretation of the exchanged symbols and actions is based on prior knowledge (including resources such as plans) and taken-for-granted ideas about how the situation has to be interpreted. Garfinkel called this the ethnomethods of the participants, while pragmatism draws heavily on ideas of socialization and routine action. However, both approaches include moments of variation and creativity (e.g., Joas 1997) in their conceptualizations. Ethnomethodology was even based on the very critique of traditional sociology, which treated individuals as "judgmental dopes" (Garfinkel 1984, 68) who only follow pre-defined rules or norms.[17] Instead, the members of a social collective are competent on their own, where social structure and order are performed always-anew and therefore also potentially always a bit different. In other words, stability of social order is not a theoretical presumption but an empirical question. This, of course, has some important consequences for the production of localized order and accounts – in this case in the use of categories and key-words – in larger communities that share standardized classification systems. The problem we faced here was that the categories so far were used very differently in different editorial teams, and the list was a product of historical processes, where some teams even had their very own categories, just for their shows. Bowker and Star (2000, 287) argue that "categories are historically situated artifacts and, like all artifacts, are learned as part of a membership in communities of practice". And this became an issue here because several hundred learned categorization practices had to be coordinated with each other. Instead of integrating everyone in a common situation where the production of accounts (and socio-technical order) could have been coordinated *in situ*, the central planning system WhatsOn became a connecting device of many different communities. Installing the editorial team as an obligatory passage point thereby was important, as "anomalies always arise when multiple communities of practice come together, and useful technology cannot be designed in all communities at once" (Bowker and Star 2000, 310). Instead of repairing the communicative production of a common order within the situation, the online editorial team was assigned the task to do *categorial work* (Bowker and Star 2000, 310), managing the different meanings in the different communities to foster cooperation. Returning to the example of Ziewitz (2017), the task was no longer to articulate one's observations in a way that the algorithm would be able to make sense of, but to coordinate the different forms of sense-making in a process that would allow a communicative logic of updating and correcting one's accounts in a way that would work for the algorithm. The discussion on whether something matches the qualification "of our understanding of a road" (Ziewitz 2017, 6) no longer took place between the situated observers but was mediated via a common infrastructure and classification system, connecting the online editors and the many other editorial teams. This all had to be accomplished, so "that a world imagined outside of the system, of conversation and exchange, of sociality and communication, could become the world in here, the social world of the algorithmic system" (Neyland 2015, 128). Producing what I call *algorithmic reflexivity* here meant not just resolving meaning of signals but also

17   Of course, this is a result of the structuralist legacy within sociology and other social sciences. That is, from the perspective of an ever-present and self-reproducing structure, conceptions of deterministic actions make sense – or are even necessary to prevail in the given paradigm.

to establish a whole organizational structure that produced accounts of the social world that could become translatable to the algorithmic technique.

Institutionalizing Algorithmic Reflexivity

The production of metadata is much more than just making a video database machine readable. Instead, what we could see is that the algorithm assumed that the references flowing in the socio-technical system were comparable to each other. Or in other words: the enactment of the world in which the algorithmic system should work had to be standardized (see also Gillespie 2014). In this chapter, I discussed different approaches to produce such a stable practice of referencing, a dominant enactment of the video database via metadata, each with its issues and problems, as the organizational structure and interdependencies at hand made it im/possible to do so. Each case that failed was part of another network of translations or functional relation, producing data and meeting affordances of specific settings and situations. Algorithms are embedded in a broader ecosystem in which they operate and are made operational. The power of the algorithm lies not *within* the algorithm but in the allies that it can mobilize in order unfold its agency (Ananny 2016; Ensmenger 2012; Neyland 2015). As such, the translation between the abstract algorithmic principle and the data-production processes need a form of institutionalized and stabilized *algorithmic reflexivity* to resolve the previously only abstractly assumed references of the algorithm. This can be understood as an inscription process of a second order, in which the assumptions of the developers about the social system are included in the concrete artifact through interpretation and scripted usage of signals – as we have seen in terms of interpreting ratings of users – or are delegated to the organizational structure, as we have seen in the case of meta-data production for the video content. Thus, the process of inscription does not just put an algorithm together but is also the process of nested forms of de-inscription, which are potentially stabilized. Understanding algorithmic agency there-fore requires us to recursively reconstruct processes of inscription and de-inscription and the involved forms of reflexivity that lead to the stabilized and institutionalized entity that we call *the algorithm*.

What does it mean to say that the algorithm is becoming institutionalized or even an institution? Within the sociological discourse over the past – roughly hundred – years, the notion of the institution has been a counter-point to the idea of anthropological givens. Instead of naturalizing observable structures by arguing that humans or society are simply like that, the notion of the institution highlights that humans are in need of developing stable and repeating forms of interaction that are durable over time and space (e.g., Parsons 1954). These forms of behavior order our everyday life, as they become unquestionable and act as if they were natural. In the phenomenological line of thinking, Berger and Luckmann (1967) even speak of the objectivation of meanings and practices that allows therefore to identify certain types of interaction as an institution. By arguing this way, the institutions become social facts in the meaning of Durkheim ([1895] 1982).[18] Social facts are for Durkheim objectively given and hard structures that are explainable out of the social realm alone. However, this understanding of an institution as durable, comparable, and traceable practices grants the notion of the institution an ontological status that acts rather as an explanation than as a starting point for the analysis of the social. Instead, it might be worthwhile to ask how institutions as fairly regular patterns – to borrow a term from Law (1994) – are being enacted and referenced in these situations. In his theory of structuration, Giddens combines these different attitudes, arguing that institutions re-produce these settings themselves, thus making subsequent practices more or less likely. Stabilized practices take, as Giddens argues, a vital role in the production of social structures, which we are faced with in concrete situations as durable obstacles to our actions (Giddens 1984). However, we encounter these structures always through the enactment of them through particular actors in the situation – they have to be mobilized. Just as Garfinkel argued that social order is to be explained rather than being used to explain, institutions and their upholding are the result of situated practices that order the situation according to an idea of the institution (see also Passoth 2021). How are ideas, rules, and customs being mobilized to uphold the institution? This also makes it necessary to look at all ordering elements in these situations. What infrastructures, algorithmic scripts, data silos, transport protocols, disciplinary codes such as journalistic ethos, have been mobilized and coordinated in order to make these fairly regular patterns of practices possible? Each of the involved actors thereby represents a set of practices that keeps itself stable, thus making it possible to trace stable practices over time and space and relate them to each other. In this sense, the video database of the archive represents an institution and the process of subsequent institution*alizing* at the same time. Thus, an institution is always necessarily both: the stable socio-technical fact and a practical achievement. Installing *algorithmic reflexivity* is a vital element in institutionalizing algorithmic systems.

As discussed, the developer team combined the scripts of the algorithmic techniques with practices and scripts of other actors, such as data producers, infrastructures, or databases. Algorithmic reflexivity had to go from explicit and uncertain to implicit and durable. However, the achieved social order produces the algorithm as a durable actor and depends also on the assembled actants, with their own resistances, assumptions, in short: scripts. In the case

---

18   Of course, we have to understand the program of Durkheim also as a political move to establish sociology as a distinct discipline and making it independent from biology, psychology, or the natural sciences.

of the recommender system, this happened in two fundamentally different ways, first, in the case of collaborative filtering, the signals of the interactions between users and video-items were questioned, re-interpreted and appropriated for the usage in the recommender system. Based on their own experiences, the developer team tried to understand the different situations to which the ratings were referring to and interpret them accordingly. Resolving the meaning of signals was here part of the development of the algorithm, and a form of algorithmic reflexivity was stabilized as part of the algorithmic script. In the second case of content-based filtering, the development team did not think about ways to interpret the signals themselves, but delegated processes of reflexivity to other organizational sites. The concerns were not in which way the signals should be understood, but how one can be sure that the references provided by the organization are comparable to each other in the first place. In both cases, however, forms of *algorithmic reflexivity* were installed and stabilized as organizational practice.

In the previously discussed example, Ziewitz (2017) was struggling precisely with these translation processes. Instead of producing taken-for-granted meanings, each occasion of a new street had to be questioned and tested. The indexicality of the algorithmic expression was not easy to resolve – and it was for sure not the result of an uninterested, i.e., routinized, process of reflexivity. Instead, the implicit procedures were made explicit by making "the "reflexive" character of practical activities observable" (Garfinkel 1984, 9). In the example of Ziewitz, the structure and ordering of the city did not follow the imagination and assumptions of the algorithmic ethnomethods. Resolving the notion of the road was not that easily translatable and involved a lot of work on the side of the mediator – here in the figure of Ziewitz and the other participants. This, however, is not only a problem of incompatibility of different interpretations but an incompatibility of different forms of ordering the world. The streets that were the subjects of inquiry for the formulated algorithm are the result and the delegation of the city and its socio-technical order. The formation of the streets is the materialization of the whole history of the city – and with it a materialization of manifold decisions, rooted in urban planning and politics (e.g., Aibar and Bijker 1997). Latour (1999a) showed that the production of scientific knowledge rests on the production and circulation of references. In his famous example of jungle soil, the jungle was made experienceable, comparable, and describable over distance by references, which could be followed forth and back. From the jungle to the publication, the chain of references is kept stable, and with it the reality enacted on each of the stations of the translation process. However, the references that circulate from the Amazon forest to the office in Paris are not only signs or symbols referencing jungle soil. They signify the whole apparatus that makes the production and circulation of references possible in the first place. They reference a socio-technical order, including apparatuses, scientists, editors, research assistants, and so on. In a similar way, the data produced within the public broadcaster was not only a problem of an external description, but every instance in which data had been produced (or failed to do so) was an issue of the entire organization. The data that were available were not only referencing singular videos but also the practices and arrangements that made the data possible in the first place. The signals that had been interpreted were not only referencing users and their preferences but also the national digital infrastructure and the tracking regime that transported them to the algorithmic script. The data represented not a detached symbol that could be easily re-interpreted. Instead, these symbols were referring to specific organizational structures, with their own performed and practically enacted functionality within the broader assemblage called the public broadcaster. Just as the roads reference the history of the city, the produced data symbols reference the becoming of the public broadcaster through time.

These organizational configurations, however, were incompatible with the taken-for-granted assumptions inscribed into the algorithmic script. And while in the case of collaborative filtering, the ethnomethods of the algorithm changed, content-based filtering needed a new distributed and organized communication structure. By implementing such a distributed communication structure, the public broadcaster did not change but extended its organizational structure, adding institutional practices coupled with an infrastructure that allowed the coordination of different practical communities and their production of accounts. Instead of using already established data silos or external solutions, the software development team added a layer of organizational and institutional practices. In the end, we made the public broadcaster bigger than it was before to solve the newly emerged problem. But by doing so, we also added a *new* organization, as the enactment of the public broadcaster – and the algorithm – within the newly installed socio-technical structure differed from all the other enactments we encountered. The practical achievement of the algorithmic system became more than just tinkering with code, development environments, or mathematical functions. The organizational structure was part of mobilizing, installing, and relating new actors and enroll them into the network that was the institutionalized algorithm.

5

Algorithmic Politics

Enlighten, educate and entertain. – Reith, 1924

Recommender algorithms and filter systems, such as Search Engines, are a general problem for contemporary democracies. Or at least this is the narrative. According to that trope, filter bubbles or echo chambers threaten the way we are being informed about political and social news within our society. This is an even bigger issue if the institution that uses such algorithms has the explicit mandate to foster democracy by distributing information equally and in its plurality. In this chapter, I will therefore discuss how the topic of filter bubbles became a problem in the development team and what ambiguity in different normative goals emerged, namely, between popularity and the orientation on successful role models, such as Netflix or YouTube on the one side, and the shared normative idea and (seeming) necessity of balancing personalization with diverse information provision. These problems did thereby not just come up in the development project of this specific broadcaster but reflect a much broader discussion about filter systems and democracy by academic scholars and the political system of Germany. I will therefore highlight the arguments in these debates to understand how this issue emerged in the local site, that is: how it was mobilized.

The discussion of filter bubbles as a threat to democracy thereby hinges on specific assumptions about the communicative structure and the normative goal of information diversity. The discussion of the public sphere rests especially on the implicit assumption that a coherent and monolithic public is to be found. I argue that a pragmatist conception of publics in a plural might serve us better in understanding the problem at hand and may help us to develop a better understanding of potential remedies. Instead of assuming that algorithms fragment a previously coherent public sphere, I argue that the public broadcasting system was a solution to specific configurations of media technologies and generative processes of publics in the plural. Diversity as a policy goal thereby has a specific function in producing a common communication sphere. The question then is not so much whether diversity is being achieved but how it is done so. In the development project, we experimented with different approaches to produce diversity and make it a tangible and actionable object. And while these approaches had their very own problems and challenges, they can still teach us something about necessary next steps. In a bigger picture, however, the question is not only how we might be able to produce a coherent public under new conditions of our media system, but how an algorithmic system, such as the recommender system that we developed, became a political actor. In reformulating a media-sensitive way of achieving the legal and political goal of diversity, the algorithm as a technological actor had to mediate between different normative systems with their different imaginations of an interaction system.

The selection of the public broadcaster as a case thereby might seem odd at first. Technology and its artifacts are political (Winner 1980), they have an impact, they regulate and enable or resist certain ways of (inter-)acting. Thus, this is nothing specific to a broadcaster, nor something specific to algorithms and machine learning. However, the sites of politics are specific. As seen in the previous chapter, the social orderings of an organization are reflected in the data production that goes into the machine learning system. That is, machine learning does not only require a certain form of data, it requires a certain form of social order. At the same time, the case of public broadcasting is not just part of implicit politics of an artifact but subject to an ongoing institutionalized political debate about democratic order and the media system. Here, the debates and the issues are not just implicit but take the form of a controversy and crisis. In the debate, machine-learning-driven mechanisms of information selection challenge the established political function of the media system and its orderings. Thus, as an institution that is born out of political debate and has been subject of it ever since, the issues that arise in the relation of social orderings, machine learning techniques, and political power are surfacing and can be studied. A question that is often raised when studying filter bubbles, bias, or injustice of algorithmic systems is the question of the normative framework against we would measure the impacts of a technology. However, this question is not always easy to answer, especially when different normative ideas conflict each other, such as liberalism and equality. In the case of public broadcasting in Germany, however, this question can in principle easily be answered. The normative and political claims are made very explicit and are even part of the German constitutional law. What makes the public broadcaster as an organization and institution therefore a case for such a study is the fact that the quarrels between algorithms and democracy are more graspable, the interplay between regulation and algorithmic design more visible. The issues of algorithmic politics, either with a small p or a big P, and its translation into political and normative reasoning are the same everywhere, but here they are very explicit. Therefore, public broadcasting is an ordinary example but at the same time a special one, as it shows what problems, politics, and design strategies have been mobilized and how they relate to each other.

Mobilizing Problems

Within the development project, two different issues became relevant for the team. First, the issue of the legal and political obligations of a public broadcaster, which differentiates it partly from private media actors. As a public institution, the public broadcaster has a specific role within Germany's democratic system. By mobilizing these issues, questions about the recommender system and its function did emerge quite soon in the project. However, secondly, the issue of competition with big players like Netflix or YouTube was made relevant in the discussions. In order to stay relevant in a changing media landscape, the need to adopt techniques developed and distributed by established big players emerged also quite soon. Both issues became matters of concerns for the developers, yet each issue pointed towards a different normative ordering system which was to be realized in a specific design of the recommender system. The legal-political obligation in form of a legal normative discourse, and for the issue of competition in the form of specific algorithmic techniques came with their own assumptions about social interactions, aims, and problems. In the following, I will therefore discuss how these issues have been mobilized, and how they point towards different orderings and normative frameworks, importing also other issues, which are seemingly incommensurable.

The Democratic Role of Broadcasters

When I became part of the development project in early 2016, the aim of the project was to find a solution for the development and integration of a video-on-demand system that mitigates the risk of producing less diversity for the video content offered for individual users. Under conditions of linear broadcasting this issue had been tackled with the selection of content by editors, but this role seemed to shift under the new conditions of non-linear broadcasting. The question was: would video-on-demand lead to a highly reduced set of topics provided and consumed by the users? And if so, how could this be mitigated? The project formulated the problem to be tackled in the project description as follows:

> Digital services of public broadcasters especially face challenges, as the developed platform strategy is not only oriented towards the demands and feedback of users, but at the same time has to consider the "principles of objectivity and neutrality of media coverage, diversity of opinions, and the balance of their services (Project proposal, 1, my translation).

The problem that is being made relevant here stems from the role of public broadcasters within the democratic system of Germany. Thus, it does reference to a specific system of normative, legal, and political ideals and imaginaries, which has its roots in the legal-historical development of that political community. The German media system and the accompanying rulings of the constitutional court attribute a certain role to public service broadcasters in Germany. This attributed role within the institutional and social setup of the German state was taken as a starting point by the project team to formulate requirements for the to-be developed video-on-demand system. Therefore, I will briefly discuss the specific legal aspects of public service broadcasting in Germany. This is important insofar as it shows the ongoing and difficile discussions on the German media system and the socio-technical systems present in it as the entanglement of legal, social, and technical issues that have to be brought into alignment with each other.

The German media system was designed based on the experiences before and during World War II. During these times, radio and TV broadcasting was primarily used as a propaganda tool (e.g., Kallis 2005). The system was used to back-up and solidify the fascist system of the National Socialists. Based on these experiences and to prevent a fallback into an anti-democratic system, the Allies designed the German media system for the newly founded Federal Republic as a decentralized and neutral structure of distributed public broadcasters. Establishing a paternalistic but independent system of information provision should serve the democratization of post-war societies and also foster creating a different imaginary of the nation state (Jauert and Lowe 2005). These broadcasters were (and are) independent of each other and from the government.[1] However, the specific principles that public broadcasting must adhere to is derived from two sources. First, the principles of objectivity and impartiality are defined in § 26 para. 2 MStV, i.e., the *Medienstaatsvertrag* (Interstate Media Agreement), to prevent an imbalance in reporting of positions and opinions. The Interstate Broadcasting Agreement is also an expression of the political and legal mandate of public broadcasting

---

1   This is also the main reason why public broadcasting in Germany is not financed via taxes but through an extra household fee.

to stabilize and safeguard democracy in the Federal Republic of Germany. By providing German citizens an overview of available political positions and opinions, the public broadcaster enables an informed, free, and democratic way to form one's opinion and decisions. This idea of the democratic role of public broadcasters is reflected in the ideal of *basic provision of information*, first and originally formulated in the German context by Günter Hermann, former legal director of the West German Radio (WDR) in 1975 (Grassmuck 2014a).

All of the so far described legal obligations of public broadcasters are, however, not codified in law but are derived from the German Constitution (*Deutsches Grundgesetz, GG*), especially Art. 5. In many decisions of the Federal Constitutional Court, Art. 5 GG became the defining element of German media law (Grassmuck 2014b). Art. 5 (1) of the German Constitution includes the right to freedom of expression alongside freedom of the press and the freedom of radio broadcasting:

> Every person shall have the right freely to express and disseminate his opinions in speech, writing and pictures and to inform himself without hindrance from generally accessible sources. Freedom of the press and freedom of reporting by means of broadcasts and films shall be guaranteed. There shall be no censorship (Art. 5, para. 1, Basic Law for the Federal Republic Germany).[2]

These rights have been interpreted by the Federal Constitutional Court in many rulings over the years and has led to a tremendous depth of regulatory details (Hagen 2013). The legal obligation of information provision has also been named the *Programmauftrag* (Program Mandate) of public service broadcasting. It is derived from the *freedom of reporting by means of broadcasts* and the right to *inform oneself without hindrance from generally accessible sources (see quote above)*. The Federal Constitutional Court derives from these two rights an obligation for public-service broadcasters to make an unhindered access to information possible. The idea of basic provision of information was first taken up by the Federal Constitutional Court in the year 1986 in what has been called the 4th broadcasting decision (*4. Rundfunkentscheidung*) (Federal Constitutional Court 73, 118). In this context, the freedom of reporting is also viewed as an obligation, as was again underlined in a decision of the court on 11th September 2007:

> The freedom of broadcasting serves the free, individual and public formation of opinion. [...] The mandate contained in Article 5 (1) sentence 2 of the Basic Law to guarantee freedom of broadcasting aims at an order

---

2 Translated by: Professor Christian Tomuschat, Professor David P. Currie, Professor Donald P. Kommers and Raymond Kerr, in cooperation with the Language Service of the German Bundestag

which ensures that the diversity of existing opinions is expressed in broadcasting in the broadest and most complete way possible (BVerfG, Decision from 11.09.2007, Rn 115, my translation).[3]

The obligation formulated by the Federal Constitutional Court aims at a media landscape that ensures the broadcasting of different political, normative, and cultural positions in order to provide a comprehensive overview of all events in the European, national, and local regions in all spheres of life, as also defined in § 26 para. 1 MStV. Thus, the mandate of basic provision of information does not just regulate the general availability of broadcasting services but is also concerned with content of the aired programs.

However, in the wake of ongoing technological developments and new forms of broadcasting news and information via the internet, the role of public broadcasters also changed. Instead of just providing TV and radio programs in a linear manner, the Internet made it possible to distribute news in a non-linear way and with a mix of different media, blurring the boundaries between print, audio, and video formats. Adapting the modes in which public broadcasters make their programs available via these new technologies created a challenge in relation to the basic mandate of public broadcasting. In the already cited ruling of the year 2007 the Federal Constitutional Court also expressed concerns about the constitutionally demanded basic provision of information under new digital technological conditions:

> New technologies allow the use of navigators and electronic program guides, whose software can be used to influence the decision of information selection of recipients (BVerG, Decision. from 11.09.2007, Rn 118, my translation).[4]

This concern of the Federal Constitutional Court reflects the fear of the emergence of filter bubbles and echo chambers through means of (although not explicitly mentioned) algorithmically recommenders as a mode of diminishing the ability and the right to inform oneself without hindrance, as formulated in Art. 5, para. 1 GG. The adaptation of the public broadcasting sector to the environment of changed technological possibilities and to how citizens consume information presents new challenges as to how public broadcasting is realized. These challenges make it necessary to re-think how public broadcasting can operate to contribute to its original role within democratic societies and a newly ordered media landscape (see also Grassmuck 2014a).

---

3   *German original: Die Rundfunkfreiheit dient der freien, individuellen und öffentlichen Meinungsbildung. [...] Der in Art. 5 Abs. 1 Satz 2 GG enthaltene Auftrag zur Gewährleistung der Rundfunkfreiheit zielt auf eine Ordnung, die sicherstellt, dass die Vielfalt der bestehenden Meinungen im Rundfunk in möglichster Breite und Vollständigkeit Ausdruck findet.*

4   *German original: Die neuen Technologien erlauben im Übrigen den Einsatz von Navigatoren und elektronischen Programmführern, deren Software ihrerseits zur Beeinflussung der Auswahlentscheidung von Rezipienten genutzt werden kann*

Especially recommender algorithms are an important element in the discussion in which democratic institutions and their role in contemporary societies are being negotiated.

The project was then started with these discussions as a backdrop. As such, the project and the involved partners were aware of the specific situation of public broadcasters in Germany and the potential issues that could arise from the introduction of a new technology. However, the discussion focused very soon on the role of the recommender algorithms that were becoming a central element of the new video-on-demand system. In a meeting, which was explicitly discussing recommender systems together with developers, academic partners, and online editors, Alice summarized the different goals of the recommender:

> Alice introduced the two different techniques of the recommender algorithm, explaining what a content-based filtering approach does and what collaborative filtering is. One of the online editors asked what kind of data the latter uses. Alice explained that it uses only interaction data. She also mentions that the filter bubble issue is a problem for the development, as especially content-based filtering tends to create filter bubbles. However, the different approaches and goals for the recommender systems can be outlined in three different ideas: first, recommending content which you would like the most, which she discussed under the heading of "Exactly for you." The second recommender approach could produce results that are surprising for the user, creating diversity – under the headline of "something different." And lastly, a goal could be recommending controversial topics. Here, Alice did not give an example or a possible headline. The editorial team member interrupted her and asked if she can send around a paper, or if she should take notes (fieldnote).

For the sake of tackling the issue of filter bubbles within an institution that was built around the idea of supporting democracy through balanced and broad information provision, the project followed the call of Crawford (2016) to think about this from a design perspective. It was also important to the developers that the design of such a recommender system must be one that is deeply embedded in the ideas and normativities of the public broadcasting system and not something that is simply bought off-the-shelf. In reaction to a discussion whether an external solution should be bought, Bob replied on Slack:

> In addition to what Charlie and Alice are discussing, I would like to emphasize again that we should raise this discussion as much as possible on a more general and reasonable level, [...] as we are working hard to produce the necessary know-how, to implement and advance

recommendations exactly for public broadcasting (Bob via Slack in #machinelearning)

It is important to note that although the problem we were tackling was – in part – the result of the specific legal setting in Germany, it was not invoked by the courts or a regulator but through the institutions involved in the research project themselves. As such, the public broadcaster wanted to proactively react to *potential or imagined* issues that might occur when developing such a product based on a general discourse and embed the discussion actively within the moral and normative framework of public broadcasting. Thus, the question whether such a recommendation engine would violate the legal obligations of the institution as a *matter of fact* becomes less relevant than the observation that the possibility became a *matter of concern*.[5] Thus, legal issues have been mobilized by the institution based on general discussions (e.g., Neuberger and Lobigs 2010). The normative idea of the specific role of public broadcasters in Germany has been mobilized in order to change the problem that had to be solved by the algorithm. The development project therefore created a direct link between the technical realization of a recommender system with a whole legal and political order. The recommender system was not just a technical realization of calculations, code, and databases but also a reference to German democracy and its institutions. However, this legal setup, which has been mobilized within the organization, was not the only issue that arose when implementing the recommender algorithm.

Competition

A second concern voiced in the development project – and beyond – was to stay relevant in a media system that is characterized by fierce competition and technological advancements from private companies. Netflix was also referred to in several occasions as a role model but also as a competitor. The following slide was distributed by Alice and Bob in the development team. It was discussed and distributed in a meeting of different public broadcasters, directly setting themselves in relation to YouTube and Netflix. Thus, it represents this ongoing discussion within the public broadcasters in which the problem of competition has been mobilized within the very institution that also formulates the problem of diversity.

Especially the younger generation is here portrayed as a consumer group or population that no longer follows traditional forms of TV consumption and that has adapted their viewing habits according to services like Netflix, which is also explicitly mentioned here. Thus, Netflix is for one seen as a direct

---

5   This formulation is taken from Latour (2004), but in a slightly different context. This also touches upon a perspective on law, which does not regulate behavior by itself but must be invoked in practical discourse to become effective.

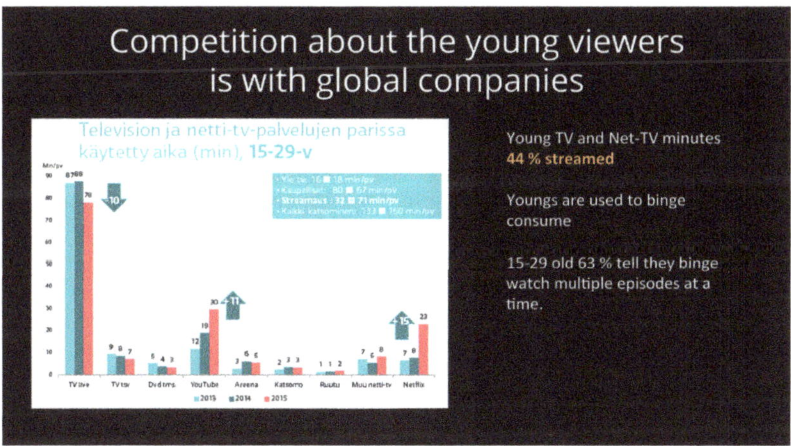

[Figure 6] Slide shared in the project team showing the market shares of different video-on-demand services

competitor but also, and this is much more interesting, as a force shaping the political economy and the population's viewing habits. The result of this perspective is that one has to become more like Netflix in order to be able to survive in the fierce competition but also to learn from their best practices and their success. In short, Netflix became a role model for the development project – and beyond. This also came up in several meetings but was best summarized by Bob in an interview:

> Yeah, I think, just as, the big role models are of course things like YouTube and Netflix. Simply, because how people interact with it, what it means to them and so on. And they are also in all aspects, what belongs to the recommendations […] textbook examples of course (Bob Interview, my translation)

Thus, Netflix became a reference point in two different ways. First, Netflix was seen as a market force, able to change the political economy, reflected in viewing habits – such as binge watching – and expectations of the users. Second, algorithmic techniques were being mobilized in the development project from exactly these actors. And these were heavily influenced by the problem definitions of Netflix and similar services.

One of the techniques that was utilized for recommender systems was Collaborative Filtering. This algorithmic technique came directly from the domain of Netflix. In the beginning of my time at the project, Alice sent me a paper explaining collaborative filtering, which directly resulted out of the so-called Netflix Competition. In that competition, Netflix provided a data set from their streaming system and asked the participants to find suitable solutions to the problem of predicting ratings. Interestingly, the paper not only described the

Netflix competition and the technique found there but was actually written by the team who won the contest several times.

> Our team's entry, originally called BellKor, took over the top spot in the competition in the summer of 2007, and won the 2007 Progress Prize with the best score at the time: 8.43 percent better than Netflix. Later, we aligned with team Big Chas to win the 2008 Progress Prize with a score of 9.46 percent. At the time of this writing, we are still in first place, inching towards the 10 percent landmark (Koren, Bell, and Volinsky 2009, 47).

According to the authors, although it was a contest, there had been discussions around the techniques in the developer community. The authors describe that their "discussions with other top teams and postings on the contest forum indicate that these are the most popular and successful methods for predicting ratings" (Koren, Bell, and Volinsky 2009, 47). Thus, the development team mobilized algorithmic approaches to the issue of recommendations that have been very successful in other contexts. If Netflix and YouTube are the main competitors and role models for the own development, it makes sense to at least have a look at the techniques that are regarded the best performing ones. Also, these companies are widely known as important and innovative forces behind the development of recommender algorithms (Amatriain and Basilico 2016). However, the recommender technique imported to the development project was the result of a normative order with very specific assumptions, goals, and environments in which they were developed and in which they were performing well. This good performance is precisely entangled with the problem that the algorithm should solve. But what exactly was the problem for Netflix to be solved? Looking at the Netflix prize website, we find that:

> Netflix is all about connecting people to the movies they love. To help customers find those movies, we've developed our world-class movie recommendation system: CinematchSM. Its job is to predict whether someone will enjoy a movie based on how much they liked or disliked other movies. We use those predictions to make personal movie recommendations based on each customer's unique tastes. And while Cinematch is doing pretty well, it can always be made better (Netflix Prize).[6]

The idea of recommendations is to match the users' unique taste, predicting the enjoyability of a movie. This might not come as a surprise, but it is still important to point out, as recommendations can serve many different purposes. The general aim of a recommender system is based for one on the

---

6   *https://www.netflixprize.com/rules.html*, accessed: 13.3.2020

narration of information overload[7] and the burden of choice in a multi-option society. Thus, recommender systems can help to manage and reduce the complexity of modern information societies. This is also reflected in the preface of the recommender system handbook, which was also provided to me by Alice. There Ricci, Rikach, and Shapira write: "Recommender Systems are valuable means for online users to cope with information overload and help them making better choices" (Ricci et al. 2011, vii). Yet, what counts as a better choice is not qualified. There are many different forms of producing relevance of recommendations, depending on the underlying goal of the recommender. As Morris (2015) points out, a Bourdieu'ian perspective would see a recommender in the form of a cultural intermediary's tasks not in recommending you things *you* like but that might reflect a certain cultural habitus, signifying a sense of belonging to a social class or milieu. Thus, the function of a hypothetical Bourdieu'ian recommender is precisely to not match the recommendations with *your taste* but to recommend items against your initial ideas of enjoyability. A recommender that would foster diversity, as suggested by Helberger (2015), would also not necessarily recommend items you like but content that would complement a diverse information diet. Thus, it is remarkable that the idea of recommender systems that recommend similar items to match the users' taste has become self-evident to a degree that questioning this form of relevance seems odd to many people. However, coming back to the paper in question, the background of these assumptions is made very explicit.

> Modern consumers are inundated with choices. Electronic retailers and content providers offer a huge selection of products, with unprecedented opportunities to meet a variety of special needs and tastes. Matching consumers with the most appropriate products is key to enhancing user satisfaction and loyalty (Koren, Bell, and Volinsky 2009, 42).

Given the strong influence of Netflix and the quote by Koren, Bell, and Volinsky (2009) above, it seems that the mode of selection might not reflect general societal needs, but is aimed at a clear market-oriented need to keep the *consumers* attention on the site of the service/product provider, and ensure that they come back. Seaver (2019) even compares recommender algorithms in this respect with traps. The goal is therefore individual consumption, not societal status ("look what fancy movies I watched"), or the orientation on information needs. Also, the choice of expressing the problem to be solved reflects this attitude. The recommender does not target citizens, individuals, or members – each category comes here with its own connotations – but consumers. This is also not surprising, given the economic origin of this technique (Amatriain and Basilico 2016) and the market value that is being created through recommender systems. By now, these technologies are central

---

7   For an overview of the concept of information overload see also: Eppler and Mengis (2004).

elements of entire business models (Smith and Linden 2017) and the prediction of users' taste is a crucial element of market formation (Poechhacker and Nyckel 2020). As a result, it seems fair to argue that the development of recommender systems is primarily driven by market interests, which is reflected in the way the algorithms are being developed. As Hallinan and Striphas (2016) argue, the algorithm is the product of a specific contest design. Or in other words, the problems explicitly formulated and the taken-for-granted approaches of a community heavily influence the construction of algorithmic techniques.

It is important to note here that this is not a critique in itself but more of a reflexive account of the origin of the algorithmic technique and its assumed problems to be solved. This reflexivity has become important in the project, as it shows that through the community efforts and the process of disciplinary delegation and displacement of inscriptions, subsequent development projects are being impacted. Problems as well as its solution were imported by specific algorithmic techniques, which are connected to services with their own, market-oriented, perspectives and visions that are inscribed into the technology. Information selection in these techniques is guided by similarity and a market logic. And they are developed and evaluated in an economic and market-driven environment. Thus, the aim is information reduction to a set of similar enough items to keep the consumer engaged with the platform.

Issues of Technology

Importing algorithmic techniques from Netflix and similar sources also imported their scripted assumptions about problems, interactions, and solutions. As we have seen in the previous chapters, algorithmic techniques are not just tools one can apply, but they are also references to entire communities and the issues formulated by them. In the context of a public broadcaster in Germany, the problem that the recommender solved created some frictions of normative ideas of how a public broadcaster should work. The recommender system was seen as introducing problematic features to the online presence of the broadcaster. Both problem definitions, the one from Netflix and Co., and the other from the public and democratic discourse have thereby not only been mobilized in the project out of the blue but also connect to larger normative orders. One being core of a widespread understanding of public broadcasting as central institutions of democracy in Germany, the other from a commercial community discussing and developing recommender systems. These two mobilized problems create a tension in the formulated goal of the recommender system that need to be tackled. As shown, the development project was caught between two very different concerns and problems imported to the development project – and two that are in direct opposition to each other. Being a public institution with the specific task to

foster democratic discourse led to the idea of producing a diverse set of information in the recommender system. The concern of competition, however,
led to the exact contrary problem definition – i.e., producing personalized and
reduced sets of information to assist media choice and keep the users on the
platform at the same time.

Understanding this tension between diversity as a driver of a holistic communication space and personalization of media services requires us to revisit
the underlying conception of the public. The democratic function of public
broadcasting services rests on the idea of providing comprehensive information in order to enable discussion in a public sphere. Reformulating the
ideas about the public might pave the way for solutions that fit the current
shift within media landscapes and to re-inscribe assumptions, issues, and
solutions in recommender techniques. Thus, we first need to understand
the underlying problem of contemporary democracy with filter systems and
reformulate it to find socio-technical answers. While I already discussed the
German situation, it shows only a specific instance of the issue which can
be problematized in a broader manner. In the following section, I will therefore discuss the scholarly discussion about filter bubbles in political theory in
general and for recommender systems in particular.

Algorithms, Discourse, and Some Issues

Since the emergence of filter bubbles or echo chambers in the scholarly
discussion, these concepts have been brought into relation with democracy
at large. The Council of Europe claimed in 2007 that "media pluralism and
diversity of media content are essential for the functioning of a democratic
society" (Council of Europe 2007 cited in Helberger 2018, 155). As discussed,
this has been taken up by the German Constitutional Court and also became
an issue within the software project. However, this also relates to other questions at large within democracy. If a broad information diet is a necessity for
contemporary democracies, as it is being claimed, then this touches to some
assumptions and presumptions about how democracy ought to work. I am
going to revisit theories of democracy that can be found in relation with the
filter problem and the role public discourse takes within them. Doing so will
shed some light as to why recommender systems and other information filters
are deemed as dangerous. In my argumentation, I will give a broad overview
of the discussion – an in-depth discussion of the communicative structure
of democracy would surely require a book of its own, if not a whole library.
However, the aim is not to provide a comprehensive discussion but to highlight central features of public discourse within political theory – and why
recommender systems seem to challenge the function of public discourse in
democratic societies. I will do so by introducing a distinction of theoretical
approaches, one that I call consensus-oriented democratic theory, and the

other as a political theory of conflict. Such a distinction is – as every analytical category – always somewhat artificial and other forms of ordering theoretical contributions can be found. I do this, however, to illustrate that *at the core* these different concepts of democratic discourse face the same challenges when introducing new and algorithmic media, although the solution would differ. I will then review the concept of diversity as being discussed in relation to public broadcasting, showing what problems this concept addresses, what problems the concept itself brings with it and how I contextualize it in the bigger frame of the theoretical perspective on democracy. In the end, I will address two shortcomings of the discussion: the assumption of a holistic public discourse and the decontextualization of diversity.

Issues of Political Theory: Fragmentation of Public Discourse

Media systems are central elements in political communities, as the very idea of a political community like a nation state is formed through and by the shared imagination and visions that are being transported via that form of communication (Anderson 2006). In order to enable a community to see itself as such, a form of communication has to be found that somehow links all members of that society together. Anderson (2006) refers to the problem of gluing together individuals that would otherwise never meet in time and space – and therefore would not be able to form a society. For Anderson (2006), the media system of a nation is therefore a crucial element in the constitution of a common identity, common goals, and common imaginaries. The latter are thereby important in the constitution of a shared understanding how things are ought to be, as Taylor (2004) formulated it. That is, they transport a normative framework for individual orientations. Writing down text or recording sound and images enables new forms of social relations that point beyond the momentarily situation, bridging geographical and temporal distances (see also Marvin 1990). This then also binds together relational conceptions of societal construction (e.g., Simmel [1908] 2009) and holistic ideas of stable social entities such as the society. Central media infrastructures are therefore important institutions of modern societies. But the role the media system is granted varies over different political systems.

The premise of liberal democracies is one of pluralism as "a permanent feature of the public culture of a democracy" (J. Rawls 2005, 36). Thus, the idea of liberal democracy is founded on forms of finding compromise between different ideas, interests, and identities through means of inclusion and discourse to find a political consensus between different positions. At the same time, and to prevent polarized and extreme positions, this calls for citizens who are able to freely and autonomously come to an informed and educated opinion. While what I call here consensus-oriented democracies include a range of different approaches and theories, this is a feature that they all share. For John Stuart Mill ([1861] 2020), an important thinker of liberal democracy, the informed citizen was an important prerequisite for participating in a liberal democracy. This was based on ideas of the Enlightenment ideal of a *politically* educated citizen who is able to make her own decisions based on rational reasoning. Not much in contrast to this idea, republican perspectives on democracy seek for the virtuous citizen who "should be enlightened and informed in order to make good decisions on behalf of the community" (Mossberger, Tolbert, and McNeal 2007, 6). But also deliberative or participatory[8] approaches highlight the prerequisite of the competent and informed citizen for successful participation. Participation requires the ability of the participants to be heard, thus be included, but also to be able to take up the arguments and positions of the others, to come to a common solution or conclusion. The need for competent members, however, creates a dilemma for consensus-oriented forms of democracy. In formulating the need for the educated and informed citizen, these theories formulate a mode of in- or exclusion based on skill, not group membership. This becomes especially problematic for approaches of participatory or deliberative democracy, as inclusion is essential for these forms of democracy. The tension has then been resolved in different ways. Barber (1988), for example, assumes that citizens already have these qualities, i.e., Barber assumes informed and capable citizens as givens. He further argues that competence to handle political issues is the result of being confronted with them. As a result, including citizens in the political discussion and confronting them with different issues enables them to participate within the democratic system. In this argumentation, representative democracy does not allow the competent citizen to emerge, as political issues are being discussed amongst experts but not with the citizens (see also Parry 1989). Other thinkers like Warren (1992) do not believe that we can simply assume these qualities, and therefore formulate the need to enable individuals to become competent citizens. In order to function as a democracy, the state has to produce its own foundations by informing and educating the people.

From these approaches to democracy, an obligation of the state to enable its citizens to take part in the political discussion via information provision can be derived. This requirement has later been formulated as a right for the citizens, for example, in the German context and has at the same time materialized in a public broadcasting system that actively enables citizens to inform themselves. Within an informed public all arguments are being exchanged, evaluated and – most importantly – are able to be seen. There is empirical evidence that such a public sphere fosters social inclusion (Huckfeldt, Johnson, and Sprague 2002) and political participation (Mutz 2006). Therefore, a liberal democratic imaginary is based on the production of a common

---

8   For a differentiation of these terms, see Schmidt (2010, 237).

communication space in which these different voices and opinions are being discussed. This perspective has been driven to an extreme by Habermas (1991), who argues that the public sphere should be a realm free of power and oppression, realizing the so-called ideal speech situation. In a Habermas'ian public discourse, the best argument wins over the others simply because of its rationality and not because of some power play. This leads to a situation in which not only every position is being heard but also to a general acceptance of political decisions. Therefore, a shared public is a vital element in realizing liberal, deliberative, and even more so rational forms of governance and democracy.

The idea of the informed citizen who can form her opinion in a rational way has been criticized by different scholars. For one, the idea of an educated citizen shows the tendency to exclude parts of the population from voting (Ten 1998). Participation can, in this perspective, not be as inclusive as it should be in a plural society. Especially, as this would extend structural inequalities into the political realm. By formulating an ideal of an educated, rational, and informed decision, socio-economic disadvantaged parts of the population would be excluded from the political system (Englert 2016). The second argument brought forward against the ideal of rational and deliberative consensus argues against the idea of a shared rationality. The ideal of the informed and educated voter hinges on the idea that a consensus can be reached via rational argumentation and compromise. However, John Rawls (2005) argues that the search for an external rationality or any other consensus-building principle would undermine the original goal of liberalism and its acknowledgment of pluralism. If there is one true rationality, pluralism would be delegitimized, as we have an external reference for evaluating political positions. Pluralistic ideals are then deviant to this one true rationality – and therefore they are wrong. This critique has also been formulated by Schumpeter ([1942] 2008), focusing on the orientation of classical democratic theories, as he names them, on the public good. According to Schumpeter, there is no single identifiable public good which a group of people could agree on, nor could be brought to agreement on through rational arguments. Not least because the ideas of public good are too different and plural. In the end, so the critique, producing an educated and informed citizen, who is therefore able to participate in the political discourse, itself favors a hegemonic idea of politics and rationality.

To others, like Chantal Mouffe (2005), democracy and the political therefore is not the search for consensus and the result of rational argumentation, as Habermas conceptualizes it, but creates the potential to "subverting the ever-present temptation existing in democratic societies to naturalize its frontiers and essentialize its identities" (Mouffe 2005, 105). That is, every form of democratic governance is a hegemonic system, favoring one position over the other based on the accumulation of (political) power. What differentiates democracies from other systems is the possibility to rearrange the distribution of power, i.e., to give power to other ideals and actors. Where such a possibility ceases to exist, there is no real democracy. Consensus-driven democracies, however, lead to a state of post-democracy (Crouch 2004; Ranciere 2005) in which participation of citizens is diminished. Ranciere (2005), for example, argues that consensus rests on the exclusion of parts of the population who are not represented in an institutionally formed political consensus. As a result, consensus suggests a commonly found decision, whereas it simply might have excluded deviant positions from the discourse. For Mouffe (2000, 62), it is therefore crucial that different "collective identities forming around clearly differentiated positions, as well as on the possibility of choosing between real alternatives." In her critique of consensus-driven democracy, she argues that a common rationality has led to a political system in which different actors were converging towards rather similar positions, and only nuances marked the difference between the different options (Mouffe 2005).[9] By not presenting real alternatives, the political system has, according to Mouffe, been weakened and allowed rather extreme parties to rise. While the idea of a conflict-driven democracy differs in essential points from liberal and consensus-driven ideas of the democratic system, the role of the public sphere is also quite important. Not in the way to educate and therefore enable citizens to take part in an informed discussion, but to make real alternatives visible and therefore offer the possibility to become part of *a different* collective identity. The ability to choose between different positions within the democratic system, no matter if they are deemed rational, hinges on the ability to *see* them in the first place. A media system that makes certain positions unavailable therefore hinders potential change – leading to the same effect as if there were no alternative at all.[10] Therefore, a shared public which echoes most, if not all, opinions is also important in this concept of a democratic political system.

A shared public is equally important for different ideas of democracy. Either in producing a common idea of public good or rational decisions, or by confronting the established system with alternative ideas and approaches. Filter systems, such as search engines or recommendation systems, are now actively challenging this function of the media system within the political system of such a society. Based on empirical studies, Thorson et al. (2021)

---

9   On this behalf it is also interesting to revisit the critique of Hannah Arendt on Western political philosophy. She writes that in this tradition, politics has always been seen as a matter for experts (Arendt 2017).

10   Just as a side note, this is also a reason why targeted, i.e., personalized, political ads are such a big issue. They can over-represent the advertised position and can make it seem as if there are not many alternatives, and presenting the alternatives is a specific framing that works for the targeted group.

argue that while individual choices have an important effect on information exposure, recommender algorithms act as mediators between collective action and individual choice, and thus shape exposure. In this co-production of information exposure, algorithms take a central role, selecting appropriate information for the user based on the observed collective behavior. Thus, while we are living in times with more information available than ever, these mechanisms reduce the amount of information available to us. This is in principle a meaningful way of reducing complexity. However, when it comes to public discourse about political issues, these technologies potentially fragment political discourse.

Departing from such a perspective, it becomes clear why the emergence of filter bubbles and a subsequent fragmentation of the public sphere seem problematic for discourse and conflict-oriented democratic forms alike. Without shared information to self-identify as part of a bigger community, the imaginary that Anderson is referring to loses its ability to glue together the highly complex and dispersed political communities, allowing a polarized and splintered public of opposing and often unconnected social groups. This not only becomes problematic for the nation state as an imagined community per se but especially for contemporary democracies (e.g., Sunstein 2009), as finding a political consensus in a shared discourse is undermined. Under the condition of filter bubbles and communicative segregation of communities, these discourses become self-referential. Through computation, a filter algorithm not only classifies content as relevant or irrelevant but also creates groups of people who – based on the observed behavior – act as a class. A consensus is reached in each of these filter bubbles, resulting in multiple enactments of democracy and society, potentially undermining participation and producing extreme and incommensurable positions.[11] This is an issue insofar as the imagined community disintegrates into many different communities. If we were now to imagine a recommendation engine that mitigates these effects, we would come to an ideal-typical approach that distributes a wide variety of information, showing what is out there. But such a Habermas'ian recommender system would also provide not only the information that other arguments exist but enable the citizen to understand and evaluate them. Thus, a Habermas'ian recommender would be an ongoing exercise of contextualizing arguments. The ideal of a rational algorithm in a discourse that is never finished, that can always be reopened, if better arguments come along.

11   This perspective becomes even more troublesome as the political as a confined space of interaction and specialized communication ceases to exist (if it has ever done so). In late modernity or reflexive modernity (Beck 1992; Giddens 1984), multiple areas of (everyday) life become political issues and places where the political is to be discussed. Without such a defined arena of politics, with or without an ideal speaker situation, fragmented communication via the media system(s) becomes even more damaging for contemporary democracies.

In political theories that do not favor consensus but conflict-oriented forms of democratic engagement, filter systems are a problem too. In reference to Mouffe, Crawford (2016) reminds us that algorithms are not necessarily equipped with the qualities that make them good mediators of public positions. Through following a logic of selection of similar content, the user is – potentially – governed in a way that delimits the possible positions one could take. While digital technology and especially the Internet can be a tool for increasing and supporting these different positions and their emergence, as Mouffe (2005) and others (e.g., Papacharissi 2010) argue, the problem is more in the actual structure of the Internet, where some filter systems, such as Google's search engine or Facebook, become central entry points into these information realms. Through producing micro-publics of homogenous content, the possibility of dissent between different positions is – if not taken away – at least reduced. Thus, the fragmentation of communication and information, as the main concern is with filter bubbles, seems to provide the means to subvert the needed subversion in "ever-evolving, ever-imperfect democracies" (Papacharissi 2010, 79). Algorithmic mitigation strategies, however, would require a different approach than a Habermas'ian recommender system. A radical democracy algorithm would rather search for alternative and confrontative positions, therefore making it possible to align oneself around clearly distinguishable positions. Thus, such an algorithm would not necessary look out for contextualizing arguments, or provide more information about a position, but highlight where it differs from others.

While the challenge posed by traditional recommender systems is at the core the same for both approaches to democratic discourse, the solutions might look different. However, in both perspectives, a policy of a common communication space is a means to prevent the domination of one group over the others (see also Karppinen 2013). Building a common, inclusive, and independent communication infrastructure therefore is an important pre-requisite to limit and distribute power in a (political) community. These general concerns also have been taken up in a public service media-specific discourse, especially focused on the question of recommender systems and diversity of information.

Diversity Discourse

The debate about public service recommenders is not a new one. To the contrary, discussion around filter bubbles and the democratic obligations of public broadcasters in relation to recommender systems sparked a vivid debate within academia and beyond. This topic has thereby not only been discussed within the German legal context (e.g., Dörr, Holznagel, and Picot 2016) but throughout a small, yet growing international and interdisciplinary community of scholars at least since 2011 (e.g., Breeman, Breeman, and Helberger 2011; Helberger 2011; Seaver 2012).

Democratic discourse, as discussed in the previous section, hinges on the idea of a common sphere of communicated ideas, ideals, and positions in their plurality. This then, however, raises the question of how such an idea could or should be addressed in terms of the media system. Subsequently, scholars like Helberger (2011) or Napoli (2011) then formulated diversity as a concept and policy goal to operationalize the idea of pluralism in a media setting. Diversity, as understood by Helberger (2019), must therefore include every significant interest within a given community, including news about political parties, positions, economic development, non-state interest groups, such as religion. This understanding of diversity is now seemingly at odds with the functionality of recommender systems. In the following, I will therefore focus on the problems that are discussed in terms of diversity, but also the shortcomings of the diversity concept.

Diversity is a central principle in the distribution of news for the public media system. However, with the ongoing transformation of media technologies, from a linear to a non-linear mode of distribution, recommender systems are becoming important elements in *broadcasting*. According to Van den Bulck and Moe (2018), this creates a dilemma for public broadcasters. On the one hand, they have a legal and political task to fulfill. On the other hand, the technology is designed to deliver content tailored to the user's need. Under conditions of linear and centralized broadcasting, the idea of diversity was rooted in the practices of the editors, who decide what the program should look like, what information need to be aired, and in which form. However, with the shift towards a new media ecology and algorithms that filter information, a tension between diversity and popularity emerges.

As a result, diversity as a policy goal in public broadcasting seems to be at odds with modern recommendation systems. While human editors produce programs that represent society's plurality, algorithms select less diverse content and potentially can put media organizations under pressure to produce popular content. Therefore, these systems do not necessarily follow the idea of diversity that is part of the ethos of public broadcasters. These potential issues of recommender systems on diversity in information provision, and the political environment in which public broadcasting services have to navigate, led, according to Sørensen (2019), to a rather hesitant adoption of recommender systems by public broadcasters.

This creates challenges not only on the political but also on the conceptual level. Diversity in itself is a concept that is hard to grasp and which is multidimensional (Napoli 1999). Helberger (2018, 154) notes that in the discussion "there is still considerable conceptual disagreement." This was true in 2018 and is still true today. Diversity in this respect has been discussed as structural diversity, content diversity, and exposure diversity (see also Joris et al. 2020) – leading to some diversity in the usage of the concept of diversity. Structural diversity means the plurality of media owners and sources, and addresses the issue of market concentration in the media sector (Karppinen 2013). Content diversity addresses the diversity of distributed content that is realistically accessible (Roger & Tang 2009; Hargittai 2000), i.e., the content made available to the users. Exposure diversity, however, addresses the diversity of the content actively consumed by the users (Napoli 2011). Yet, there are also other forms of diversity, raising the question of representation. Malik (2018) makes us aware that diversity can also be applied to the community of content producers or the represented societal groups within the recommended content, e.g., in the form of racial and gender bias. Thus, diversity as a concept has been applied to almost every level of the media system: production, organizations, distribution, and consumption. Diversity is therefore an umbrella term for very diverse notions of plurality.

In relation to recommender systems, diversity has mostly been discussed in terms of content and exposure diversity, the first focusing on the supply side, the latter on the consumer side. There is a debate as to which one represents the ethos of public broadcasting and therefore fulfils the democratic function of a public media system. The original issue with recommender systems is the reduction of available information – and thus the reduction of choice. Thus, creating diversity within recommendations makes it possible to empower the viewer to choose from different and presumably unknown content. Bennett (2018) argues that presenting new, surprising or challenging content via a "serendipity window" (Bennett 2018, 118) would put public broadcasting services apart from commercial competitors. For the realization of the right to information, as formulated by the German Constitutional Court, content diversity and serendipity as proposed here surely seems sufficient. However, other scholars like Napoli (2011) and Burri (2015) argue for exposure diversity. They base their argumentation on the observation that there is no conclusive or causal connection between diversity of provided content and diversity of content that has been consumed by the users. Thus, against the background of the informed citizen as a policy goal, exposure diversity is to these scholars more important than content diversity. The latter approach is about enabling citizens to be informed, whereas the first one actively wants to produce the informed citizen. As a result, and as Sørensen and Hutchinson (2018) show, the problem definition of a recommender system depends on the question of the underlying imagination of society and the specific role assigned to public service recommender systems, raising "the sticky question about PBS paternalism in the PMS context" (Sørensen and Hutchinson 2018, 97). Thus, the level of diversity one would address depends on the normative assumptions made.

Some Shortcomings in the Debate

In this section, I briefly revisited the discussions about filter bubbles in algorithmic systems, the role of the public sphere within democracy, and the role of diversity in this discussion. This discussion, however, falls short in an important aspect. Both, the public sphere and diversity are being discussed as static elements within a given society. However, to fully grasp the relation between media technology, democratic discourse, and diversity, it might be helpful to shift our attention to the generative processes of these elements – especially under the changing conditions in a new media ecology.

At first, it might be productive to shift our perspective on the public as a given to something that is achieved in a specific socio-technical environment. Doing so addresses the public as a result of practices and interaction between heterogeneous actors – including communication infrastructure. The formation of the public then changes under different technological and social configurations – it is dynamic and contingent. While for Anderson – amongst others – the mass media system as it developed in the 20th century is able to produce such a public, this is only true for a specific configuration of communication channels and structures. Under conditions of linear broadcasting, a centralized and linear communication platform was established and (public) broadcasters acted as an information reduction agent. Diversity was there produced via the expertise and knowledge of editorial teams, putting together different and meaningful media content. Under current conditions of digital and networked communication, however, the system shifted to a non-linear and often decentralized system with newly emerged actors that select, reduce, and distribute information via novel means, including search engines or recommender systems. Thus, the production of a common public – if this was ever really achieved – has to adapt the newly emerging communication infrastructures and patterns.

At the same time, a discussion on diversity abstracts the relation between information distribution and information consumption away into the notion of the algorithm. Discussions around search engines or recommender systems tend to root the filter bubble effect in the algorithms alone. While the original contributions on this topic were of theoretical nature, the search for empirical evidence continues. Empirical studies on YouTube found a strong polarization effect based on the recommendation algorithm of the platform (O'Callaghan et al. 2015). Also, in search engines, scholars argue that we can observe a bias in search results towards already popular content (Halavais 2017; Introna and Nissenbaum 2000; Rogers, Becker, and Stalder 2009). This is then problematic in terms of information selection. Unkel (2019) showed in an empirical-experimental setup that ranking of search results has a strong influence on information selection. Thus, these findings would support the so-far formulated filter bubble hypothesis. However, other studies come to the conclusion that there is no or no strong filter bubble effect (Courtois, Slechten, and Coenen 2018; Puschmann 2019). Especially, Bakshy, Messing, and Adamic (2015) found in an empirical investigation that the influence of social networks on the emergence of filter bubbles is not as strong as often assumed, as these bubbles are more a result of users forming their own environment and selection logics. Puschmann (2019) comes to a similar conclusion after investigating potential filter bubbles in the representation of political parties in Google Search and Google News. In addition, the phenomenon of confirmation bias has been identified as an important element in explaining the emergence of echo chambers, as Quattrociocchi, Scala, and Sunstein (2016) observed on Facebook. Additionally, empirical tests have shown that personalization does not necessarily produce less diversity (Möller et al. 2018) or even shows an increased diversity of news consumed (Beam and Kosicki 2014).

These different findings hint at the problem that filter bubbles and biased information selection is (also) a result of platform-specific logics and interaction patterns between heterogeneous actors involved. The emergence of filter effects cannot just be attributed to an algorithm but should also take into account platforms and the broader media environment (Helberger 2018) in which they are embedded. Search engines work differently than social networking sites. YouTube, itself a platform, includes features of both worlds. Information exposure therefore is a multi-dimensional process in which active choices and algorithmic curation work together to create exposure. A constant shift and adaptation of practices and expectations, both in content provision and algorithmic selection processes creates highly volatile filter results, based on exclusion and inclusion of information sources. Thus, the results of an algorithmically computed public always emerge out of the complex interactions of consumers, providers and algorithmic systems (Mager 2012).[12] This, however, also includes "individuals, institutions, and industries [that] have emerged to attempt to 'game' search algorithms" (Crawford 2016, 82). Users shape their environment through choice and behavioral patterns, the providers try to game the algorithm, and the algorithm reacts to these processes itself though re-computation. But the algorithm is also constantly adapted by the platform service provider in order to circumvent unwanted effects (Mager

---

12   Here we also see one of the fundamental problems of radical transparency in algorithmic terms, as algorithmic transparency would create a new power distribution in the process of adaption. In these terms, algorithms are not stable entities, but should rather be seen as ever-changing actors in a process or reciprocal adaptation, where a cybernetic equilibrium can never be reached, as the definition of a stable and favorable state differs amongst the involved actors. Different to the reflexive turn in cybernetics (see Hayles 1999), there is not one system observing itself and adjusting the internal operations accordingly, but the interaction system is observing itself from multiple perspectives, with different normative attitudes, resulting in not one favored stable state, but multiple ones. Which one can be realized – with the according algorithmic system – then is a question of distribution of means and power.

2012). Yet, not everyone is equally empowered to influence the selection process. While mathematically there is no distinction between the different interactions, the technical know-how and the design of the platform can distribute the power to influence the news feed results differently, allowing a few to push certain contents, increasing an echo-chamber effect (Jamieson and Cappella 2008; Meraz 2009). Additionally, media scholars criticized that emerging communities can be addressed through the Facebook ad system. As such, Facebook allowed them to specifically target groups they labeled as "emotionally unstable teenagers" and "jew haters" (Angwin, Varner, and Tobin 2017), or to target people with specific political interests allowing to advertise tailor-made content for these groups – and potentially influence voting behavior (Kim 2016; Kim et al. 2018; Kreiss and McGregor 2018). So instead of trying to include these co-produced sub-groups into a wider public or news exposure, these mechanisms potentially reinforce existing polarizations and build new forms of collective action (Bimber 2003; O'Callaghan et al. 2015). This, however, is not necessarily the result of the algorithm, but in case of ad-targeting a specific logic of the platform and its business model. The problem of filter bubbles must therefore be contextualized for specific forms of information provision, may it be search engines, social media sites, video portals, etc. Filter bubbles are not just a result of an algorithm but are co-constructed between users, algorithms, platforms, and economic interests – and require platform-specific expertise in navigating between all of them (Allgaier, Geipel, and Morcillo 2019; Cotter 2019).

These findings show that we cannot talk about *the recommender algorithm* in isolation. Instead, the context in which specific techniques are being applied matters. To account for the effects of filter technologies, we have to acknowledge the algorithmic techniques and their history as well as the platform logics in which they operate. These aspects of the discussion point towards an understanding of the public and diversity as practical achievements within a situated order of interactions. Approaches to the role of the public should not just assume that there is a public out there, which the algorithm is now disturbing or damaging. Instead, understanding the public as an achievement rather than a given shifts the question to the generative processes of the public discourse. Shifting to such a perspective then also enables us to see how diversity as a normative concept interacts with these generative processes and how we can change them in order to produce a specific normative goal of diversity. This therefore calls for a nuanced and contextualized discussion of recommender systems and the normative goal of diversity. Media technologies are an important element in these generative processes, and the technological developments within the last decades have changed the ways how the public is being constituted. Thus, redesigning media actors also changes the way how publics are being produced. To do so, we must first change our concept of the public and ask ourselves how spaces of political information and communication are being produced. Therefore, in the next section, I will discuss a different approach to public(s) based on the pragmatist philosophy of John Dewey.

Practical Publics

The question of public discourse and information provision is not a new phenomenon that came up only after the Internet was invented. Turning to practice-based conceptions of *the public*, especially ideas from American Pragmatism[13] and its uptake in STS can add something to the discussion about the role of digital technologies and the management of a splintering public. In the following, I will base my argument on the conception of democracy and the public sphere of John Dewey and its uptake within STS. Based on the pragmatists' focus on the practices of individuals, Dewey formulates a theory of public involvement that is based on two basic assumptions. First, political involvement is mediated via issues and problems that arise *in actu* (see esp. Marres 2007). And second, people are quite competent in identifying relevant topics by themselves. Public discussion therefore evolves not (just) around topics produced by experts but around topics, objects and problems encountered by the people in their (inter)actions. It is important to note here that, for Dewey ([1927] 2006), problems for the individual are the result of the collective and unintended action of other individuals or institutions.[14] Thus, in a practice-oriented approach, a public is the result of the consequences of collective action.

> The public consists of all those who are affected by the indirect con-
> sequences of transactions, to such an extent that it is deemed necessary
> to have those consequences systematically cared for … This supervision
> and regulation [of these consequences] cannot be effected by the primary
> groupings themselves. … Consequently special agencies and measures
> must be formed if they are to be attended to (Dewey 1927, 15–16 cited in
> Marres 2007, 767-768).

For Dewey, the public is therefore the group of people that are affected by the results of (collective) action and for whom these effects become a problem. While Dewey believed that these problems can be identified objectively, Marres (2007) argues that they must be articulated in order to become an issue. Thus, only problems that are being communicated are issues in the sense of a modern Interpretation of pragmatism. In the articulation of problems as issues, we also turn the notion of objectively given problems

13   Of course, Habermas' theory of communicative action relies to a great deal on pragmatist ideas and Habermas virtuously brings them in conversation with the legacy of the Frankfurt School of critical theory.

14   In this regard, Dewey's conception already formulates an important element in the later published theory of Giddens (1984), i.e., unintended consequences of social practices.

towards issues and its corresponding public as a practical achievement. The process of collecting different actors around an issue is a problem of communication, interpretation, and local practices. An issue definition can be taken up by a person and applied to the own situation – or not. As a result of this reasoning, a pragmatist perspective sees a public and the corresponding issue as the result of a chain of interactions. A public is not just given but practically constructed.

This notion of the public bears an important conclusion – there is not one public. Instead, the publics are the result of relating people to issues that emerge from collective action (Dewey [1927] 2006). If public is defined as the association of individuals with a given articulated problem, then there are as many publics as there are issues. The public as singular does not exist but re-configures itself always anew around different issues, forming what Dewey ([1927] 2006) called issue-publics. Therefore, we are dealing with publics in a plural. Not everyone must be part of every discussion, but only the people that (think that they) are related to the discussed issue at hand. The public is therefore also not bound to a common imaginary holding a fixed community like the state together.[15] Instead of assuming a common imaginary as an explanatory cause for a shared public, the question is rather how a coordination of practices is able to produce and stabilize such a public through practical means. Dewey shifts the focus of attention from the (seemingly) independent public toward the local and practical processes that constitute different publics.

An important mode of political inquiry now makes issues visible (Barry 2001). Barry argues that political protests do not necessarily have the function of preventing interventions but to put issues on the political agenda and to make them visible. Thus, "telling of a truth in public […] is always intended to have effects on, or challenge the minds or effect the conduct of others" (Barry 2001, 178). By making own identified issues heard by others, these topics become a problem to others insofar as they are confronted with it – and gives them the chance to make them an issue themselves. This issue-making, however, is not only realized via voices or protests but is enabled and mediated through technological and material infrastructures (Marres 2012) that are essential in building communities (Callon 2004). For Marres (2007), it is therefore crucial to focus on the question of how issues are made public as a condition of democracy. By making them publicly available for scrutiny, actors can attach themselves to it and make the issue stronger.

In such a conception of public discourse, the role of experts and expertise must be reinterpreted. Democracy hinges on the necessity that public media

---

15   It is important to note here that this does not exclude the possibility of a common imaginary of a social collective – it is just not related to the production of a public.

is not selective regarding which issues are being made public. Instead, it should find ways of making a wide variety of issues available to a broad audience – and therefore potentially enabling the issue to shift in scale. Dewey defined the public as the sum of individuals that are affected by the consequences of collective action. Through distributing these issues broadly, the institutionalized actions of media actors extend the consequences of collective action further and make them available for reflection within a broader population. By doing so, the emerging public is being opened up for other members of society, making emerging issue-publics potentially stronger but also confronting it with other agonistic ideas and positions. The role of experts is therefore a crucial one, but in a radically different way. Instead of *just* informing the emerging publics, it also becomes an essential feature of these experts to connect and relate different discussions and provide relevant information.

What is relevant, however, is contingent not only but especially when it comes to algorithms. This often means popular or trending and therefore follows an economic impetus, and more often so in an opaque way (Gillespie 2014). In democratic discussions, however, relevance has another meaning. What is relevant for a democracy is also the antagonistic position which I can learn about and try to counteract – either through rational discourse, as Habermas suggests, or by open agonistic dissent, as Mouffe argues. Thus, relevance is also defined as the information that would foster conflict and debate, which might scrutinize the actual existing order. And therefore, relevance defined by the individual or a confined collective around an issue must be broadened to include agonistic positions. Through mediating actions, different collectives are confronted in debate by connecting different issues and groups. In her rather positive account of digital technologies as part of liberal democracies, Papacharissi (2010) argues that the multiplicity of spheres does not hinder democratic discourse because they produce an in-between-ness, thus connecting people according to their preferences, values and imaginaries. However, given the potential polarizing impact of filter systems and the ever-ongoing co-construction of publics, caught in hegemonic orderings and unequal power distribution, a call for a mediating entity to enable discussion and conflict seems reasonable. One of the central institutions of contemporary democracy – the so-called fourth power – has to administer a fragile balance between enabling the construction of dissent by connecting opposing publics but at the same time aiding these emerging publics with facts and verifiable knowledge *relevant* to these discussions.

It is important to keep in mind that Dewey's formulation of democracy as a bottom-up approach of issues is the result of a discussion at the beginning of the 20th century. The debate addresses the fate of democracy in the new industrialized society (Marres 2007). According to Marres (2007), two factors were relevant for the debate: a new media system, including newspapers and broadcasting, and secondly the increasing complexity of industrial societies. Thus, the debate was a reaction to a specific media system and its challenges and possibilities for democracy. The solution that has been found for constructing a common communication sphere, in which issues are being selected and represented, was a radically different one than we find it now.

The media system of the 20th century represents a rather centralized and linear form of taking up and distributing issues. Newsworthiness and the connected idea of diversity had been discussed in the offices of editors and program designers. They were composing a collection of media items that was in principle the same for everyone. Thus, a small group of experts were selecting and putting together information sets and the available information was (in principle) accessible to everyone via central distribution centers, such as newspapers, or broadcasters. The media infrastructure did not only function as a tool for sending information, but the organizations themselves were aggregators of information. The production of diversity happened ex-ante. However, in times of non-linear streaming, the program is not fixed for a given timeframe. The user can enjoy the content whenever she wants. Of course, there is still a moment of control, as media-on-demand websites normally show curated areas. However, sites with strong personalization find other ways to select and curate content: by datafication of media content and users alike. The content that is shown is in case of automated information selection not provided by experts but by an algorithm. Based on observed behavior of the users, the recommender calculates what video ought to be shown next. The process of co-production of relevance therefore gradually shifts expertise of curating from editorial teams toward metric and algorithmic means of information selection (see also Jones and Jones 2019; Sørensen and Schmidt 2016). Thorson et al. (2021) therefore conclude that the selection of information made visible shifts from the organization towards the algorithm. Topics – as potential issues – therefore do not emerge based on actions of editors but based on my own behavior and the behavior of other users.

The production of calculated publics is now for one at the core of the problem for the old media system. Algorithms produce collectives through calculations that did not exist before (Gillespie 2014). As such, it is not clear who sees what information. But secondly, editors cannot put together corresponding information that would produce a diverse information diet. Thus, an *ex-ante* production of diversity is undermined. But a pragmatist account also opens up the possibility to think about the emergence of calculated publics in a different form. Algorithmic filter systems calculate the different publics based on collective behavior to make certain information relevant for an individual. However, pragmatist theory conceptualizes the emergence of issue-publics in exactly the same way. Issues become relevant for an individual based on the consequences of others' behavior. The role of a public service algorithm then would not be to prevent filter bubbles but to identify them and connect "diverse audiences to shared content" (Bennett 2018, 117). To do so means to rethink the role of technology and infrastructures in producing a shared information space. As boyd (2010, 39) argues, referring to the older term of networked publics: "While networked publics share much in common with other types of publics, the ways in which technology structures them introduces distinct affordances that shape how people engage with these environments." By this, she and others (Itō 2008; Varnelis 2008) conceptualized how social media sites *enable, shape and hinder* the emergence of new publics. Thus, the contribution of recommender systems to emerging issue-publics can – and should – also be read in a media-sensitive way, raising the question of how different algorithmic techniques are entangled differently in the making of publics.

The emergence of issue-publics in digital information environments is a complex process on which power relations have an immense impact. Marres (2007) argues that we should extend our understanding of democracy to how objects are part of the formation of democracies and publics. By this turn, she extends the program of STS into political theory. For pragmatists, the question whether issues enable public participation was crucial. Making issues public means opening them up for more associations and allow different positions to connect with them. It becomes apparent now, why the configuration of the media system is essential for the distribution of issues. By taking up and distributing different articulated problems, a media system can allow others to build new associations with it. Thus, intervening in the production of issues also means intervening in the digital infrastructure and the algorithms that co-construct the emerging issues in a way that the normative aim of a democratic system is met. As a result of these conclusions, the pressing question in respect to the filter bubble discussion is not whether they exist or not but how the formation of issue-publics is prescribed, transformed or modulated by algorithmic filtering systems within democratic societies and its institutions, and how media environments are to be designed in a democratic society.

According to some scholars, it is thus imperative to intervene in this complex assemblage in order to fulfill the policy goal of diversity. Recommender algorithms do not necessarily threaten the democratic ideal but can also be used to support the democratic role of public broadcasting services and foster diversity. Through *Diversity by Design,* broadcasters can fulfill the ideal of a diverse information provision even better. Reviglio (2019), for example, argues that serendipity, i.e., surprising content that the user did not expect, in recommender results can be a powerful design principle to counteract on filter bubbles. Potentially, this can even be achieved by employing the same technologies that create the problem of filter bubbles in the first place. As Helberger (2015) argues:

> In short, it is possible to design electronic program guides or other search intermediaries, such as search engines, in a way to help users find the content they are interested in, then the same technology also can be used to do potentially the opposite and point users toward more diverse choices (Helberger 2015, 1329).

Thus, by actively producing diversity through algorithmic means, recommender systems could become a means to mitigate filter bubbles (Helberger, Karpinnen, and D'Acunto 2018). Nudging users into content diversity has therefore been discussed as a viable option to stay true to the public broadcaster ethos (Burri 2016). Nissen (2006, 69) even argues that "influencing the listener's or viewer's choices, and thus media consumption pattern is the very reason why public media were established and why their existence has been upheld even in times of abundant media supply".

There have been some voices evoking the issue of paternalism in developing these technologies (e.g., Sørensen & Schmidt 2016). This position has some appeal, as an intervention in the production of publics is the result of a specific political ideal and a powerful institutional and hegemonistic infrastructure. However, if we discuss the role of public broadcasting within contemporary democracy, it only makes sense to do so if we share the assumption that these public media infrastructures fulfill a function within our democratic society. If this presumption is lost, then the need for a public media system as such vanishes. Thus, if the ethos of a public broadcaster is accepted as something valuable, the question of whether public broadcasting services should intervene in the production of a common public is futile. Instead, such intervention becomes a necessity.

Based on the pragmatist perspective on publics, the question of how a public sphere is constructed changes. Instead of mitigating filter bubbles that originate within the digital condition of our contemporary societies, the process of designing algorithmic systems and media landscapes adapts the role of public broadcasting to mitigate the tendency of human communication to (re-)produce filter bubbles and bias under new socio-technical conditions. Understanding the generative processes of publics, on the one hand, and applying new technologies within our media systems to fulfill their normative obligations under changed conditions is therefore imperative for democracies in the 21st century. The debate about the political and democratic impact of recommender systems thereby not only sparked discussions about the role of algorithms in a public media system (Helberger 2019) but also how these recommender systems can be built according to the formulated policy goal of diversity (Helberger 2011; Pöchhacker et al. 2017).

As shown in this section, the digital turn of journalism, not only in public broadcasting services, has been discussed as a disruption of the media system and its established practices (Caswell 2019). The increasing delegation of editorial tasks to algorithmic systems can create opportunities (Helberger 2015) but must also operate in a distinct legal and normative setting. Both perspectives, however, urge us to turn to the design of journalistic technologies (Diakopoulos 2019, 2020). As Hunt & McKelvey (2019) argue, media policy should also consider processes of deployment and development of (media) algorithms. The political struggle described in this section also became relevant in the development project, by trying to *reformulate* the recommender algorithm in a way that made it compatible with a normative perspective of communication in a public political sphere. The implicit assumptions of what the communication of a recommender algorithm should look like, i.e., how we define relevance of information, became problematized within the very institution that utilized already well-known algorithmic techniques. The whole research and development project around the public service recommender system, which I was lucky to be part of, mobilized issues of diversity, popularity and expert knowledge, and started to tackle them with different approaches that I will further discuss in the following section. The different normative tensions described so far on a macro-level also became visible in the micro-cosmos of the development project, making it necessary to navigate and align the algorithm between different normative and political claims and necessities.

(Un)Probable Solutions

Algorithms are no unchangeable facts – nor can we neglect them purely as constructions. Instead, the design and implementation of algorithms represents a normative ideal of what the problem to a given community is and how one should and could tackle it. Recommender algorithms are no different from that. As discussed in the previous sections, recommender algorithms operate in the difficile tension between economic origin of the technique and the normative demands of a public media environment. This tension and the potentially resulting issues for democratic societies call for a design approach of public service algorithms (Helberger, Karpinnen, and D'Acunto 2018). In the software development project, this was one of the goals: construct a recommender that is appealing and up-to-date with the current developments but also realizes the democratic obligations of the public broadcaster. However, during the development process, it became clear that issues were not only resulting from this tension, but more specifically in the collision of different local orderings realizing these normative claims differently. Thus, if we shift our perspective from abstract normative obligations towards the practical and situated forms of ordering, things become even more complicated. In the following, I will therefore discuss three different vignettes of our attempts to build and or evaluate a recommender system based on the idea of a diverse information diet. These approaches are situated on different levels of inquiry: changing the algorithm and its parameters, reinterpreting the model produced by the algorithmic learning procedure, and evaluating the existing information diet.

Noise

As part of our journey to learn about the recommender system and its different techniques, I also came across different formulas and optimization metrics. In short, every machine learning approach needs a function that measures how good the calculated model predicts the available data. The optimization function is thereby different for different techniques and sometimes also for different goals. A question that comes up very frequently is for what the machine learning model should be optimized – which leads to different forms of evaluation. While we were discussing the optimization function for the collaborative filtering approach used, we came up with another idea. If we do not know what diversity is, then maybe we can just produce noise, which would eventually produce diversity, as the accuracy of the algorithm would go down. In the following, we discussed the idea of tinkering with single parameters of the formula, which look like this:

$$\min_{x_*,\, y_*} \sum_{u,\,i} c_{ui}\left(p_{ui} - x_u^T y_i\right)^2 + \left(\sum_u \|x_u\|^2 + \sum_i \|y_i\|^2\right)$$

[Figure 7] Optimization function for the collaborative filtering algorithm (Hu, Koren, and Volinsky 2008)

The formula from figure 7 shows an optimization formula for collaborative filtering. What the formula does is to compare the measured rating, here the value p, with the calculated values of the predicting model, here x and y. The closer the calculated values are to the measured rating, the better the fit of the model to the observed data. Interestingly enough, the parameter c_{ui} represents the confidence that the algorithm has in the measurement and normally takes a value between 0 and 1. That means a higher value of c makes the algorithm value the calculated error margin more, whereas a small c means that the error made by the calculated model is not so important and can be neglected to a certain degree. Our idea then was to lower c_{ui} claiming that the errors made by the model are not that important in general. By allowing a higher margin of deviation from the original rating behavior, the algorithm, so the idea, would produce diversity in the recommended sets by itself. That way models that might otherwise not be accepted for deployment would be considered by the recommender system. As a result of that, the recommender system would produce models with less precise predictions, i.e., produce more surprising and non-fitting results. This, however, created two problems. First, the model would produce a random diversity, meaning that it is hardly controllable how the diverse set of information would be assembled. This idea of diversity, however, was explicitly addressed in the interview with the online editorial team. Asked how important diversity is in the results of the recommender, they answered:

> Diversity is important to me. But it should not be that diverse. So, a thematic connection is certainly important to me. So not, when the crime series is named "bunny in the pit," then showing a documentary about rabbits (Interview with Online Editors, my translation).

The idea of diversity realized through the algorithmic script was not in line with the institutional expectations of the editors. The idea of randomness did not correspond with the editors' needs. In a workshop held by us later, the editors argued again that they need to be able to direct the behavior of the recommender, as for different sites the recommender would need different ways of recommending elements. Noise, however, took away the possibility to control the output, as the predictions become less accurate.

In addition, we, the development team, were a bit worried about the randomness of the results. By producing random results that the users would not understand, we thought it would be very unlikely that the users would actually stay on the platform. Therefore, this intervention would not create a higher exposure diversity because people would simply dismiss the recommender as malfunctioning – especially because users' attitudes towards diversity are diverse themselves over different subpopulations (Bodó et al. 2019). The developers were pre-assuming the expectations of the users. The algorithmic script would have worked technically, but the institutional expectations of the editors and the expectations of the developers regarding the expectations of the users, i.e., expectations of a second order, did not fit this form of changing the algorithmic script. Although it would have been able to adapt the algorithm, other forms of ordering made the development team reconsider and dismiss the idea in the end.

Anti-Recommender

Producing noise showed to be problematized within the development team, as the calculated recommendations – including unpredictable noise – diverted from what the development team expected to be the users' expectations. In the wake of these developments, we applied another idea, which was connected to not adapt the model creation of the recommender, but to utilize the same model for the recommendations of dis-similar items. The recommendation algorithm was therefore changed so that it was using the same computed model in two different ways. In the traditional way, it would recommend items that were predicted to be similar to the items the user would normally watch. The second mode, however, would search for items with a large distance in the calculated vector space, i.e., that the recommender would show you items that are very dis-similar to the items the user would normally watch. This approach was called an anti-recommender and was shown in the beta version of the video-on-demand platform under the heading of "something different." The anticipated advantage of this approach was that the calculation, which is the computational expensive part of the recommender system, would be left unchanged and only the subsequent item selection through the recommender system would be re-scripted in order to adhere to the normative idea of diversity. As Helberger (2015) argued, the same technology that potentially produced filter bubbles and a reduced information exposure can be used to actively produce diversity. In addition, this approach was based on *collaborative filtering*, and therefore not bringing the approach into conflict with how meta-data was produced. In *collaborative filtering*, the n-dimensional vector space is calculated only with the ratings observed by the users, not the meta-data produced by the organization. However, the idea of the anti-recommender also produced problems in terms of translatability into diversity. This time, the results are not random, which does not create problems in terms of (expectations of) user expectations. In addition, the recommendation results of an anti-recommender have been shown in a different section, fulfilling the classical task of recommendations while providing an additional opportunity to diversify one's own information diet. However, as the project went on, we were confronted with a central feature of collaborative filtering as a huge problem in terms of evaluating diversity. Alice and I were discussing the output of the collaborative filtering technique relatively early in the project.

> The normal distribution based on the factorization is creating nice bell curves. But why? What is the factor referring to? Today I was sitting next to Alice and she showed me an example calculation for collaborative filtering. She calculated the features in 10 dimensions, and we were looking at them. Alice told me that she calculated the latent factors. They are all a normal distribution, i.e., a bell curve. Alice asked me how we should interpret this. "Maybe you as a sociologist, can you tell me what that means?" I have no idea myself what we were looking at here exactly (fieldnote).

The problem here is actually twofold. First, the calculated dimensions of the recommender system are not really intuitive or easily graspable. Since the output of the matrix factorization are *latent dimensions*, their meaning is not transparent. Instead, the vector space that describes the items and users is defined by dimensions that emerge out of usage patterns. Possible exam-ples could be "movies in which Antonio Banderas has a beard" – only that the recommender system would not tell you the description of the dimension. The same problem emerges from content-based filtering. While it is easier to grasp what diversity would mean based on the meta-data of the video items, the vector space produced here is very big. (Almost) every word in the description is being used as a dimensional descriptor in the vector space calculated – which creates a highly complex system that is not easily understood, and which cannot be easily interpreted in terms of diversity. That is, translating a rule set of diversity composition seems hardly possible.

Especially, when asking the editors how they judge content, the answers were implicit and referred to the editors' experience in the field. "They are all journalists and have worked in many editorial offices and they have a good overview" (Online-Editors Interview). This explanation was, however, not only referred to when it came to judging content and its quality in general but was also applied to the idea of diverse content and the moral and legal obligation of the public broadcaster.

> They are all curators, who have been part of the house for a long time, and they are absolutely aware of the public service mandate. [...] Every-one has also for a long time now been part of the [institution]. But they also have their professional training. [...] That is an inherent part of them and it is [...] somehow self-evident. Therefore, it is not necessary to dis-cuss this every day because it is a part of us (Online-Editors Interview, my translation).

The editors were referring to implicit knowledge that had been developed over time on the job. Thus, translating their expertise in relation to diver-sity and judging content and content compilation was not translatable into an algorithmic metric. What diversity is in the institutional setting was not directly accessible, and therefore not translatable into a working metric def-inition of diversity. Thus, in the end, we were stuck in a situation of two forms of expertise and knowledge which were hard to formulate explicitly, but relied more on an implicit training[16] and understanding of the different actors. The two approaches to order and understand the world relied on knowledge – one professional, the other machinic – which were not easily translatable into each other.

Diversity Calculations

The previous section hints towards a problem of translating normative ideas about diversity into a metric that can be used to create an interface between organizational and political norms and algorithmic reasoning of recommender

---

16   It is indeed interesting that both, editors and algorithms, are being trained to acquire implicit knowledge. Thus, training machine learning models could be seen as a (simple) form of machine socialization.

systems. For that we have to consider how diversity can be calculated and what this means in terms of (e)valuation. In the most abstract definition, diversity of a given item set can be calculated by comparing every item with every other item and adding up a similarity score. Mathematically, this can be expressed as the following:

$$\text{Diversity} = \frac{1}{2} \sum_{i_j \in u} \sum_{i_k \in u} \text{sim}(i_j, i_k)$$

[Figure 8] Diversity calculation as defined by Yadav et al. (2020)

Thus, the definition of diversity in a mathematical formulation hinges on the further definition of the similarity function. However, how similarity is defined relies on the operationalization of the term. Yadav et al. (2020), for example, propose diversity calculation and recommendation based on ratings of other users of a particular genre-specific cluster (calculated via k-means clustering) to enable cross-genre recommendations. Thus, the calculation of similarity depends on the ratings of other users. Möller et al. (2018) applied a different method, using the technique of topic modeling, based on the LDA algorithm. In doing so, Möller et al. (2018) calculated latent topics based on full text articles and their meta data description of news items. Similarity of the recommended items was then expressed as the metric distance of items in the resulting vector space. In these two examples alone, we can already see that similarity and the inferred attribute of diversity rests on very specific ideas and choices how to operationalize diversity. An open question then is how different metric versions of diversity interact with an understanding of this term in a given community.

At the time when we as a project team were tackling this issue, Alice pointed me towards the chapter on evaluations (Shani and Gunawardana, 2011) of the recommender systems handbook she gave me earlier, where diversity as a concept was being discussed. The authors there suggest a metric to calculate diversity based on the distance of the items in the vector space used to describe the items. The vector space that was the basis of this calculation was produced by the content-based recommendation algorithm. Thus, the metadata to describe the different items was important. One of the suggestions there was "we take each recommendation list that an algorithm produces, and compute the distance of each item from the rest of the list, averaging the result to obtain a diversity score" (Shani and Gunawardana 2011, 288). Diversity is the average distance between the recommended items, as diversity is reflected as the inverse of comparability. And as we have learned, the closer two items are placed in the calculated vector space, the more similar they are. As part of a side project, Alice implemented such a metric of diversity and ran it against different recommender outputs and different shows.

> Alice was presenting the results of the diversity scores. The project leader
> on our side, Marvin, and I were already sitting there. Alice was connecting
> her Macbook to the beamer and stands in front of us presenting the
> results. She showed us some graphs of the different diversity scores
> based on output of the recommender prototype, she implemented on
> the iPython notebook and the meta-data that was available for the video
> content. In general, the diversity scores are rather low to average. What
> is, however, surprising is the fact that the show, a soap opera is rated very
> high. I asked Alice how this could be. Everyone was amused. Alice thinks
> that this is because in every episode something different happens. This
> explains the distance of the single episodes (fieldnote).

Measuring diversity as proposed is rooted in the logic of the recommender
system, and within that logic it is absolutely accurate. However, as we all
were amused by the thought that the single episodes of a soap opera could
represent diversity shows that there is a divergence between mathematical,
data-driven ideas of diversity and the way we resolved the concept on a more
reflexive, qualitative basis. Based on the data considered, diversity therefore
was maybe achieved calculatively but not in the way as it was intended by the
organization or the law. The metadata description, e.g., title, keywords, text
teasers, of the selected items was diverse, as many different terms were taken
up. However, the interpretation of the project team was totally different.

The problems in measuring and visualizing diversity were instructive in more
than one way. First, the metric based on a rich set of available metadata
was not very helpful because the metric was not able to contextualize the
meaning of them. As we have seen in the previous chapter, algorithms need
to develop a form of algorithmic reflexivity in order to handle data in a way
that is appropriate in the social system where they are placed. The algorithm
that calculated the metric of diversity, however, failed to account for the situated and institutionally accepted way of diverse content. Similarity derived
from an abstract n-dimensional vector space was not enough to evaluate how
others would account for similarity and diversity. The calculative definition
deviated from how it is defined in the institutionalized understanding and
the normative imagination of diversity in public broadcasters. The problem
is defining a metric that reflects an understanding of diversity (Sørensen and
Schmidt 2016) as applied in the context it is being observed and experienced.
Again, the data production regime in place worked against the intuitive idea
from Alice regarding diversity production. To apply the formulated form of
diversity in the organization, the meta data of the single episodes should
have been more similar to each other. This, however, was incompatible with
the idea of good meta data as discussed by the newly formed online editorial
team. In an interview, a colleague told us:

So. Now we also have the problem that they name all their episodes the same way. The byline is always, well, the byline is always the same. That is ok, but. This here is also always the same. This means, this is actually, in short. What would you tell the editors? [asking her colleague] (Online Editors Interview)

To which her colleague answered: "Actually, only mean things are coming to my mind" (Online Editors Interview). That is, the working practices and the formulated needs, how the editorial teams needed and wanted the meta data was not compatible with the aim of the metric to measure diversity. How similarity or diversity is defined differs between the algorithmic logic of similarity and the ones applied by professionals, which subsequently make recommender systems being experienced as problematic agents in the process of information distribution. Thus, the adaptation of the algorithmic evaluation of diversity failed as the institutional logic was not compatible with the algorithmic idea of diversity. Calculating diversity became problematic in itself by colliding with at least two different implicit understandings of the term – our intuitive grasp of diversity within the project team and the established working practices of the editors.

Valuing Algorithms

Public broadcasters are always working in a situation of constant struggle to balance between their societal role as democratic institutions and the need to maximize their reach (Nissen 2006). The assumed normative ideal of diversity in the development project had the concrete goal to adhere and connect to a normative system, established some time ago. This normative system we referred to is assembled by laws and legal principles, courts, contracts, oversight boards, and a public and academic discussion. Thus, the organization and, as part of it, the development team formulated a problem to be solved – fulfilling the legal obligation of presenting a diverse information diet to the audience via a recommender system. This problem, locally derived from a general policy goal, created a tension between the issue imagined by the project and the problem that an off-the-shelf recommender algorithm would solve – i.e., to recommend items that are similar or popular. Yet, the tension is not only the result of the economic origin of these techniques and the legal obligation of a public institution. Instead, new configurations and condition of the contemporary media ecology challenges established forms of producing a public information sphere, serving democratic discourse. Instead of assuming that recommender algorithms are a threat to democracy, I proposed in this chapter that we should focus our attention on the conditions of possibility of a common public sphere and conceptualize it as a practical achievement (partly) of the public media system. A pragmatist conception of issues and publics in plural, and the way each of these emerge from collective interactions may help us to evaluate possible ways to produce a shared and open information space. In such a conception, the work of a public media infrastructure and its experts is predominantly to make different issues available to a broader audience and give them the chance to make them their own – and therefore stronger – or to oppose them in an agonistic or rational discussion, scrutinizing them and confronting these issues with other perspectives and opinions.

Applying a pragmatist perspective of issue-publics to recommender systems creates the need to revisit the algorithmic techniques and reformulate them in order to make them compatible with the democratic idea of distributing and broadening issue-publics. By doing so, we focus on the generative processes of calculated publics and search for ways to intervene in their production and how to relate them with each other. Within the recent discussion about recommender systems, this has been named with the need to produce diversity within recommendation results. Within the software development project, we tried to do exactly that and explored different ways of intervening in the production of publics via recommender systems.

In the project, neither the problem nor the solution experienced radical re-formulation but rather adaptation of already known techniques. The problem of measuring diversity was utilizing the same model that the recommender system was using anyhow, but interpreted and applied differently. By measuring diversity based on the calculated distance of items in the n-dimensional vector space of the model, the logic prevailed in principle but with an inverse interpretation. The same happened with the adaptation of the recommender system itself. The two examples given demonstrate two different steps of intervention, one within the model production itself – producing noise by tinkering with the parameters –, and another with the different application of the calculated model by applying a different logic of selection.

However, the translation of the policy goal into algorithmic means was not as straightforward, as we encountered some problems in the process. Measuring diversity, as the algorithmic metric tried, assumed a different form of meta data production which led to interesting results of what the algorithm presented as diverse. This meta data production that conflicted with the assumptions of the metric was even enforced and fostered through the central online editorial team, following a journalistic ethos of good and presentable video descriptions – which had primarily the user in mind. The same conflict was observable with the production of noise, by which the control over how the recommended videos were selected was undermined. Also, the expectations of the developers that the user would expect other – more coherent – forms of recommendations, made an adaption of the calculated model difficult. And lastly, the implicit knowledge on which the profession and the algorithm were depending could not be translated into each other – as none of them could be made explicit. Both actants – as the result of their own disciplines[17] – had an idea what comparability, compatibility, and diversity "meant" to them, but in both cases an explicit formulation of these principles and understandings was not possible. The here described incommensurability of different forms of evaluation and implicit knowledge, however, produces serious problems for the democratic role of recommender systems, as described earlier. As argued, the role of Public Broadcaster Services changes within a digital information ecology, making new forms of expertise necessary, connecting different and opposing issue-publics. This, however, requires an understanding of the qualitative assessment of these publics. Since algorithmic forms of evaluation introduce forms of comparability that is not graspable from an institutional and professional perspective, the task of relating these issues with each other becomes harder. Some form of translation between these different expressions of comparability seems necessary. Thus, translating algorithmic outputs and models into accounts that are understandable and interpretable within a given normative setup poses a necessity if these actors are to be integrated into a normative ordering, such as democratic values. E.g., the anti-recommender could have been a successful tool for realizing diversity from a pragmatist understanding of emerging publics. However, to include editorial experts and their (often implicit) understanding of diversity would require a department of data scientists, translating clusters within latent vector spaces into political categories and vice versa. Diversity therefore is not just a set of diverse content but refers to a normative order that defines what this concept is, and lets it emerge. Keeping the democratic ideal of our public media systems under new socio-technological configurations therefore means to re-align the orderings with them accordingly.

All of these issues are not just technical but refer to different formations of social order, institutional practices, and professional knowledge. The development of the algorithm had to navigate between three different normative ideas of the public broadcaster, which materialized in three very different problems that the algorithm should solve: popularity, democratic ideals, and journalistic ethos. Navigating and reconstructing the messy processes of inscribing assumptions in the algorithm shows how different normative ideas had to be negotiated, prioritized and balanced with each other. Thus, the democratic quality of the algorithm was the result of these negotiations and balances. Instead of just being a recommender system, the algorithm was the projection field of an ongoing political struggle.

17   While not in the focus of this discussion, it is noteworthy that discussions about realizing diversity within recommender systems begin to feed back into the professional sub-discipline within computer science. The local matter of concern is now delegated within another context to foster social and technological change.

6

Ordering Algorithmic Democracy

[T]here is order at all points. – Sacks 1984, 22

How can we think about algorithms in general and machine learning specifically in terms of democratic order, and what does doing so even mean?
What is the connection between this seemingly purely technical topic and one
of the oldest questions within the social sciences? And are we even qualified
to make such calls? Something in the nature of algorithms, AI, and digital
technologies provokes some unease, a feeling that society and its issues
and the development of new technologies are not detached. Of course, this
is not only true for digital technologies. In a now canonical article, Winner
(1980) argued that artifacts are political in their consequences for human
(inter-)actions. Another well-known mantra within the studies of society/
technology relations states that "[t]echnology is neither good nor bad; nor
is it neutral" (Kranzberg 1986, 545). Technology is an essential building block
of our social structures and our moral interventions within the social fabric.
And so are algorithms and machine learning techniques. Thus, it should not
surprise us that a rich and ongoing discussion about the "social power of
algorithms" (Beer 2017) started some time ago and is now intensifying with
the increasing number of promises and applications of this technology. This
is not only reflected in the increasing number of publications but also in the
newly emerging institutions specifically focused on the social implications of
AI and digital technologies, such as the *AI Now Institute*, or the *Data & Society
Institute*. The discussion around algorithms, AI, and digital technologies
thereby revolves around different topics and theoretical approaches, which

highlight several different issues and sometimes also potentials for intervention (e.g., Benjamin 2019; D'Ignazio and Klein 2020). Of course, the debate around algorithms is extensive and fluid, and it is hardly possible to list all contributions. However, one can see some patterns emerging from the discussion, what perspectives are being applied and what dominant theoretical perspectives are being utilized in order to shed some light on the phenomenon on the algorithm as a socio-technical phenomenon. In my work I identified four different perspectives on the topic. First, a problem-oriented approach, which is not primarily concerned with theoretical or conceptual questions. The question here revolves around problems of transparency of algorithmic systems (Pasquale 2015), bias and inequality reproduced through algorithmic systems (Eubanks 2018; Noble 2018) and the notion of seeming objectivity of algorithms (Beer 2017; G. Rieder and Simon 2016). In the contributions that are more focused on the development of a theoretical and conceptual approach, three perspectives seem dominant within the contemporary discussion: a Foucauldian approach, Marxist perspectives, and cybernetic theories. Other perspectives, like ANT (the one I am promoting in this book), a phenomenological perspective, or pragmatist approaches do exist as well but as it seems rather on the margins of the discussion, and mostly not connected to the question of social order or power relations of and with algorithmic systems, esp. in democratic institutions.

In the accounts of the algorithm, as being discussed in the literature so far, the political quality of the artifact is either naturalized (algorithms *are like that*) or explained away by an overarching normative structure of society, like the capitalist rationality. Algorithmic power is treated either way as a social fact – to borrow the expression from Durkheim ([1895] 1982) –, an objectively given force within contemporary social configurations. This, however, created some unease and raised the question as to what the algorithm that we talk about actually is (Seaver 2017; Ziewitz 2016). As Mager (2014, 30) states: "However, all these contributions cannot explain why search engines have become powerful actors in the first place and how they – and the algorithmic ideology – are stabilized in contemporary society." What then would be a perspective that explores the notion of algorithmic power without relying on these often very productive but still somewhat paradoxical notions of object and structure, essence and construction? In the previous chapters, I reconstructed from empirical observations the way that *the algorithm* is formed by various domain-specific enactments that *make* the algorithm but, at the same time, must also integrate its technical attributes into these practices of *making the algorithm*. First, the algorithm exists as a *disciplinary enactment*. It references back to a whole discipline and community of practice that enables, distributes, and explains the algorithmic techniques that are then being implemented. As such, it provides the intellectual and material infrastructure in the form of textbooks, lecture slides, conference panels but also in standardized development environments, programming libraries (that include many of the aforementioned techniques) and so on. The diffusion of algorithms and their techniques is an important element in understanding how they travel into almost all areas of social life, and also how that process and structure diffusion already limits the possibilities of subsequent integration of these actors into organizational or institutional settings. Second, the algorithm has been produced as an organizational enactment, where the organized and organizing practices of the public broad-caster co-shaped the final implementation. This has been shown especially in the ways in which the data necessary to run the algorithm has been produced within the organization. While the algorithmic technique of content-based recommendations requires standardized, homogenized, and quickly produced meta-data for video-content, the organization practices – based on the operational logic of the broadcaster – followed another logic of diverse descriptions and long processes of ex-post meta-data production. This lack of alignment between data production and algorithmic data usage became also obvious when applying collaborative filtering. While no meta-data from within the organization was needed, it showed the need to understand or to control the situation of the users when they were watching the broadcaster's video content. Within the development team, there was a considerable degree of uncertainty on how to interpret the signals of the users. When is a rating good or when is it bad? Did the user watch the full video on purpose or did she fall asleep? Thus, the algorithm needed a way to reflexively make sense out of the data signals that it computed – which either included controlling the data production or having enough insights to interpret them "correctly". I call the process of implementing this interpretability of data signals an ex-ante *Algorithmic Reflexivity*. The last enactment of the algorithm constructed it as a political challenge that needed to be tackled. Public broadcasting in Germany has a very specific function in terms of the democratic system. Following the insights of the Enlightenment that citizens are able and required to become competent members within the political discourse, the aim of the public broadcaster is to enable them to do so.[1] In general, this has been interpreted as the obligation of public broadcasting to provide a broad information diet to the citizenry. This duty is endangered by the introduction of recommender systems that are, by design, selecting and tailoring the information that is made available. This was the reason that *the algorithm* became a problem in and of itself that requires intervention. What followed were different attempts to change the basic functionality of the recommender algorithm in order to bring it in line with the democratic ideal of diversity in information provision, including introducing noise or using the calculated data model in a different

---

1   There is an ongoing debate about whether public broadcasting should effectively educate or just offer the possibility for the citizens to educate themselves (Sørensen and Hutchinson 2018)

way. This all resulted in a synchronous enactment of the algorithm in three different ways, where each way was present at all times during the project, while also needing to be simultaneously coordinated with each other.

With this chapter, I will bring these empirical observations together and discuss them under the notion of social order and through the conceptual lens of ANT and ethnomethodology. For this, I first suggest that the discrepancy in addressing algorithms as either powerful actors in themselves or as structural epiphenomenon resembles an ongoing discussion within social theory, especially in the discipline of sociology. This will then be the point of departure for discussing the notion of social order as proposed by ANT, which is partially based on insights of ethnomethodology, and to show how it provides a possible perspective on this discussion but also complicates the picture of social order. I argue further that this complex idea of social order and the structure of socio-technical action can provide us a better understanding on the relation between social order, democratic institutions, and machine learning or algorithms. Reconstructing the difficile notion of algorithmic power thereby rests on our attempts to understand how different situated networks of social order are coordinated with each other, and how different enactments of *the algorithm* are bound together by practices of software developers.

Structure and Agency: The two Sociologies

The problem of structure and action is by no means a new issue for social research. With that the discourse about algorithmic power reproduces – to a certain extent – problems that sociology and other social sciences have been tackling for a long time now: how to account for the observable social behavior based on a larger normative or historically given structure (e.g., O'Donnell 2010; Sztompka 2014)? Especially in sociology the distinction between structure and action is one that accompanies the theoretical discussions since its founding. As Archer (1982) formulated it: "The fundamental problem of linking human agency and social structure stalks through the history of sociological theory" (Archer 1982, 455). Sociological reasoning was either focused on self-regulating structures or the local and unhinged (social) action. This development led to the formulation of "[t]he two sociologies" (Dawe 1970, 207). This distinction – and the paradox it poses – mirrors our everyday experience of us being able to act but still encountering constraints that restrict, regulate, and influence our possible actions.

> While we never cease to experience ourselves as acting, choosing, purposeful, aspiring human beings, we also never cease to be aware of the factory gates closing behind us, the office days that are not our own, the sense of oppression by organizations nobody runs, the "not-enough world" we are forced to inhabit most of the time (Dawe 1978, 365).

According to some scholars, this distinction therefore is imminent not only to social experience but must also be an essential characteristic of social theorizing (e.g., Archer 1982). However, there was (and is, one might add) a growing dissatisfaction with this differentiation of structure/action, system/individual, or discourse/subject. As Sztompka (1994, 273-274) argues: "Social wholes and human individuals have only virtual existence, their separation and mutual opposition is the product of false, distorted imagination: common-sense illusions, and theoretical as well as meta-theoretical fallacies." Thus, the issue of the theorizing of algorithmic power mirrors a discussion that sociology (and other social sciences) has been having since the moment it became a science in its own right (e.g., Vargas et al. 2008).

Different sociological approaches have dealt with exactly that issue to reformulate the actor/structure problem and find a solution that starts the observation neither from a metaphysical perspective, nor from the assumption of an ever free and omnipotent actor. Instead, the agency/structure problem is being resolved by a chain of practices that appear as if they were an external force, but are ultimately the – often unintended – result of interactions and their resulting and assumed interdependencies (Elias 1991; Giddens 1984). This perspective then also has some serious implications on our understanding of (democratic) institutions, and organizations. We no longer can take them for granted but also have to understand how institutions emerge from practices. As a result, the often-cited differentiation between micro, meso, and macro structures starts to dissolve. Callon and Latour (1981) offer a perspective that does not need an *a priori* differentiation between macro and micro level. Instead of assuming a difference between macro and micro actors, between structure and agency, they argue that precisely this difference needs explanation. They resolve the micro/macro divide by ignoring it altogether.

> The paradox with which we ended the introduction has now been resolved. We end up with actors of different size even though they are all isomorphic, because some have been able to put into black boxes more elements durably to alter their relative size. [...] [B]y directing our attention not to the social but towards the processes by which an actor creates lasting asymmetries (Callon and Latour 1981, 285–286)

Instead of taking micro and macro, structure and agency as given entities, both are part of the same coin, made relevant and visible only by circulating references (Latour, 1999b). However, ANT does not only offer a perspective to dissolve the structure/agency issue but also sees non-human actors – such as algorithms – as vital elements in the production, enactment, and stabilization of structured practices. The answer to the question how institutions become powerful, and how algorithms acquire agency is according to ANT the same: through their practically installed associations with other actors. Taking such a stance then turns the question around: it is not how the algorithm exerts power, but how the figure of the algorithm – as a practical achievement – was able to create an ordered and durable environment, which makes itself appear as if it is this powerful entity, and which asymmetries are created by ordering processes. In the following, I will therefore discuss how enacting algorithms (Seaver 2017) relates to *doing order* – and how this (hopefully) can offer a perspective of algorithmic power that sheds some light on how the algorithms in question have "become powerful actors in the first place" (Mager 2014, 30). This question becomes even more pressing, when algorithms are becoming imminent elements of democratic institutions.

Before we go on, there is an elephant in the room that has to be addressed. So far, I have mixed notions of power and social order as if the two concepts are interchangeable. Thus, a few words on the relation of power and social order might be necessary. Power and social order are for sure two of the most used concepts and words in social theory. The latter is even said to be a defining question of sociology. How is social order possible? How can we explain that this thing that we call society does not fall apart? Such questions have driven sociological theorizing for many decades and led to the formulation of functional-structural or system's perspective, treating social order as an independent entity.[2] At the same time, power has been used as a tool to unveil unequal distribution of means to act and to formulate resistance (e.g., Foucault [1975] 1995). Both perspectives can thereby be understood as a reaction to the development of enlightenment. Metaphysical or divine forces as ordering principle were discarded and replaced by the insight that the social world and its order is made by humans (Dawe 1970). Both approaches have been criticized, as they replace the cause with the outcome. As Law (1992, 380) argues: "If we do this we close off the most interesting questions about the *origins* of power and organization" (emphasis in original). ANT offers an interesting link between social order and power. Both are generated by relations, or to put it in more classical sociological vocabulary, by actions between a heterogeneous set of individual entities. Order is the result of interaction patterns that aligns different actors, and therefore provides them with the ability to act. Power is then an effect of these interactions, as it is the product of the position of an actor within the interaction patterns, within the actor-network. Practices produce (local) social order, and at the same time construct the ability to (forcefully) act, i.e., power. This also resembles the definition of power drawn from Weber:

---

2   Sociology as a discipline is surely too young to talk about it in terms of centuries. Although Auguste Comte used the term sociologie already in the year 1851 (Comte [1851] 2014) for the first time, we are not even looking back to a history of two hundred years of our discipline.

> Power (Macht) is the probability that one actor within a social relationship
> will be in a position to carry out his own will despite resistance, regardless
> of the basis on which this probability rests (Weber [1922] 1978, 53).

It is only that the basis of this probability rests on the local production of
orderliness and on the position of an actor within that pattern of interactions
that allows her to carry out her own will. Social order and power are two
sides of the same coin, linked by the production of agency – if we focus on
the practice that brings them into being. In shifting the focus, we therefore
do not look at an omnipotent principle or actor but rather at the idea of *doing
order* and *doing power.* This (and this is one of the great contributions of fields
like STS) also includes elements that are traditionally left out of sociological
reasoning, the domain of things and technology (e.g., Graham and Marvin
2001; Latour 1990; Marres 2012). Technical artifacts enable or limit agency and
thus also contribute to the production of order and power alike. So, what
we are referring to when we talk about order and power is not *social* but
socio-technical.

With the formulation of *doing order* I already hinted at one of the most
important influences of ANT: Ethnomethodology and its conception of a
locally produced and practically achieved order. Latour (1999b) wrote that
ANT "was simply another way of being faithful to the insights of ethnomethodology: actors know what they do and we have to learn from them not only
what they do, but how and why they do it" (Latour 1999b, 19). This reflects the
fundamental critique formulated by Garfinkel (1984, 2002) of the Durkheimian
legacy within sociology. Basing the analysis of the social in the generalized
normative or structural systems reduces according to Garfinkel the individual
actors to "judgmental dopes" (Garfinkel 1984, 68). In contrast, interpretative
paradigms ask how the social world is constructed through interaction and
interpretation – assuming the members of an *always already ordered* world as
competent actors who know how to produce order. Social order in terms of
Garfinkel is always locally produced and enacted through practices – therefore
a practical achievement. To Garfinkel and other ethnomethodologists, there
is no unordered situation (Sacks 1984). Order can be found in the "orderliness
of practical action" (Livingston 1987, 13). In other words, the world is always
already ordered, albeit not according to one big paradigm that an external
observer, like a fellow sociologist, is applying, but to an internal and situated
logic which is enacted through and in local practices.[3] Ethnomethodology
therefore does not focus on the question of how an objectively given world,
identified as a structure or a system, determines the interactions within a

---

3   This insight is derived from Garfinkel's studies of Schütz and his sociological
    phenomenology. The problem of applying external observational categories to social
    actions is impressively dealt with, amongst others, in his discussion of Parsons theory of
    social action (Schütz and Parsons 1978).

given situation, but how such a structure is accomplished within situated actions. As Suchman argues:

> The outstanding question for social science, therefore, is not whether social facts are objectively grounded but how their objective grounding is accomplished. Objectivity is a product of systematic practices or members' methods for rendering our unique experience and relative circumstances mutually intelligible. The source of mutual intelligibility is not a received conceptual scheme, or a set of coercive rules or norms, but those common practice that produce the typifications of which schemes and rules are made (Suchman 2006, 76).

Social order, consequently thought as from a practice-oriented perspective, therefore is a locally enacted *doing order*, which also creates the classifications, subjectivations, and relations that sociology normally takes as structuring elements (see also Law 1994). And in this doing, the practices *show* their orientation towards ideas, actors, structures, etc. that are not actually present but are enacted within the situation. Thus, doing order also refers to other situations in which order is also achieved practically and locally – but this happens in potentially always different and anew forms. In anticipating other situations and their orders, a connection between situations in time and space is created by what Schütz, an important influence on the thinking of Garfinkel and the formulation of ethnomethodology, called the process of typification (Schutz 1976). For example, I might stop in front of a red light even if no policewoman is present. In anticipating other orders and making them relevant in the situation changes the situation and my interpretation of it. This, however, creates other problems.

Schütz, drawing immensely from Husserl and Bergson, was interested in formulating a general theory of the social that radicalizes the notion of understanding and consequently takes the subjective perspective into account (Schütz [1932] 1993). For him, the processes of understanding a situation, anticipating the reaction of an alter ego and taking into account for the design of my action *to be taken* (Schütz, [1932] 1993) is already part of a social action itself. An important implication to this reasoning is that these parts of designing one's own action are not available for empirical scrutiny – neither for a participant in the interaction, nor for the social scientist observing interaction processes. What is not being expressed can also not be understood by another person (Eberle 2008). As a result, Garfinkel neglects the subjective and cognitive design of action, and focuses on the question of how social order is practically achieved by the exchange of accounts.[4] As a result, the link between order and individual action is for Garfinkel the

---

4   Here we see the influence of Parsons, who also rejected the idea of taking psychological processes as the starting point of an analytic perspective of social phenomena. In fact, Parsons called this an ontological and psychological problem, in which he – as an analyst

process of *understanding and making oneself understandable* through what he called ethnomethods.[5] By applying the ethnomethods, competent members of a social group actively order the social, instead of following an abstract principle of social order. Thus, the aim of interpretative perspectives[6] is to explain the social based on the different, localized practices that created and reproduce social order bottom up, without assuming a given idea of a social normative structure that determines social interactions. Norms and values are not translated into social action, but social action lets the norms emerge out of a localized interaction situation. Normative accounts, organizational structures, or societal interdependencies are enacted and performed in the different situations (Drew and Heritage 1992). Structure in that perspective is not some meta-physical entity that stands against observable practices. Instead, "structure exists [...] only in its instantiations in such practices" (Giddens 1984, 17). Social structure is not only the product of practices but must also be enacted in these practices. This is also true for political ideas or visions as diversity or equality. These values have to be enacted, also in and by technologies.

Of Networks and Orderings

Creating order always also refers to methods of (local) social control and negotiation of possible actions. If the sequence of actions diverts from a known or assumed order, actors can try to *repair* the situation through interventions or re-interpretations of the situation. Garfinkel famously showed this in his breaching experiments. This also refers to the notion that interactions happen always for "another first time" (Garfinkel 1984, 9). Each interaction has the potential to fail, to divert from known or assumed chains of practices – and therefore needs reinterpretation or intervention to bring it back to known territory. However, human actors are not the only ones that potentially limit or enable possible actions. Latour demonstrated in many examples that the material and technological world is also element of a locally enacted order (Latour 1990). A speed bump can make us drive slower, and a door closer can motivate us to adjust our pace. Yet, just as plans or normative accounts, the presence of material actors does not deterministically enforce a certain behavior but becomes part of the enactment, where different actions seem possible. Coming back to the notion of the algorithm, it is surely an actor that

of social structures and relations – was simply not interested in (Schütz and Parsons 1978).

5   It is noteworthy that this turn towards observable actions is not too far from Parsons' idea of social action. He argued that we are socialized into a schema of terms, which we apply to reflect about ourselves and to understand the actions of others (Schütz and Parsons 1978, 104).

6   I summarize them here, as pragmatism, ANT, and ethnomethodology share this empirical orientation (e.g., Emirbayer and Maynard 2011)

can enable or limit possible interactions, e.g., by filtering away important information which one would need for a diverse information diet. However, just as human actors, these technical entities have to become part of the situation in which they subsequently can become part of the local order. Latour (2005) calls this process delegation and translocation, where technical and material actors are put into a social situation, and a specific normative task is delegated to them. Engineers and developers (amongst many other actors) actively send these actors to other situations to have an effect, which is based on the anticipation of assumed interactions that will unfold (Callon 1987). Thus, situations are being connected with each other through processes of delegation and mobilization. ANT extends the perspective of ethnomethodology by treating local non-human actors of the situation as *references to other situations*.

In their discussion of institutional order, ethnomethodologists argue that local interaction can reference ideas, actor, or situations that are not local and translate them into resources for the local production of order, e.g., by orienting their practices on organizational rules (Drew and Heritage 1992), codes of conduct (Wieder 1974), or plans (Suchman 2006). By taking a semiotic stance[7], these interactions can then be understood radically relational – and thus can be followed. Whatever is mobilized and integrated into the locally practical achievement of social order references to something else. Normative frameworks are thereby not only practically achieved locally but are better described as being re-enacted. What is being mobilized through accounts – even if it's absent – becomes part of the situation and thus part of the inter-actions that are framed by and frame the situation. In discussing the micro/macro issue, Callon and Latour (1981) argue that

> "[t]he ethnomethodologists forget to include in their analyses the fact that ambiguity of context in human societies is partially removed by a whole gamut of tools, regulations, walls and objects of which they analyse only a part" (Callon and Latour 1981, 284).

These actors, the tools, regulations, material and technical elements, are part of the situation and therefore become part of the interpretation – they frame the situation. Additionally, they are being mobilized from somewhere else, e.g., the category list which has been produced in a team meeting, we can follow the resource through time and space. Thus, the methodological credo *follow the actors* (Latour 2005) does not impose a structure outside but follows the relational structure which unfolds in an actor-network (Latour 1996).

---

7   This is then also where Greimas (1983) and his semiotics become relevant for the analysis of social order. The given accounts of institutional or organizational rules or normative systems that are narrated references to something. Making them (intersub-jective) relevant in the situation by producing accounts about them means to integrate them into a shared narration.

The algorithm is not a single entity but the (practically achieved) result of the mobilization and relation of manifold actors – and manifold situations of constructing them. Thus, the black boxes, present as tools, techniques, books, and articles, each of them referenced to a different network of associated situations, which themselves were enacting and stabilizing specific versions of that entity that we were dealing with. Bringing together all these entities, including algorithmic techniques, made the emergence of the algorithm possible but also restricted the following actions. And these tools were often used in a way that was taken for granted, i.e., they were not problematized. The algorithm was locally enacted, within the offices of the software developers, but each of the mobilized items was referring to something else, beyond the actual situation. A paper about recommender techniques was not just put together by signs, but it became a sign itself. Thus, through understanding actants and narrations, such as normative frameworks, as references, we connect a chain of practices that exceeds the local situation. Without the discipline of computer science or the community of software developers, the algorithmic techniques would not have been available in the project that designed the recommender algorithm for the public broadcaster. As Callon and Latour (1981) showed for other "macro" actors, the algorithm achieved durability by assembling many different black boxes. This has also been shown in a similar way for data production. A singular data point mobilized in a situation of producing and technically stabilizing social order references not only an object out there, like a video in the storage servers of the broadcaster, but the (chain of) practices that produce the data. This included at the end a whole new organization. The contribution of ANT to the understanding of practically achieved social order is therefore the provision of the means to follow the practical production of social order (and therefore power and agency) through time and space without bringing back the need for a metaphysical idea of a generalized structure of system rationality. This has profound impacts on our understanding of the notions of structure or social order.

If a certain actor-network, and with it a certain order, is durable and stable is a question of force and power, as Latour argues: "The consistency of an alliance is revealed by the number of actors that must be brought together to separate it" (Latour 1993a, 185). At the same time, the extent to which such an actor-network unfolds is an open and (basically) an empirical question. Thus, notions like society, organization, or even democratic institution are only important insofar as we can observe how these entities are being enacted and achieved within a chain of practices mediated by actants. When we go back to the archive, the data production followed a locally enacted reason or problem that the department was solving. They were describing themselves as an institution that organizes video material according to the needs of the editors. The production of a discursive description of their department was recursively applied to their own practices. What the colleague from the archive was telling us was not only how things are being done but also enacted a certain rationality. The same is being discussed with algorithmic techniques (B. Rieder 2017). The techniques come with the imaginations of a (relatively abstract) problem to be solved. And they come with many *pre-scriptions* (Akrich 1992)[8], i.e., resources that allow the users to imagine the setting in which the piece should be used, here in the form of handbooks, tutorial videos, or class syllabi that teaches the software developers how to read and use them – and how to relate them with other actants. Thus, the discourse there is an expression of making ideas and rationalities accountable. Both entities, the algorithm and the archive, exist only, as they are expressions of different chains of practices. However, these practical enactments of the algorithm or the archive can differ, depending on which situated perspective we are looking from.

Multiple Orderings

By aiding the idea of relationality and associations, ANT offers a perspective that connects the idea of locally produced order with the notion of a social structure – represented as a chain of translations and/or practices. The simple but powerful answer is: they are the same. There is simply no difference between the locally achieved order and a broader social structure that would explain this order, as the former and the latter are the product of always newly established associations and interactions. As Latour argues: micro and macro level do not exist by themselves but are identified by circulating references that address them as such (Latour 1999a). Instead of explaining local actions by a bigger structure, each interaction is already embedded in a (rhizomatic) network of practices and actants, *which connect situations through time and space*. This poses to some extent a radicalization of Gidden's argument that we are confronted with social structure always through and by local practices (Giddens 1984) – and has even been applied to state institutions (Callon and Latour 1981; Passoth and Rowland 2010). However, the relationality combined with locality of associations produces problems in the conceptualizing of *the social*. Our object of inquiry is not only locally produced, but it is also multiple.

The generative element in ANT are neither actors nor structures but processes of associations and translations. The actors as well as structures are made objective through stabilizing these chains of associations. Yet, since the idea of a deterministic translation between culturally stabilized symbols or norms has been replaced by situated and localized practices of practically achieving normative accounts, the resulting order and the resulting actors

8   There is some terminological issue here, as the concepts and terms defined by Akrich (1992) and Akrich and Latour (1992) are not always coherent. While Akrich (1992) talks about pre-scriptions, this exact term is not included in the terminological framework proposed by Akrich and Latour (1992). There you find a pre-inscription and a pre-scription, which, however, differ heavily in the proposed meaning.

can vary. This, of course, creates a situation of a multiplicity of social orders. In this perspective, a singular and unique explanation of how social order is achieved will never be able to account for "every topic of logic, meaning, method, reason, and order" (Garfinkel and Wieder 1992, 202). Instead, Garfinkel and Wieder introduced the notion of order* to highlight that *social order* is an umbrella term, referencing to this multiplicity of locally enacted orders. Thus, institutions, organizations, and entire societies can be part of a system of normative accounts or interdependencies. These, however, are not being translated into behavior one by one but are mere resources for a practically achieved order.[9] This has two important implications: first, the enactment of involved actors varies with the practically achieved localized order. And second, depending from which situation one starts, different actor-networks as inter-situational orders emerge.

This multiplication of social order has profound implications for the idea of delegated technologies and artifacts as well. In the process of designing material and technological artifacts, developers realize their assumptions about how the situation will unfold. According to Callon (1986), the developers become social scientists themselves.[10] The aim is not only to design an artifact but to design the situation. This process has been conceptualized by Akrich (1992) as inscription. However, the scripts of the designed technologies do not deterministically define the consequent interactions. If this were the case, we would just have replaced the mechanism to produce Garfinkel's judgmental dopes. Instead, the translation processes can deviate from the assumed inter-actions – the process of subscription or de-inscription, as Akrich and Latour (1992) call them, can vary. That is, the process of making the ontology of the technological artifact enacts it in a different way. Even the technical object of the algorithm changes based on the interactions of which it is part of. Different enactments are part of different actor-networks. That is, in the multiplicity of locally enacting ontologies and subjectivities, we can also observe the different locally achieved enactments of social order, and how it unfolds and connects semantic entities in different situations through time and space. Identity or subjectivity as something that is achieved and not naturally given is by now a commonplace within the social sciences. Identity, normativity, etc. are not previously given but achieved in interaction. They emerge from the practices, not the other way around. This has been most impressively reconstructed in Garfinkel's analysis of Agnes, a transgender person, whose gender identity was enacted throughout different situations in producing

---

9   As a side note, one may argue that exactly this insight exemplifies why sociology relies on statistical analysis with probabilities and not deterministic formulas to calculate "the social".

10   Of course, this is only true for a specific form and imagination of sociology. If not trained as social scientists, it is rather unlikely that the developers will discuss the terms of the situation to be designed with in theoretical terms.

accounts that were identified with a *female* gender identity (Garfinkel 1984). However, producing accounts alone is not enough. They must be taken up and interpreted by the other interactants, who themselves then react with the production of accounts, which Agnes had to interpret as being successful or having failed. And, of course, Agnes had to decide how to follow up with appropriate accounts after that. Thus, the practice of producing accounts is not only a doing on the side of one actor, but also involves the application of similar (enough) ethnomethods to interpret these accounts on the side of the interacting partner. Practices stand between the involved partners. In the assumption of an always already ordered situation, Garfinkel then shifts the perspective and argues that the emergence of these accounts produces identities. Consequently, he also speaks of actors instead of individuals or the self. Actors are the result of practices, they are not previously given. Following the idea of radical symmetry, this idea then has also been extended not only to role understandings but to bodies, and the materiality of non-human actors. Mol (2002) reconstructs how atherosclerosis is being diagnosed and treated in a Dutch hospital (throughout the book she only talks about hospital Z). Visiting different sites, she reconstructs how every site and every situation differs in how they approach the disease. By applying different techniques, different instruments, or learned typifications, the disease is in every situation something else – because the practices to deal with it are different in each site.

> Instead, objects come into being – and disappear – with the practices in which they are manipulated. And since the object of manipulation tends to differ from one practice to another, reality multiplies (Mol 2002, 5).

Not only actors are being produced through situated enactments but also bodies, instruments, and materialities. However, it also creates some problems for our understanding of social order. Earlier I described the mechanism of delegation as sending technical actors to a situation as a regulatory force. Yet, if they are enacted locally – in the situation – this regulatory force is put into question. Enacting multiple realities also means multiple ways of interacting with the actant – and thus the multiplication of its ontology (Mol, 2002). This creates some complications in this outline of *doing transsituational order*. If the delegated artifacts are enacted differently, how can we understand them as producing order at a distance? The local practices simply undermine the imaginaries and assumptions of the developers put into the artifact. It is true that the notion of multiple ontologies does complicate the picture of delegation, yet it still does have an effect. The actors are multiple, depending on the practical ordering which they are part of, but they also do have reality and materiality which is part of the enactment. As Mol (2002) formulates it: they are *more than one, but less than many*.

Coming back to our algorithms, what does that mean for the perspective on algorithmic power discussed here? Instead of explaining algorithmic power, it seems that our object of interest is being lost, decentered. Instead of describing an algorithm and its power, we are now talking about multiple algorithms in multiple situations. Our recommender system is dissolving in its different situated enactments and in its multiple ontologies. Is the practical production of algorithmic agency leading us to relativism? Yet, it is exactly not that I argue that algorithms are random, without any impact on the situation, nor that they are this solid block of forceful action. If I were to do so, I would end up at the point that created this unease that I described earlier. They are something in between, but this in-between-ness is important. The whole reason why the recommender algorithm was hard to integrate into the organization of the public broadcaster was its resistance, the inbuilt ideas and assumptions about the configuration of the social world it should interact with. It would just not have been possible to change these assumptions by including the algorithmic technique in different practices. No matter how hard we would have tried, without replacing the algorithmic technique with another one, we would not be able to make it work with e.g., graph-based data. The multiplicity of the algorithm had been reduced by the associations built in its disciplinary enactment.

On the other side, however, there was room for multiple implementations. Different practices associating the algorithm differently, the identity of the algorithm would have changed dramatically. Let's assume for one moment, the data from the archive would have been used for the algorithm. It would have been a different actor, producing other results. It would still be a recommender – but rather with historic data. The local practices that were constructing the meta-data change the identity of the algorithm if we include it in the generative practices. By establishing an entirely different actor-network, a chain of practices, a specific ontology of the algorithm has been enacted. Thus, the algorithm in the local enactment is more than one, but it is also very much less than many.

Law (1994) takes this now a step further, introducing different *modes of ordering*, i.e., a specific (discursive expressible) rationality of relating heterogeneous actors. These modes of ordering are "fairly regular patterns that may be usefully imputed for certain purposes to the recursive networks of the social. In other words, they are recurring patterns embodied within, witnessed by, generated in and reproduced as part of the ordering of human and non-human relations" (Law 1994, 83). It is important to add two comments to contextualize the notion of modes of ordering. First, they are not deterministic mechanisms to produce social order – that would bring us back to structuralism. Instead, they are *fairly regular* – including the possibility of variation. And secondly, they are locally produced. In other words, modes of ordering do not produce orderings, but the orderings are observable as different modes of ordering. Thus, we can observe them without granting them causal power. The modes are the result of ordering practices, not the other way around. What these modes of orderings do and why they do it is both part of the local enactment of social order(ing). However, the notion of modes of ordering allows us to identify the local rationalities and their connection to other normative ideas or imaginaries of other situations. In the case of the development of the recommender algorithm, we also encountered different modes of ordering, which allowed or prevented the extension of the actor-network that constructed the algorithm.

The Algorithm as Disciplinary Enactment

The recommender algorithm has been enacted as a technical object, which was mobilized from a community of computer scientists and developers – and thus resembles a collective and disciplinary enactment. In their work, the developers of the project mobilized many different black boxes in order to make and do the recommender algorithm. This included, of course, the algorithmic technique that was brought into the development process. From textbooks and influential academic papers, the idea of the recommender algorithm was imported to our work, the meetings, and the discussions. This is what is normally identified as the algorithm. Bits and pieces of code but also mathematical formulas, description of calculation processes, and the discussion of potential issues and challenges, when implementing this algorithm. These came with the names of collaborative filtering recommendations, based on LDA techniques, or content-based recommendations. However, these were only the elements, the black boxes that would be opened, questioned, tinkered with. At the same time, many other elements, actors, and black boxes were mobilized and linked with it – to make it something that would be runnable. Only in the interplay of different tools, environments, and imagined problems did the algorithm as an actant in the development process begin to take shape. In manipulating, mobilizing, and relating tools like iPython notebooks, libraries, and text books, the algorithm could be tinkered with. By mobilizing different techniques, the development team was also mobilizing solutions to imagined and abstracted problems – solvable in a specific actor-network. Thus, the development project was not only trying to come up with a solution to a given problem but mobilized an actor-network and its orderings into the process of constructing the recommender system. And all of that followed a specific rationality, a set of taken-for-granted ideas on how to start a development project, how to *do* the recommender algorithm as the technical entity it is. Ideas on how to change the performance and how to adapt the algorithm to the local constraints often happened in reference to other sites, other situations, other actors – and other practices. Coming back to an episode that I already discussed earlier, Alice introduced me to the world of recommender systems. Step by step, she showed me how these mysterious things work, what I can expect from them, and where they might fall short.

> Hi! After you have read this article you understand what collaborative filtering with explicit feedback is. But: we are actually dealing with implicit feedback (users don't rate videos directly) and so we have to use different approaches :simple_smile: This article explains how to do collaborative filtering with implicit feedback and why it is different. If you feel like it is useful now, you can read it. But probably what you are doing now with clusters is more important - I didn't get around to try it myself yet. See you on Friday! (Alice via Slack Private Message)

But she did so by referencing to something else, to slides from a course in Stanford or to a paper written by a group of developers who won the Netflix Prize. This seems awfully obvious for anyone who has ever learned a new subject. We rely on external references, books and manuals. But it points to something different. By relating all these elements together in the local practice of making the algorithm, we do not only import texts or books. Instead, these entities are references to a whole other configuration of social orderings. We do not only mobilize a technique but a whole discipline. However, in doing so, we also import a specific form of reasoning into the local production of order. We become part of a larger actor-network which also enacts what Kuhn (1996) famously called a paradigm, or what Fleck ([1935] 1981) named a thought style. The local practices become part of a collective in which the rationality of an entire discipline is circulating. And the practices that enact this mode of ordering also enact the algorithm as a technical object, as a technical issue.

The Algorithm as Organizational Enactment

Algorithms are not just technical objects, but also organizational actors. Starting from the notion that software is algorithms combined with data (Wirth 1975), the process of making the algorithm had to build new associations that – again – went beyond the situation of the developers' offices, their daily SCRUM meetings, and their iPython notebooks. Instead, the search for data was leading to different organizational departments, institutions, and even to how the users of the recommender system were tracked. Based on Ziewitz' (2017) elaboration of the algorithm's ethnomethods, the quest was not just to find data sources but also to find data sources that would be compatible with the algorithmic techniques mobilized from the disciplinary enactment. As Ziewitz (2017) notes, we have to formulate observations in a way that makes them relatable to the algorithmic technique and its ways of seeing the world.

> As we had to parse our observations in a constant struggle to respecify
> the situation in the image of the self-imposed constraint, the walk was
> not so much a case of recognizing patterns, but an exercise in explicating
> observations in the language of the algorithm while figuring out whether
> and to what extent they could facilitate the job at hand – a determination
> that itself was subject to the contingencies of real-time navigation (Ziewitz
> 2017, 10).

This was then also an issue for the recommender system. We were looking for
data to power the algorithmic system in different places of the public broadcaster. However, the data found in different instances was also not just there
but was referencing a whole apparatus of practices that constructed them
according to a local rationality, to a *local and fairly regular* way to practice
data production. The algorithmic technique – and its chain of associations –
needed to be translated into something that is compatible with and relatable
to organizational processes of data production. To do so, the development
team visited different institutional settings in which the algorithm could
become an active part of the enactment of the organization – and therefore
the algorithm.

This happened by establishing a new group of online editors. This group was
acting as a watchdog for the newly installed process of producing meta-
data. The thematic editorial teams were entering meta-data into the central
planning system exclusively for the recommender system. For this, fields in
the database scheme of this central planning system that were not used by
anyone saved the entered data. And in addition, several discursive elements,
such as a fixed category list or additional guidelines, were produced to guide
the practices of data production. Coming back to the online editorial team, I
was told in an interview:

> In relation to the metadata, there will be a style guide, so that the editorial
> boards have something they can stick to. And then we have to look how it
> works (Online Editors Interview).

Similar to the textbooks, articles, and slides, the local production of social
order(liness) was accompanied by delegated actors to frame the local situation. Guidelines and category lists were sent in order to steer (not deter-
minate!) local practices. In the case of our recommender system, the actor-
network unfolded throughout the organization, as the enactment of the
algorithm was showing a specific mode of ordering. As a result, the algorithmic
technique started to construct its own ordering, occupying infrastructural
elements that were not used yet, and establishing new (practical) institutions –
thus, adding an enactment of the organization next to the already established
ones. The enactment here followed a specific idea as to how data should be
shaped and produced in order to make good recommendations. In other

words, a specific rationality was at work. The production of data as part of the imagined algorithm referred back to an entire socio-technical organization on its own. In this socio-technical configuration, accounts in the form of data are being produced that can be reflexively interpreted by the algorithmic eth-nomethods in place. And once the association is established, the algorithmic technique becomes part of that actor-network, resulting in the organizational enactment of the algorithm. Change the order, and you change the algorithm.

The Algorithm as Political Enactment

And last, but not least, the algorithmic system was enacted as a political problem. The main issue to be tackled by the research project I was part of was filter bubbles. Public broadcasters have a special legal obligation to provide a broad and diverse information diet to their viewers. By doing so, these institutions should enable citizens to make informed decisions, especially in their role as voters. This reflects the public broadcasters' function within a democratic system. As described, recommender systems are, by their very design, the anti-thesis to a broad information diet. However, exactly this broad information diet was an issue that got mobilized by the research project I was part of. And it did so by referencing an ongoing discussion in politics, legal institutions, and academic disciplines. Thus, the algorithmic system became part of another actor-network that grappled with the technical details of the recommender system and its democratic qualities. As a result, we tried to formulate a mathematical definition of diversity, change the algorithmic script in order to produce noise, and build an anti-recommender. In each of the instances, a specific logic of interpreting and relating the behavior of the algorithm to a normative idea of its political qualities was enacted. The algorithmic system was not only a technical tool that should be used, but it became a political issue that needed to be solved. A third rationality that guided the development project.

Each of these occasions can be seen as a different mode of ordering in which the algorithm got enacted, narrated, and put in relation with many different actors. And in each of the situations the algorithm was something else. A technological technique integrated into an ecosystem of an entire com-munity, an organizational actor that needed to be integrated into the different practices of data production, or a political issue that needed awareness and solutions. However, in each of the situations many different actors were present, but the central figure this book and the development project revolved around was exactly that: the figure of the recommender algorithm. The question in all these cases was how to deal with the concreteness and multiplicity of the algorithm in making it a functional and durable actor that would have agency – i.e., that would *do* something. And not just do *something* but act accordingly to the role of the democratic imaginary, enacting an algorithmic democratic order. And this against the background of different enactments with very different constraints and assumptions about possible and following practices.

Interfering Orderings: Coordinating Algorithms

Social order is produced not by actors, and not from structures, but from practices of translations and associations in which actors are being narrated and constructed in the act. However, as Mol (2002) has shown, these different enactments of bodies, materialities and other actors can become subject of many different orders. In the case of enacting atherosclerosis, different medical practices enacted the same body in different ways – producing different ontologies. Becoming part of many orderings therefore produces the need for coordinating these different versions of the enacted actor. As we have seen in the preceding chapter, the algorithm to be developed also became part of different orderings. For one, the algorithm was part of the network of disciplinary enactments, including a material environment and the discursive objectivation. But the algorithm was also part of an organizational enactment, where data had to be produced for the mobilized algorithmic techniques. And then, in the end, the algorithm had to navigate different social orderings of technological assumptions, editorial ethos, and a political discourse. In each of these occasions, the algorithmic technique was mobilized, narrated, and practically realized as a member of the socio-technical collective *that was the algorithm*. Understanding the algorithm without the different relations is not possible. However, these moments of translation were precarious and instable. Every single heretofore discussed enactment of the algorithm relates to another mode of ordering. Yet, if we look closely, the enactments or translations of an algorithm belong not just in a specific set of an ordered and ordering interaction-system, but they always existed on the edge of these different orderings. The algorithm as the end-result is part of all of these ordering systems and their specific logics and modes. While the disciplinary enactment clarifies where the algorithmic technique originates from and how we can understand them as objects of social orderings, institutional and political dimensions describe not just different modes of ordering, but more importantly, the (failed) coordination of different enactments of *the* algorithm. What the algorithm is or was, is the result of manifold negotiations, discussions, and compromises. The algorithm, as it was achieved in the end, was not the practical achievement of one situation, nor was it one enactment, but it was the coordination of many different enactments, many different situational and practical achievements and many different orderings.

Algorithms are not only the algorithmic techniques that are being applied, but they must also be understood as an actor-network that includes processes of data production, information infrastructures, and the enactment of a new and different organization. However, before this actor-network could be stabilized in the case of the public broadcaster, we encountered many problems along the way, as we were searching for data in the archive, or as we tried to produce the data ourselves via speech-recognition software. In the archive, the mode of ordering related the different human and non-human actors in a way that made it impossible to translate data into something that would be compatible with the algorithmic technique of content-based filtering as imagined by the development team. The practices of the archivists were associated with the issue of producing a video archive suitable for the practices and needs of the editorial teams, thus producing new and interesting video formats. However, the resulting format of the data that was provided by the archive was not compatible with the action program inscribed into the algorithmic technique. The data produced was too dense for calculation. At the same time, the timing of data production was not suitable for the imagined functionality of the recommender system. The archive simply took too long to produce meta-data, a timing that was very suitable for editorial tasks but not so much for the fast pace of the recommender system. The archive was not a data pool for the recommender but a resource of research for the editors. Thus, we can understand the issue at hand as a problem of reference, translation, and social order. The data that was produced did not reference an apparatus that had an algorithm in mind, as for that the way the videos were tagged would have needed to change. Instead, the normative idea of the practices, and their functional self-description, aimed at being useful for the work of the editors, who were putting together new shows and formats. At the same time, the algorithmic technique was referencing the set of practices and expectations of the developer community, the computing resources, and the assumed expectations of the users, to find the newest videos for the recommended list. In order to fulfill the latter, the archive would have needed to change. However, it was stabilized by its integration into the organizational structures that served the aforementioned rationality. The algorithm and its allies were not powerful enough to bring about this change within the local process of social ordering.

This issue of power and social order could also be observed in our second approach to produce data, an approach that led even beyond the boundaries of the broadcaster. As described, an idea was to instantiate a speech-recognition software to translate the audio tracks of the videos. These textual data then could have been used for the algorithm's calculations. However, this failed, as the algorithmic technique had to mediate two different orderings and their use of language. The most prominent TV show of the broadcaster was using the local dialect, which was simply not understandable for the speech-recognition software. While this episode could be seen as a pure technical issue, it hints at something very important. Taking a material-semi-otic stance of social orderings, each of the actors here, the TV show and the speech-recognition software, is the product of specific networks and ordering. For the broadcaster, the TV show was important, as it also defined the local identity of the broadcaster. Thus, the script writers, the actors, and the audience deemed the way it was presented important – and therefore changing the language was not an option. At the same time, the speech-recognition software can be understood as a reference to *the practices* of training the software. If I had followed this reference, I would have ended up in the offices and other sites of a big North-American company, in which developers were putting together this piece of software with a specific imagination of its application. This obviously involved a so-called standard German, which is (at least) understood in all German speaking communities. Combining the two actors, the TV show and the speech-recognition software, failed not because it was a technical issue (this is 'only' an epi-phenomenon), but because the processes or ordering were incompatible with each other – *and the local software project did not have the power to adapt either of them.*

A central element of the research project was to align the recommender system with a political and legal system – and thus to enact it as a political issue. By reducing the available information via means of personalization and filtering, it was seen as posing a threat to the democratic function of the public broadcaster. In these situations, we tried to align the technical artifact with an idea of diversity by design. Our attempts included the adaptation of the algorithmic technique itself, trying to change the optimization formula in order to produce noise in the recommendations of the algorithm. This, however, failed, as the developers and the online editors expected that the users would be confused by a recommender that produces random lists of videos, and as a result would see it as malfunctioning. Thus, the adaptation of the algorithm's optimization function failed, as the ordering processes of the entire video-on-demand system were mobilized in the expectations of the users' expectations, i.e., expectations of a second order. By narrating these expectations, the developers were referencing another situated production or social order – and showed an orientation towards known normative settings. In a second attempt, we tried to utilize the calculated model of the recommender system in a different way, translating the calculated description of users and items into two different actors, a) a list of recommendations that would favor the classical approach to recommendation, i.e., popularity, and b) a so-called "anti-recommender," which presented video items that are very different to the ones shown in the first box, producing diversity via showing people videos that would normally not have been recommended. However, this form of diversity was based on implicit knowledge of the algorithmic model, which was incompatible with the implicit knowledge of the editorial teams. The latter had their own ideas and practices of safeguarding diversity in the program, referring to their experience and training. However, since the production of diversity of the algorithmic actor was based on latent variables and reasoning, it was not tangible for the editors and we therefore could not align these two ideas of diversity. Again, each of the two implicit knowledges I found in the broadcaster were the result of specific localized forms of producing order. The algorithmic model of the machine-learning-powered recommender was referencing to manifold and successfully aligned practices in the software development project and its allies in the organization, whereas the implicit knowledge of the editors was referencing the formation of an entire professional community, with their training programs, team meetings, and daily conversations on how to create a good program. And in addition to these issues, we even had trouble explicating diversity via calculative means. When trying to do so, we found that a prominent soap opera was already very diverse by itself – simply because the show portrayed a different narrative in each episode. Therefore, also the words used were diverse. This evaluation of diversity, however, was not compatible with our – or the legislator's – concept of diversity, a concept that rested more on a qualitative assessment. In order to fix this specific metric and to align it with our understandings, we would have needed to adapt how meta-data was produced for the videos. This collided with the idea of good meta-data of the online editorial team – who insisted that a diverse description of different episodes of a show is important for the user. Again, the assumption of the algorithm and the production of data – understood as a reference to a whole and complicated set of practices – would not fit each other. The enactments of the value of diversity were incompatible, and so the enactment of the democratic recommender system became a problem.

In all of the discussed instances, the different visions and versions of the algorithm needed to be coordinated. The mobilized technique from the computer science universe had to be translated into an organizational and political actor and the conditions of possibility provided in each of these settings. This, however, produced a shift in the identity of the algorithm. John Law (2002) argues that these objects, caught in between different orderings, are fractal, that they exist in many different states at once. Based on his report on the making of a military aircraft, he notes:

> I am saying, then, that an object such as an aircraft – an "individual" and "specific" aircraft – comes in different versions. It has no single center. It is multiple. And yet these various versions also interfere with one another and shuffle themselves together to make a single aircraft (Law 2002, 2–3).

Thus, in order to produce a singular object, something that can be delegated into other situations as a stable actor, different versions of the same actor need to be coordinated with each other. In the case of the algorithm, this means to bring these different orderings into coherence with each other in the figure of the algorithm. In order to become a recommender system and a successful recommender according to the ideas of the developers, the algorithmic technique had to be coordinated with the different practices of producing data and evaluating its normative dimensions. However, this proved to be difficult, as the modes of ordering of the local institutional practices of data production were not easily related to the inbuilt script of the algorithmic technique. The archive or the speech recognition software simply enacted other ideas how the socio-technical world was configured. At the same time, the script of the recommender technique had to be adapted. Building algorithmic reflexivity meant to align different enactments of the algorithm with each other in a way that they would add up to something different – to something coherent. John Law (2002) notes that

> [...] fractal coherences are coherences that cannot be caught within or reduced to a single dimension. But neither do they exist as coherences in two or three separate and independent dimensions. In this way of thinking, a fractionally coherent subject or object is one that balances between plurality and singularity. It is more than one, but less than many (Law 2002, 3).

However, the coherent object of the recommender system does not just balance different enactments with each other. In fact, the development process was the establishment and institutionalization of another, an additional, enactment of the algorithm. In this enactment, the other enactments – and their modes of ordering – were included or excluded, changed in the process, or kept stable. Thus, in order to produce a stable and coherent recommender system, different versions of the algorithm, the organization, and politics got aligned with each other, changed, and negotiated different modes of making the algorithm tangible and durable. Especially two modes of doing so have been highlighted in the examples discussed. For one, the alignment of the algorithmic technique with different forms of data production changed the way the algorithm was enacted, and therefore poses also a moment of intervention. The second one was the mode of translating algorithmic and machine-learning-powered mode of reasoning, or better: to give accounts in a form that is translatable to the normative system of another enactment. As we saw, each of these alignments came with important decisions as to what relations are to be kept stable, e.g., between the archive and the editors, and which one could be changed, in our case the relation between the editors and the central planning system. Algorithmic agency – and therefore its power – is the result of putting these different enactments into black boxes, i.e., stabilizing them, and relating them to each other via an additional practically achieved order, including normative assumptions, imaginaries, etc. that have been locally enacted somewhere else.

These enactments put in relation keep the actor that we normally call *the algorithm* stable. Thus, they influence possible forms of translation for subsequent orderings that mobilize this (always already) stabilized algorithm.

The algorithm is still more than one, but certainly less than many. And with each integration into further orderings, possible translations, and possible ontologies decrease in number.[11] In the object of the socio-technically realized algorithm, multiple social orderings want to inscribe their locally enacted and imagined forms of social order – and, at the same time, only so many of them can co-exist, and some of them are mutually exclusive. As described, our attempts of producing a recommender algorithm sensitive to diversity interfered with the normative ideas of good editorial work and the way data was produced. The potential scripts to solve one problem were simply incompatible with other practices in the organization. The same happened in the case of producing metadata for the algorithm. The orderings within the organization were simply not fit for the requirements of the algorithmic technique mobilized from the software development community. The technical enactment of the recommender system needed to find a way, how it could be translated into the organization of the public broadcaster.

However, order is not only to be found in the different sites discussed so far. The alignment of different enactments was a production of social order itself – and followed its own rationality, a rationality that was itself normative and political. And often enough, it also was the art of the possible. Software development projects then become a moment of negotiating different social orderings with each other and realizing the result of these interactions in the algorithmic system. In the end, the installed and institutionalized algorithmic system then is the result of a very own enactment of a social order, in which the different orders are being coordinated. The algorithm has become a structural element itself. By closing and coordinating different enactments as black boxes, it became a social fact.

Delegation of Algorithmic Power

A specific conclusion of this process of negotiating different – always already present – orderings in the process of inscription can be drawn for the notion of delegation. Latour described with this the process of delegating normative power to an actant, often material or technological. And this is the starting point for our question of algorithmic power and agency in general and in democratic institutions specifically. However, observing the process of how this black box is initially being made shows the different normative assumptions and ideas that need to be balanced within the process of delegation. Close to never, delegation happens in a tabula rasa place where one can build a system from scratch. Close to ever, there is the already always ordered world there, which does not only incorporate one normative

---

11   In fact, this resembles very much the idea of reduction of complexity found in other social theories.

dimension but many different orderings that interfere with each other – and which need to be coordinated in the process of constructing the action program of an artifact. Thus, an *action program* is not only the result of the engineers' assumptions but is also born out of the conditions of possibility to inscribe them into the artifact – and which is updated in the process of implementing these techniques in specific software projects. The durable artifact becomes the materialization of a compromise that resembles and reproduces the social orderings. Coherence and durability are the product of the activity of mediating between different enactments, ontologies, and orderings. Thus, the idea of inscription, de-inscription, and delegation is being complicated. It is not a straightforward process of designing values and norms like diversity into an artifact. Instead, the process of producing a normative artifact is the result of nested and linked processes of de-inscription and re-inscription. The algorithmic technique as it was being mobilized from the realms of software development and computer science had specific scripts inbuilt. It came with stabilized assumptions about the interaction process in which it would operate. However, by embedding it into different enactments, organizational and normative, the material actor got applied differently, i.e., varying processes of description, and was changed in the process in its technical properties, thus experiencing a process of re-inscription. De-inscription and re-inscription therefore became two sides of the same coin. Combining the algorithmic technique with different forms of data put it into a specific context but also extended the artifact. At the same time, tinkering with the parameters of the optimization formula was a de-inscription of the technique – using it differently – but also inscribing different ideas, norms, and assumptions about the context of its usage. This, then, has some profound implications on our discussion of algorithmic power. By looking at the idea of algorithmic power and agency through the notion of social ordering, some conclusions can be drawn that do not reduce the issue at hand to the omnipotent algorithm nor to a metaphysical principle of societal structure. And, which can point us to the moments and sites of intervention to align and adapt algorithms to democracy.

The algorithm is not an element in a singular rationality. Instead it is the manifestation of different rationalities and institutionalized logics that are being negotiated with each other. And with that, the algorithm itself is already the result of a power play or an attempt to produce order. Evaluating algorithmic power refers to different moments of ordering and enacting what is to be ordered in the constant process of making and re-making the actor that is normally attributed with the notion of the algorithm. However, instead of being just this one element, it is a culmination point of a fight of normative ideas. Thus, finding algorithmic solutions – and their problems – is not a straightforward process but needs to be related to the diverse ecologies embedding the algorithm. The question then is no longer just how we can assess the power of a singular algorithm, e.g., by looking at its code base. Instead, it gets a bit more complicated. Which ordering systems have been neglected, which ones were included? How did one ordering system interfere and change the other one in the negotiation of the concrete form of the algorithm? In the example of the recommender system at hand, one ought to ask why did the archive not just change the way they worked? Sure, they had their own discursive definition of their purpose and the problem they should solve, but they could also discard this definition and change their practices according to the formulated needs of the algorithm. If they had done so, the work of the editors would also have changed quite dramatically. Thus, the mode or ordering that we found at the archive was an expression of a power play. Was the actor-network of the archive-editor collective strong enough to resist the expansion of the recommender system's actor-network? In our story it was, but it could have also been differently. Thus, this already reflects the power to re-structure the social world and its practices. But this then also makes a strong point to not attribute all the power to the algorithm, nor to take away all the explanatory power from it. Algorithms do something, they sort, recommend, search, and sometimes beat us at chess. However, they do so because they were able to co-exist in different ordering systems, because they were able to coherently coordinate their different enactments into one durable actor-network.

As different enactments need to be coordinated, this also sheds new light on the role of software development projects. If we follow the here presented narrative, then they are no longer just sites where technologists put together different bits and pieces, like communication protocols, database designs, and algorithmic techniques. Instead, their role shifts towards a site in which these different enactments are being coordinated, negotiated, and stabilized. Software development projects therefore enact a different socio-technical order in which they reach out to and negotiate with other institutionalized orderings, and balance assumptions and ideas relevant for the project, including the legal system, ethical considerations, practical data production, an organizational idea of broadcasting, and so on. This also shifts the idea of an intervention in these settings. It is not only to provide ethical guidelines or best practices. It is also not the diversification of developers alone (although this is an important topic!). Instead, intervention means to understand and multiply (or sometimes even exclude) relevant modes of ordering that need to be coordinated within these project settings. On the other hand, it can also tell us about the presence of social orderings that contradict each other, making us aware of the choices we have to make or think about ways to make them compatible via new and inventive methods. In addition, it also leads us beyond the borders of the development project and could lead us to other surprising sites, like the offices of a big North-American company. When talking about algorithmic power and algorithmic order, aiming at the singular algorithm therefore misses its target, as does the idea of an omnipotent societal rationality. Instead, the relevant question is: what are the *infra-structures* of our algorithms and who controls them?

Now we found our way back to our starting point. Neither the individual level, nor the structural perspective *alone* can help us to understand, explain, and interact with algorithms in our society. Instead, by focusing on the generative processes of algorithmic actors, we see how these two levels blur their boundaries. Algorithms are social facts only because we are confronted with them in such a way where they are enacted in a situation of achieved social order. Yet, at the same time, these techniques, databases, and communication infrastructures that are combined in the notion of the algorithm *do* something, they are real and often resist our attempts to game or challenge them. Describing potential problematic (or even positive) effects of algorithms and machine learning, we can rely on their individual power granted to them by a structure. However, as soon as we want to intervene in the construction of our social world's co-inhabitants, we must unpack the processes of stabilization and have a good look at what orderings and rationalities are being included, excluded, and changed in the process of digitally ordering our societies. This in itself becomes the democratic question of inclusion and representation that goes beyond a normative expression of values via computer code. Discussing democracy in the digital era therefore also requires us to realize how democracy gets engineered in these projects and how already existing orders allow or hinder an algorithmic enactment of democratic values. In the past, in the name of innovation, democratic states willingly weakened the structures of public institutions and allowed big tech players define the modus operandi of these public arenas, leading to phenomena that we now call control societies or surveillance capitalism. Yet, these developments are not a natural given or unavoidable. Instead, we can ask ourselves the question: how far do we open up our democracies for big digital players and under what conditions are we willing to do so? Because in the end, IT could be otherwise.[12]

12   I am very thankful that I am allowed to borrow this wonderful phrase from the Technology in Practice Group, IT University Copenhagen, who developed it in a workshop in 2017.

Conclusion

Making a (democratic) algorithm was a challenge for the public broadcaster. It required the coordination of multiple sites and rationalities in which the algorithm was enacted in an already established and always already ordered world. What the algorithm became in the end reflects not only the technical details of some thousand lines of code, or the applied calculations. It also reflects the different social orderings that made these calculations possible in manifold established and institutionalized infrastructures and practices. Instead of thinking that an algorithm is doing something (which is true), it might be more productive to take a closer look at what *doing algorithms* means when we want to start to understand and potentially also regulate the power of algorithms. Focusing on the in-between-ness of the different involved actants, that is, asking what connects them and how the identity of algorithms and its subjects change can provide us with the means of doing algorithms differently. The description of the emergence of the recommender algorithm then also can leave us with some important implications and insights into the processes of ordering our digital societies. First, software development projects, and this includes the development of machine learning and AI applications, cannot just be understood as a technical endeavor. Instead, these development projects are sites in which different societal, normative, legal, and organizational demands and structures come together. A dev-team therefore not only organizes their own disciplinary version of the algorithm but must coordinate different demands, imaginaries, and realities with each other in order to make the algorithmic system happen. The algorithm is then not only a few lines of code alone but is an actor that can only exist because it could successfully integrate different actors into its existence, to an extent that it reaches out to entire organizations or legal apparatuses. This is for sure also the result of a society that increasingly relies on digital technology to a degree that was not conceivable some decades ago. Problem definitions change, from issues that are purely in the domain of computer science, into domains of economy, medicine, public media, or even warfare. But this also makes it necessary to change our attitude towards software development projects. These sites of coordination and algorithmic reflexivity must be populated by many different people, able to translate the rationality of an n-dimensional vector space into tangible legal or political claims. At least three demands can be derived from such an insight: a) new forms of translating calculative rationality into qualitative accounts needs new structures of social ordering; b) value by design approaches need durability and c) let us not just focus on algorithms but also the platforms and environments that make them. Each of these points is a broad and potentially bold demand, maybe even born out of the necessity of academic prose, but I am convinced that every one of them is important and worth further research and effort if we want to understand the complex relation between machine learning and democracy.

Translating Rationalities

First, new forms of translating a calculative rationality into something that is relatable in political or legal debates are highly necessary. As shown in the discussion about diversity, the possibility to express certain ideas and norms in an algorithmic logic failed, partly because the discourse on diversity always operated with an implicit understanding of what we mean by it, and which therefore was part of our taken-for-granted repertoire in our conversations. Even the translation between the legal formulations, as found in the decisions of the German Constitutional Court and the related laws, and the implicit understanding of the term by the editors shows that the expression of diversity is something that is learned through examples and practices, not by mathematical formulations. If something violated the assumed ideal of diversity, there were procedures to come back to an acceptable state. Or to use the notions from ethnomethodology, the competent participants had ways to bring the situation back to a state that was considered normal. With algorithmic systems, such procedures to normalize the situation are still scarce. Especially, as the methods are missing to reflexively resolve the accounts produced by algorithmic systems. Paradoxically, the answer could be more data science, not less. More quantitative analysis, not less. But data science that is born out of different ordering systems and where the experts have knowledge from different domains. It is not without irony that data science experts themselves started to search for external expertise (Ribes 2019; Ribes et al. 2019).

Taking the issue of diversity and recommender systems as a point of departure, data science methods would have to be combined with more qualitative and interpretative modes of inquiry, translating implicit knowledge of the editors into forms of algorithmic reasoning. For example, connecting different thematic clusters via rules that a recommender would have to follow, like: If user1 was shown many videos from Cluster 1 ("national politics"), show her videos from Cluster 54 ("international culture"). This would, however, require methods to identify that there are such clusters and then formulate rules that are understandable to the algorithmic system – and it requires expertise from at least two different domains.

Governing algorithmic systems then becomes a problem of coordinating different moments of translation and ordering, not only a process of realizing straightforward normative assumptions and ideas. In the end, we can ask ourselves whether we do not overburden developers if we want to make them realize many different normative accounts in the scripts and ontologies of the algorithm in the narrow sense – and maybe we should also look for solutions by changing the algorithmic system in a broader way. In addition, the nature of machine learning makes it seem like it is not enough – although it is important – to include different forms of expertise during the development process. Instead, a more durable solution might be necessary. Which brings me to my second conclusion.

Institutionalizing Value By Design

Value sensitive design is and has been an important branch of the discussion for a long time. Helen Nissenbaum (2001) argued relatively early that computer systems and digital applications do embody values (see also Friedman and Nissenbaum 1996). This led to the insight that values of digital systems can be adapted through processes of co-design and value sensitive design. At this point of the book this should not come as a surprise. And there are many interesting and valuable projects and attempts to build more responsible and ethical systems – including the very project that this book is based on. Zhu et al. (2018), for example, formulate proposals for including different stake-holders and their expertise early in the design process of algorithms. Méndez Fernández and Passoth (2019) even conceptualize software development as an *interdiscipline*, which necessarily must include different theoretical, disciplinary, and societal perspectives. Other scholars proposed to make team compositions and contributions of different societal groups visible via data visualization (D'Ignazio and Klein 2020) in order to make issues in team compositions visible. Diakopolous (2019) also argues that employing a value by design approach is essential in the realization of algorithmic accountability. There is an already very vivid community that seeks to realize value sensitive design in digital technologies. However, Diakopolous (2019) also argues that evaluation is an essential element of algorithmic accountability (see also Jones and Jones 2019) – going beyond the development stage of algorithmic systems. This is even more true – as I would like to add here – because of the networked nature of machine learning and algorithmic systems.

Machine learning depends heavily on the ongoing process of calculating and applying models based on observational data. However, as we have seen, the data itself needs heavy investment of interpretation and rationalization. What I call *algorithmic reflexivity* is the process of aligning data and algorithms in a way that includes and enables the understanding of the processes of data production. These processes are thereby never detached from a broader practically achieved order – and therefore in itself historically contingent. Thus, even in applications where models are being trained only once and then applied without further change, a shift in the configuration of related social order(ings) can change the entire identity of the algorithmic system. The algorithmic reflexivity is simply no longer adequate for the situation referred to – the algorithm is no longer a competent member so to speak. This is then even more problematic for applications that are continuously learning, just like the recommender system. The model is being re-calculated regularly and therefore reacts to the users' practices.[1] Thus, in both cases, also a normative evaluation has to occur continuously. Each calculation has to be evaluated against the normative framework as if it were for another first time – and if the algorithmic system deviates, bring it back to a state that we deem acceptable. This, however, requires us to radically rethink value by design approaches for machine learning and think of institutionalized and organizational solutions.

The governance of software development projects that I mentioned in the previous section therefore must become a permanent state in the domains that are defined as sensitive to our democracies. In the case of the recommender system of the public broadcaster, such a solution could be a separate department that tries to continuously monitor the diversity of recommendations. Thus, algorithmic normativity is not achieved by including experts on ethics or social sciences in the process of developing an algorithm, as these alliances are only temporary and will come to a natural end. Instead, we must counter durable algorithms with durable structures to change their identity. To create democratic algorithms we have to build and extend our democratic institutions. As such, democratic algorithms are becoming democratic processes of calculation.

It's the Platform Economy, Stupid!

It might be a strange ending for a book on algorithms to argue for more platform studies. However, I do not believe that this is an 'either or' matter. What I discussed throughout the book is the networked nature of algorithms and that we should understand them as emerging from different ordering systems – which also takes their technological resistance into account. However, in the case of the recommender system I discussed, it became clear again and again that the realization of the algorithm was prevented – or at least substantially diverted – through the established orderings that already existed. What the algorithm turned to be in the end was the art of the possible, as other ordering systems were simply more durable, more powerful. And while this is very visible in the case of a public broadcasting organization, it is an insight that can be applied to all occasions where algorithms or machine learning are involved. To take up a rather prominent example, we could ask ourselves if the case of Cambridge Analytica, where millions of user profiles were scraped from Facebook to target US citizens in order to influence their voting behavior, would have been possible in a different environment. The application of the

---

1   Strictly speaking, it would react to the practices that are between the users and the platform, as the practices, not the individuals, are the unit of analysis.

algorithm described is highly problematic. Just as problematic, however, is the environment that provided the means to make it possible in the first place. That platforms are important is not a new insight (see e.g. Gillespie 2018; Zuboff 2019). However, the case of the public broadcaster illustrates how platform politics and the conditions of possibility for algorithmic systems are entangled. Thus, regulating or intervening in the production of algorithms is important, but as important is the intervention into the central platforms of our everyday and political life. Understanding the power of algorithms without understanding the socio-technical order of platforms will lead us to a place where we would grasp neither of them. This could, however, go into different directions. Coordinating different enactments as a form of organization would also open up the possibility to integrate different platforms into a common structure, where auditing, democratically installed infrastructure, and means of translating normative accounts into technological means is provided by an institution that is politically and democratically legitimized. Through such a public algorithmic infrastructure, the environment that provides the conditions of possibility for algorithmic power in sensitive domains would be open to interventions and ethical, moral, and legal reasoning.

Modern Algorithms

As discussed, algorithmic systems pose different challenges if we want to understand and intervene in the ways they co-construct our society. However, they do not only pose an irritation for our normative systems but for our understanding of modernity at large. Lyotard (1984) famously proclaimed that we are entering a state of postmodernism, as the grand narratives are vanishing. Our times, so the argument, no longer have a common construction that drives them, may it be progress, the domination over nature, or enlightenment. Against such an argument, Latour (1993b) also very famously coined the phrase that we have never been modern, thus nothing can be lost but the *narrative* that we had a common narrative. Machine learning, it seems, is the logical continuation of these debates. What the discussion on AI and machine learning in general, but also the vignettes of this book specifically, show is that we hardly can keep up the idea of domination of nature or the narrative of a common and universal rationality. Algorithmic systems are, in all the issues and problems that they produce, rational in their calculative logic. But it is a logic that is not tangible to us, so that we sit in front of our computer screen looking at neural networks or a visualization of a vector space of latent factors and ask ourselves: *And what does this mean?* Mostly it means that it works. That it solves a problem. Machine learning techniques are not evaluated by the arguments they make or the general laws we deduce by them, but by the fact that they perform one percent better than the other models with a given dataset and problem, such as the MNIST database for image recognition of handwritten numbers. This then raises many questions in epistemology and social theory alike. One is the question of algorithmic objectivity. As G. Rieder & Simon (2016) argue, algorithms are seen as objective and neutral entities translating the trust in numbers (Porter 1995) into the algorithmic realm. However, objectivity is, as Daston and Galison (2010) illustrated, a collective achievement, one that requires communication, coordination, and discipline. Given the issues we have in understanding the reasoning of machine learning, and even fail to compare them to each other outside of heavily controlled settings, how does this then impact the notion of objectivity in our contemporary society? What counts as objective and why? And what means do we have to maybe construct objectivity anyhow?

The second, and maybe much bigger, question touches central sociological theories, especially in relation to theories of social differentiation. With the insight that the self-description of modernity is challenged by the emergence of these new technologies, we can also conclude that this is true for sociological reasoning, which is, according to Eisenstadt and Curelaru (1976), a product of modernity. What I have discussed throughout the book could be read as a story of different social subsystems and their issues because of their different system-internal codes. Each of these systems, let's call them that for a moment, fulfills a function, either within the organization or in the political system, or in the scientific system. However, at the same time, these different systems interact with each other via specific configurations of actors, making specific forms of actants, i.e., objects and subjects alike, possible. Thus, what form of differentiation are we observing here, and how are different subsystems integrated? These questions get even more complicated, as the notion of differentiation has to be differentiated a bit. In classical approaches, such as Durkheim's ([1893] 2014), the major form of differentiation is the separation of work within complex societies. Through an ongoing specialization of singular actants within the community, productivity rises and more complex forms of social structures become possible. However, this also requires new forms of integration, as these singular elements of modern societies become dependent on each other. Durkheim emphasized the role of organizations and the state to foster integration in modern societies. Norbert Elias starts from a different theoretical conception, namely, the different configuration of relations of individual actants, which he calls figuration, and how this results in a historical process in a monopoly of power. Contrary to Durkheim, Elias ([1939] 2000) argues that differentiation is the result of such a monopoly, as it now can in a self-referential manner begin to define different standards of production and relate them towards each other. Yet, the mechanism of integration is in principle the same for both. If we take a practice-oriented and material semiotic stance as discussed in this book, we could raise the question of what material and infrastructural forms of integration emerge in digitized societies – and whether integration is not even overemphasized under observable conditions of multiple ontologies and orderings. Similar observations can be made in other notions of differentiation, which are characterized as systems theory approaches, first and foremost by Parsons and Luhmann. Both theoreticians formulated a theory of social systems, albeit in different ways. For Parsons (1971), a society had to fulfill certain functions in order to maintain a stable equilibrium and ensure its survival. This led eventually to the famous AGIL schema of Parsons. The clou of the theoretical conception was then that every subsystem has to maintain the same functions for itself – leading to infinite recursion of functions. This made it possible to order action systems within each modern society to a functional subsystem that helps to maintain societal structure. Different to the approaches of Durkheim or Elias, integration is not a higher-level ordering system but a function next to the others. Luhmann (1996), a late student of Parsons, criticized Parsons' approach later and formulated his own theory of social differentiation based on cybernetic ideas of autopoetic and operationally closed systems. Differentiation in the sense of Luhmann no longer hinges on structures that have to be maintained but on the differentiation of various communication systems that are the product of an overarching and self-observing societal system.[2] What systems emerge is the result of an evolutionary process and cannot be predetermined. Yet, each system works with its own communication codes and operations, such as 'paying'/'not-paying' in the economic system or power/no-power in the political system. Both approaches to systemic differentiation, however, raise questions in term of the role algorithms and machine learning play in them. Machine learning stands, as I have illustrated throughout the book, between these different subsystems, connecting different rationalities and different forms of commutation codes. With this, it multiplies the frame of reference, i.e., the organization or a larger community, which is a vital element for Parsons, and at the same time builds a bridge between operational structures of different socio-technical subsystems.

These short spotlights on theories of differentiation – of course – do not do justice to the much more complex and nuanced theories. And there are many more that I cannot touch here. However, what I tried to show is that there is something to ask and explore, that algorithms and machine learning raise questions in regard to our theorizing of modern societies. And these questions are already getting attention, mostly in the German context, where the notion of 'the society' is questioned from a pragmatist perspective (Renn 2006), or where Gesa Lindemann (2019) proposes a theory of differentiation that takes technological developments more into account. An approach that is mostly in accordance with the questions raised here is probably the notion of fragmental differentiation (Passoth and Rammert, 2019). This also resonates

---

2   This reflexive turn even led to the formulation of the society of society (Luhmann 1997), as 'the society' only exists as the result of a self-observation. Nassehi (2019) later formulated digitalization as a processes of (digital) self-observation.

well with the work of Latour (2013) who described different *modes of existence* in a way that could be read as a social theory of differentiation. There he identifies distinct modes like politics, science, or law – which creates a promising bridge between approaches in STS and social theories of differentiation. Thus, there are interesting branches in formulating new theories of not just social but socio-technical differentiation that would make an interesting point of departure to ask about the role of machine learning in modern societies. I have no answer to any of these questions here, and trying to formulate an answer would well deserve – at least – a book on its own. But it is worth asking them and many others as machine learning and AI pose serious challenges to our contemporary societies *and* our social theories.

Finally, and as a hopefully positive ending of this book, I would like to say that all of these questions, arguments, and illustrations are born out of a genuine fascination with the topic. The aim is not to warn humanity about algorithms, nor to save us from Skynet. I enjoy programming, sitting over mathematic formulas, diving into piles of data, or to make geeky jokes about /dev/random. In the end, I want to understand what drives these entities that we call algorithms, and how they are part of a much bigger system that we call democracy. However, to paraphrase Kranzberg (1986): Algorithms are neither good nor bad; nor are they neutral. Therefore, we should find ways to live with them in a way that we deem positive and that is compatible with our contemporary democracies.

Acknowledgements

This book is based on my PhD thesis "Rule(s) of Recommendation. What the making of a recommender system can tell us about the difficult relation between social order and machine learning", which I defended in the summer 2021 at the Technical University of Munich. As some of the readers might know, such a book is always a challenging and fragile endeavor. Much like the algorithms I discuss in this book, the final manuscript is an achievement of a whole collective, and not just the result of my isolated and detached thinking. Instead, it implicitly references so many people, places, and situations. And while everyone who has ever written a PhD thesis knows that the process of making such a book is not always enjoyable, I would not want to miss a minute of it. In the following, I want to make visible some of the persons who especially helped me throughout this endeavor.

First, I want to thank Prof. Jan-Hendrik Passoth. It was – and is – incredible working with him. I will always remember the manifold occasions when I dropped by his office to get a signature, just to find myself standing there for at least an hour discussing media theory, social theory, or the latest *Star Trek: Discovery* episodes. During my time under his supervision and in his team, I learned so many things, and he really opened up the geeky space of material-semiotics in a way that was beyond my imagination before that.

I also want to express my deepest thanks to Prof. Sabine Maasen. She was always a great mentor to me and encouraged me to think more and to think bigger. I am, however, especially thankful for her never ending engagement for the MCTS (now: STS Department) and the thriving and intellectual environment she was able to foster (along with all the great colleagues there!). This book, and much of my thinking, would not have been possible without this great place and her guidance.

I also want to thank Prof. Iris Eisenberger for pushing me towards (and beyond) the finishing line. We all know that ending the writing process is scary. This moment when you have to say: this is it. However, a project like this is never done. There is always something that could be explained better, needs more details, could be contextualized more, especially, as you grow with the writing process. At the end you know more than when you started. Your thinking has changed, maybe got more nuanced. And you want your work to reflect that. But this is impossible. At some point you have to act *as if it is done*. Prof. Eisenberger always reminded me of that and always had an open door for me to talk about these fears and challenges. And in the end, she would always tell me: just finish it, it will be good.

Dr. Marcus Burkhardt also needs a special mentioning here. Not only did he always have an open door for me when I was stuck with my arguments, but also was always very critical – in the best way imaginable – of my writings, pushing me to be more precise. I am especially thankful that he introduced me to the world of media theory and helped me to explore this fascinating academic field.

Thanks also go to Dr. Andrea Geipel for her emotional support and for scouting the unknown and opaque labyrinth of TUM bureaucracy. At the end, she helped me tremendously in navigating the emotional and organizational difficulties of handing in a thesis and was a great friend in the more troubling times that come with writing a PhD thesis.

Peter Kahlert also deserves thanks for our engaged and engaging discussions about pragmatism and Luhmann's systems theory over the obligatory beer. There are not many persons on this planet more knowledgeable than him when it comes to the work of George Herbert Mead.

This list of people already shows that this book has been produced in a great variety of places. In its entirety this book was written in my offices at the Technical University of Munich, the University of Graz, and the University of Klagenfurt. I am grateful that all of these institutions provided me with the opportunity to dedicate a substantial part of my time to this project. Thus, I thank all the people, groups, and institutions that provided me with shelter and food for thought. This also includes the Technology in Practice Group (ITU Copenhagen), which I was lucky to visit in January 2020. Special thanks to Rachel Douglas-Jones and Baki Cakici. I also have to thank the Data Science Institute at Lancaster University for giving me the opportunity discuss my ideas with colleagues from computer science. Special thanks to Victoria Neumann.

And finally, I want to thank all of my former and actual colleagues at these institutions, especially at the STS Department (former MCTS) of TUM and the members of the former working group Innovation Law, now located in Vienna, Graz, and even New Zealand. Thinking is always better and more entertaining in a group.

References

Aibar, Eduardo, and Wiebe E. Bijker. 1997. "Constructing a City: The Cerda Plan for the Extension of Barcelona." *Science, Technology & Human Values* 22 (1): 3–30. https://doi.org/10.1177/016224399702200101.

Akrich, Madeleine. 1992. "The De-Scription of Technical Objects." In *Shaping Technology / Building Society: Studies in Sociotechnical Change*, edited by John Law and Wiebe Bijker, 205–24. Massachusetts: MIT Press.

Akrich, Madeleine, & Bruno Latour. 1992. "A Summary of a Convenient Vocabulary for the Semiotics of Human and Nonhuman Assemblies." In *Shaping Technology/Building Society*, edited by Wiebe E. Bijker and John Law. 259–64. Massachusetts: MIT Press.

Allgaier, Joachim, Andrea Geipel, and Jesús Muñoz Morcillo. 2019. "Climate Protection Policy in Germany: YouTubers and Scientists United against the Government?" Naturevolve. November 14, 2019. https://www.naturevolve.com/post/2019/11/12/climate-protection-policy-in-germany-youtubers-and-scientists-united-against-the-governme.

Amann, Klaus, and Stefan Hirschauer. 1997. "Die Befremdung Der Eigenen Kultur. Ein Programm." *Die Befremdung Der Eigenen Kultur. Zur Ethnographischen Herausforderung Soziologischer Empirie*. Suhrkamp-Taschenbuch Wissenschaft. 1318. Frankfurt, Main: Suhrkamp.

Amatriain, Xavier, and Justin Basilico. 2011. "Recommender Systems in Industry: A Netflix Case Study." In *Recommender Systems Handbook*, edited by Francesco Ricci, Lior Rokach, Bracha Shapira, and Paul B. Kantor, 385–419. Boston, MA: Springer US. https://doi.org/10.1007/978-0-387-85820-3_8.

———. 2016. "Past, Present, and Future of Recommender Systems: An Industry Perspective." In *Proceedings of the 10th ACM Conference on Recommender Systems*, 211–14. RecSys '16. New York, NY, USA: Association for Computing Machinery. https://doi.org/10.1145/2959100.2959144.

Ames, Morgan G. 2018. "Deconstructing the Algorithmic Sublime." *Big Data & Society* 5 (1): 2053951718779194. https://doi.org/10.1177/2053951718779194.

Amoore, Louise. 2009. "Algorithmic War: Everyday Geographies of the War on Terror." *Antipode* 41 (1): 49–69. https://doi.org/10.1111/j.1467-8330.2008.00655.x.

———. 2011. "Data Derivatives. On the Emergence of a Security Risk Calculus for Our Times." *Theory, Culture & Society* 28 (6): 24–43. https://doi.org/10.1177/0263276411417430.

———. 2013. *The Politics of Possibility: Risk and Security Beyond Probability*. Durham: Duke University Press.

Ananny, Mike. 2016. "Toward an Ethics of Algorithms: Convening, Observation, Probability, and Timeliness." *Science, Technology, & Human Values* 41 (1): 93–117. https://doi.org/10.1177/0162243915606523.

Ananny, Mike, and Kate Crawford. 2018. "Seeing without Knowing: Limitations of the Transparency Ideal and Its Application to Algorithmic Accountability." *New Media & Society* 20 (3): 973–89. https://doi.org/10.1177/1461444816676645.

Anderson, Benedict. 2006. *Imagined Communities: Reflections on the Origin and Spread of Nationalism*. Revised. London ; New York: Verso.

Aneesh, Aneesh. 2009. "Global Labor: Algocratic Modes of Organization." *Sociological Theory* 27 (4): 347–70. https://doi.org/10.1111/j.1467-9558.2009.01352.x.

Angwin, Julia, Jeff Larson, Surya Mattu, and Lauren Kirchner. 2016. "Machine Bias: There's Software Used Across the Country to Predict Future Criminals. And It's Biased Against Blacks." ProPublica. May 23, 2016. https://www.propublica.org/article/machine-bias-risk-assessments-in-criminal-sentencing.

Angwin, Julia, Madeleine Varner, and Ariana Tobin. 2017. "Facebook Enabled Advertisers to Reach 'Jew Haters.'" ProPublica. 2017. https://www.propublica.org/article/facebook-enabled-advertisers-to-reach-jew-haters.

Aradau, Claudia, and Tobias Blanke. 2017. "Politics of Prediction: Security and the Time/Space of Governmentality in the Age of Big Data." *European Journal of Social Theory* 20 (3): 373–91. https://doi.org/10.1177/1368431016667623.

Archer, Margaret S. 1982. "Morphogenesis versus Structuration: On Combining Structure and Action." *The British Journal of Sociology* 33 (4): 455–83. https://doi.org/10.2307/589357.

Arendt, Hannah. 2017. *Artifacts of Thinking: Reading Hannah Arendt's Denktagebuch.* Edited by Ian Storey. New York, NY: Fordham University Press.

Austin, John L. 1975. *How to Do Things with Words: Second Edition.* Edited by James O. Urmson and Marina Sbisa. Revised. Cambridge, Mass: Harvard University Press.

Bakshy, Eytan, Solomon Messing, and Lada A. Adamic. 2015. "Exposure to Ideologically Diverse News and Opinion on Facebook." *Science* 348 (6239): 1130–32. https://doi.org/10.1126/science.aaa1160.

Barber, Benjamin R. 1988. *The Conquest of Politics: Liberal Philosophy in Democratic Times.* Princeton, N.J: Princeton University Press.

Barlow, John Perry. 2016. "A Declaration of the Independence of Cyberspace." Electronic Frontier Foundation. January 20, 2016. https://www.eff.org/de/cyberspace-independence.

Barocas, Solon, and Andrew D. Selbst. 2016. "Big Data's Disparate Impact." *California Law Review* 104: 671.

Barry, Andrew. 2001. *Political Machines: Governing a Technological Society.* New York: Athlone Press.

Bauman, Zygmunt. 2000. *Globalization: The Human Consequences.* Revised. New York: Columbia University Press.

Beam, Michael A., and Gerald M. Kosicki. 2014. "Personalized News Portals: Filtering Systems and Increased News Exposure." *Journalism & Mass Communication Quarterly* 91 (1): 59–77. https://doi.org/10.1177/1077699013514411.

Bechmann, Anja, and Geoffrey C Bowker. 2019. "Unsupervised by Any Other Name: Hidden Layers of Knowledge Production in Artificial Intelligence on Social Media." *Big Data & Society* 6 (1): 2053951718819569. https://doi.org/10.1177/2053951718819569.

Beck, Ulrich. 1992. *Risk Society: Towards a New Modernity.* London: SAGE Publications.

Becker, Howard S. 1997. *Outsiders: Studies in Sociology of Deviance.* New York: Free Press.

Beer, David. 2009. "Power through the Algorithm? Participatory Web Cultures and the Technological Unconscious." *New Media & Society* 11 (6): 985–1002. https://doi.org/10.1177/1461444809336551.

———. 2015. "Productive Measures: Culture and Measurement in the Context of Everyday Neoliberalism." *Big Data & Society* 2 (1): 2053951715578951. https://doi.org/10.1177/2053951715578951.

———. 2017. "The Social Power of Algorithms." *Information, Communication & Society* 20 (1): 1–13. https://doi.org/10.1080/1369118X.2016.1216147.

Benjamin, Ruha. 2019. *Race After Technology: Abolitionist Tools for the New Jim Code.* Medford, MA: Polity.

Bennett, James. 2018. "Public Service Algorithms." In *A Future for Public Service Television,* edited by Des Freedman and Vana Goblot, 91–101. London: Goldsmiths Press.

Berg, Sebastian, & Hofmann, Jeanette. 2021. "Digital democracy." *Internet Policy Review* 10(4). https://policyreview.info/articles/analysis/digital-democracy

Berger, Peter L., and Thomas Luckmann. 1967. *The Social Construction of Reality: A Treatise in the Sociology of Knowledge.* New York: Anchor.

Berry, David. 2011. "The Computational Turn: Thinking about the Digital Humanities." *Culture Machine* 12.

Beverungen, Armin, Timon Beyes, and Lisa Conrad. 2019. "The Organizational Powers of (Digital) Media:" *Organization* 26 (5): 621–35. https://doi.org/10.1177/1350508419867206.

Bimber, Bruce. 2003. *Information and American Democracy: Technology in the Evolution of Political Power.* Cambridge: Cambridge University Press.

Bishop, Sophie. 2019. "Managing Visibility on YouTube through Algorithmic Gossip." *New Media & Society* 21 (11–12): 2589–2606. https://doi.org/10.1177/1461444819854731.

Blumer, Herbert. 1954. "What is Wrong with Social Theory?" *American Sociological Review* 19 (1): 3–10. https://doi.org/10.2307/2088165

———. 1986. *Symbolic Interactionism: Perspective and Method*. Berkeley, Los Angeles, London: University of California Press.

Bodó, Balázs, Natali Helberger, Sarah Eskens, and Judith Möller. 2019. "Interested in Diversity." *Digital Journalism* 7 (2): 206–29. https://doi.org/10.1080/21670811.2018.1521292.

Bogard, William. 2006. "Welcome to the Society of Control: The Simulation of Surveillance Revisited." In *The New Politics of Surveillance and Visibility*, edited by Kevin D. Haggerty and Richard V. Ericson, 55–78. Toronto, Buffalo, London: University of Toronto Press.

Bourdieu, Pierre. 1984. Distinction: A Social Critique of the Judgement of Taste. Cambridge, Massachusetts: Harvard University Press.

Bowker, Geoffrey C. 2006. *Memory Practices in the Sciences*. Cambridge, Massachusetts: The Mit Press Ltd.

———. 2014. "Big Data, Big Questions| The Theory/Data Thing." *International Journal of Communication* 8 (2043): 1795–99.

Bowker, Geoffrey C, and Susan Leigh Star. 2000. *Sorting Things out: Classification and Its Consequences*. Cambridge, Massachusetts: MIT Press.

boyd, danah. 2010. "Social Network Sites as Networked Publics: Affordances, Dynamics, and Implications." In *Networked Self: Identity, Community, and Culture on Social Network Sites*, 39–58. New York, Oxon: Taylor & Francis.

boyd, danah, and Kate Crawford. 2012. "Critical Questions for Big Data." *Information, Communication & Society* 15 (5): 662–79. https://doi.org/10.1080/1369118X.2012.678878.

Bozdag, Engin. 2013. "Bias in Algorithmic Filtering and Personalization." *Ethics and Information Technology* 15 (3): 209–27. https://doi.org/10.1007/s10676-013-9321-6.

Breeman, J.M., V.E. Breeman, and Natali Helberger. 2011. "On the Regulator's Plate: Exposure Diversity in a Changing Media Environment: Workshop Report and Highlights of an Expert Discussion." *Journal of Information Policy* 1: 370–77. https://doi.org/10.5325/jinfopoli.1.2011.0370.

Bucher, Taina. 2012. "Want to Be on the Top? Algorithmic Power and the Threat of Invisibility on Facebook." *New Media & Society* 14 (7): 1164–80. https://doi.org/10.1177/1461444812440159.

———. 2016. "Neither Black Nor Box: Ways of Knowing Algorithms." In *Innovative Methods in Media and Communication Research*, edited by Sebastian Kubitschko and Anne Kaun, 81–98. Cham: Springer International Publishing. https://doi.org/10.1007/978-3-319-40700-5_5.

Burke, Adam. 2019. "Occluded Algorithms." *Big Data & Society* 6 (2): 2053951719858743. https://doi.org/10.1177/2053951719858743.

Burrell, Jenna. 2016. "How the Machine 'Thinks': Understanding Opacity in Machine Learning Algorithms." *Big Data & Society* 3 (1): 2053951715622512. https://doi.org/10.1177/2053951715622512.

Burri, Mira. 2015. "Contemplating a 'Public Service Navigator': In Search of New (and Better) Functioning Public Service Media." *International Journal of Communication* 9: 1341–59.

———. 2016. "Nudging as a Tool of Media Policy." In *Nudging - Possibilities, Limitations and Applications in European Law and Economics*, edited by Klaus Mathis and Avishalom Tor, 315–41. Cham: Springer International Publishing. https://doi.org/10.1007/978-3-319-29562-6_16.

Butler, Judith. 1997. *Excitable Speech: A Politics of the Performative*. New York: Routledge.

Callon, Michel. 1986. "The Sociology of an Actor-Network: The Case of the Electric Vehicle." In *Mapping the Dynamics of Science and Technology: Sociology of Science in the Real World*, edited by Michel Callon, John Law, and Arie Rip, 19–34. London: Palgrave Macmillan UK. https://doi.org/10.1007/978-1-349-07408-2_2.

———. 1987. "Society in the Making: The Study of Technology as a Tool for Sociological Analysis." In *The Social Construction of Technological Systems: New Directions in the Sociology and History of Technology*, edited by Wiebe E. Bijker, Thomas P. Hughes, and Trevor J. Pinch, 83–103. Cambridge, MA; London, England: MIT Press.

———. 2004. "Europe Wrestling with Technology." *Economy and Society* 33 (1): 121–34. https://doi.org/10.1080/0308514042000176766.

Callon, Michel, and Bruno Latour. 1981. "Unscrewing the Big Leviathan: How Actors Macro-Structure Reality and How Sociologists Help Them to Do So." In *Advances in Social Theory and Methodology: Toward an Integration of Micro- and Macro-Sociologies*, edited by Karin Knorr-Cetina and Aaron V. Cicourel, 277–303. Boston: Routledge & Kegan Paul. https://kops.uni-konstanz.de/handle/123456789/11424.

Callon, Michel, and Fabian Muniesa. 2005. "Peripheral Vision: Economic Markets as Calculative Collective Devices." *Organization Studies* 26 (8): 1229–50. https://doi.org/10.1177/0170840605056393.

Campbell-Verduyn, Malcolm, Marcel Goguen, and Tony Porter. 2017. "Big Data and Algorithmic Governance: The Case of Financial Practices." *New Political Economy* 22 (2): 219–36. https://doi.org/10.1080/13563467.2016.1216533.

Cantador, Iván, Alejandro Bellogín, and David Vallet. 2010. "Content-Based Recommendation in Social Tagging Systems." In *Proceedings of the Fourth ACM Conference on Recommender Systems*, 237–40. RecSys '10. Barcelona, Spain: Association for Computing Machinery. https://doi.org/10.1145/1864708.1864756.

Caswell, David. 2019. "Structured Journalism and the Semantic Units of News." *Digital Journalism* 7 (8): 1134–56. https://doi.org/10.1080/21670811.2019.1651665.

Cheney-Lippold, John. 2011. "A New Algorithmic Identity Soft Biopolitics and the Modulation of Control." *Theory, Culture & Society* 28 (6): 164–81. https://doi.org/10.1177/0263276411424420.

———. 2016. "Jus Algoritmi: How the National Security Agency Remade Citizenship." *International Journal of Communication* 10 (March): 1721–42.

———. 2017. *We Are Data: Algorithms and The Making of Our Digital Selves*. New York: NYU Press.

Chun, Wendy Hui Kyong. 2008. "On 'Sourcery,' or Code as Fetish." *Configurations* 16 (3): 299–324. https://doi.org/10.1353/con.0.0064.

Clark, David. 1992. "A Cloudy Crystal Ball: Visions of the Future." Plenary presentation at 24th meeting of the Internet Engineering Task Force, Cambridge, Mass., 13-17 July 1992. https://groups.csail.mit.edu/ana/People/DDC/future_ietf_92.pdf (Accessed: 28.8.2023)

Clifford, James. 1986. "Introduction: Partial Truths." In *Writing Culture: The Poetics and Politics of Ethnography : A School of American Research Advanced Seminar*, edited by James Clifford and George E. Marcus, 1–26. Berkeley, Los Angeles, London: University of California Press.

Coletta, Claudio, and Rob Kitchin. 2017. "Algorhythmic Governance: Regulating the 'Heartbeat' of a City Using the Internet of Things." *Big Data & Society* 4 (2): 2053951717742418. https://doi.org/10.1177/2053951717742418.

Comte, Auguste. (1851) 2014. *Systeme de Politique Positive; Ou, Traite de Sociologie, Instituant La Religion de L'Humanite Volume 01* - Primary Source Edition. Paris: Nabu Press.

Cooper, Roger, and Tang Tang. 2009. "Predicting Audience Exposure to Television in Today's Media Environment: An Empirical Integration of Active-Audience and Structural Theories." *Journal of Broadcasting & Electronic Media* 53 (3): 400–418. https://doi.org/10.1080/08838150903102204.

Cooper, Rosalind. 2020. "Pastoral Power and Algorithmic Governmentality." *Theory, Culture & Society* 37 (1): 29–52. https://doi.org/10.1177/0263276419860576.

Cormen, Thomas H., Charles E. Leiserson, Ronald L. Rivest, and Clifford Stein. 2013. *Introduction to Algorithms*. 3rd edition. Cambridge, Mass: The MIT Press.

Cotter, Kelley. 2019. "Playing the Visibility Game: How Digital Influencers and Algorithms Negotiate Influence on Instagram." *New Media & Society* 21 (4): 895–913. https://doi.org/10.1177/1461444818815684.

Couldry, Nick, and Ulises A. Mejias. 2019. "Data Colonialism: Rethinking Big Data's Relation to the Contemporary Subject." *Television & New Media* 20 (4): 336–49. https://doi.org/10.1177/1527476418796632.

Council of Europe. 2007. "Recommendation CM/ Rec (2007) 3 of the Committee of Ministers to Member States on the Remit of Public Service Media in the Information Society." Council of Europe.

Courtois, Cédric, Laura Slechten, and Lennert Coenen. 2018. "Challenging Google Search Filter Bubbles in Social and Political Information: Disconforming Evidence from a Digital

Methods Case Study." *Telematics and Informatics* 35 (7): 2006–15. https://doi.org/10.1016/j.tele.2018.07.004.

Cox, Geoff, and Alex McLean. 2012. *Speaking Code: Coding as Aesthetic and Political Expression.* Cambridge, Massachusetts: The MIT Press.

Crawford, Kate. 2016. "Can an Algorithm Be Agonistic? Ten Scenes from Life in Calculated Publics." *Science, Technology, & Human Values* 41 (1): 77–92. https://doi.org/10.1177/0162243915589635.

Crouch, Colin. 2004. *Post-Democracy.* Malden, MA: Polity.

Curchod, Corentin, Gerardo Patriotta, Laurie Cohen, and Nicolas Neysen. 2020. "Working for an Algorithm: Power Asymmetries and Agency in Online Work Settings." *Administrative Science Quarterly* 65 (3): 644–76. https://doi.org/10.1177/0001839219867024.

Custers, Bart, Toon Calders, Bart Schermer, and Tal Zarsky. 2013. *Discrimination and Privacy in the Information Society Data Mining and Profiling in Large Databases.* Berlin; Heidelberg: Springer.

Danaher, John. 2016. "The Threat of Algocracy: Reality, Resistance and Accommodation." *Philosophy & Technology* 29 (3): 245–68. https://doi.org/10.1007/s13347-015-0211-1.

Danna, Anthony, and Oscar H. Gandy. 2002. "All That Glitters Is Not Gold: Digging Beneath the Surface of Data Mining." *Journal of Business Ethics* 40 (4): 373–86. https://doi.org/10.1023/A:1020845814009.

Daston, Lorraine. 2010. "The Rule of Rules, or How Reason Became Rationality." Wissenschaftskolleg zu Berlin, November 12. https://vimeo.com/18497646.

Daston, Lorraine J., and Peter Galison. 2010. *Objectivity.* New York; Cambridge, Mass.: Zone Books.

Dawe, Alan. 1970. "The Two Sociologies." *The British Journal of Sociology* 21 (2): 207–18. https://doi.org/10.2307/588409.

———. 1978. "Theories of Social Action." In *A History of Sociological Analysis*, edited by T. B. Bottomore and Robert A. Nisbet, 362–417. New York: Basic Books.

Deleuze, Gilles. 1992. "Postscript on the Societies of Control." *October* 59: 3–7.

Desai, Deven R., and Joshua A. Kroll. 2017. "Trust but Verify: A Guide to Algorithms and the Law." *Harvard Journal of Law & Technology* 31: 1–64.

Dewey, John. (1927) 2006. *The Public & Its Problems.* Athens: Combined Academic Publ.

Diakopoulos, Nicholas. 2019. "Towards a Design Orientation on Algorithms and Automation in News Production." *Digital Journalism* 7 (8): 1180–84. https://doi.org/10.1080/21670811.2019.1682938.

———. 2020. "Computational News Discovery: Towards Design Considerations for Editorial Orientation Algorithms in Journalism." *Digital Journalism* 8 (7): 945–67. https://doi.org/10.1080/21670811.2020.1736946.

Diakopoulos, Nicholas, and Michael Koliska. 2017. "Algorithmic Transparency in the News Media." *Digital Journalism* 5 (7): 809–28. https://doi.org/10.1080/21670811.2016.1208053.

D'Ignazio, Catherine, and Lauren F. Klein. 2020. *Data Feminism.* MIT Press.

Dörr, Dieter, Bernd Holznagel, and Arnold Picot. 2016. *Legitimation Und Auftrag Des Öffentlich-Rechtlichen Fernsehens in Zeiten Der Cloud.* Studien Zum Deutschen Und Europäischen Medienrech 62. Frankfurt a.M: PL Academic Research. https://www.tlm.de/fileadmin/user_upload/Infothek/Veranstaltungen/data.pdf.

Dourish, Paul. 2016. "Algorithms and Their Others: Algorithmic Culture in Context." *Big Data & Society* 3 (2): 2053951716665128. https://doi.org/10.1177/2053951716665128.

———. 2017. *The Stuff of Bits. An Essay on the Materialities of Information.* Cambridge, Massachusetts: The MIT Press.

Draude, Claude, Goda Klumbyte, Phillip Lücking, and Pat Treusch. 2019. "Situated Algorithms: A Sociotechnical Systemic Approach to Bias." *Online Information Review* 44 (2): 325–42. https://doi.org/10.1108/OIR-10-2018-0332.

Drew, Paul, and John Heritage. 1992. *Talk at Work: Interaction in Institutional Settings.* Cambridge: Cambridge University Press.

Durkheim, Emile. (1895) 1982. *Rules of Sociological Method.* New York: Free Press.

———. (1893) 2014. *The Division of Labor in Society*. Translated by W. D. Halls. Simon and Schuster.

Eberle, Thomas. 2008. "Phänomenologie und Ethnomethodologie." In *Phänomenologie und Soziologie: Theoretische Positionen, aktuelle Problemfelder und empirische Umsetzungen*, edited by Jürgen Raab, Michaela Pfadenhauer, Peter Stegmaier, Jochen Dreher, and Bernt Schnettler, 151–61. Wiesbaden: Springer-Verlag.

Edwards, Lilian., and Michael. Veale. 2018. "Enslaving the Algorithm: From a 'Right to an Explanation' to a 'Right to Better Decisions'?" *IEEE Security Privacy* 16 (3): 46–54. https://doi.org/10.1109/MSP.2018.2701152.

Eisenstadt, Shmuel N., and Miriam Curelaru. 1976. *The Form of Sociology: Paradigms and Crises*. New York: John Wiley & Sons Inc.

Elias, Norbert. 1978. *What Is Sociology?* London: Columbia University Press.

———. 1991. *The Society of Individuals*. Oxford: Basil Blackwell.

———. (1939) 2000. *The Civilizing Process: Sociogenetic and Psychogenetic Investigations*. Translated by Edmund Jephcott. Revised edition. Oxford ; Malden, Mass: Blackwell Publishing.

Emirbayer, Mustafa, and Douglas W. Maynard. 2011. "Pragmatism and Ethnomethodology." *Qualitative Sociology* 34 (1): 221–61. https://doi.org/10.1007/s11133-010-9183-8.

Englert, Gianna. 2016. "Liberty and Industry: John Locke, John Stuart Mill, and the Economic Foundations of Political Membership." *Polity* 48 (4): 551–79. https://doi.org/10.1057/s41279-016-0002-8.

Ensmenger, Nathan. 2012. "Is Chess the Drosophila of Artificial Intelligence? A Social History of an Algorithm." *Social Studies of Science* 42 (1): 5–30. https://doi.org/10.1177/0306312711424596.

Eppler, Martin J., and Jeanne Mengis. 2004. "The Concept of Information Overload: A Review of Literature from Organization Science, Accounting, Marketing, MIS, and Related Disciplines." *The Information Society* 20 (5): 325–44. https://doi.org/10.1080/01972240490507974.

Erwin, Sean. 2015. "Living by Algorithm: Smart Surveillance and the Society of Control." *Humanities and Technology Review* 34: 28–69.

Eubanks, Virginia. 2018. Automating Inequality: How High-Tech Tools Profile, Police, and Punish the Poor. New York: St. Martin's Press.

Fisher, Eran, and Yoav Mehozay. 2019. "How Algorithms See Their Audience: Media Epistemes and the Changing Conception of the Individual." *Media, Culture & Society* 41 (8): 1176–91. https://doi.org/10.1177/0163443719831598.

Fleck, Ludwig. (1935) 1981. *Entstehung Und Entwicklung Einer Wissenschaftlichen Tatsache. Einführung in Die Lehre Vom Denkstil Und Denkkollektiv*. Frankfurt am Main: Suhrkamp.

Forsythe, Diana E. 1993. "Engineering Knowledge: The Construction of Knowledge in Artificial Intelligence." *Social Studies of Science* 23 (3): 445–77. https://doi.org/10.1177/030631279302300 3002.

Foucault, Michel. 1971. *L'ordre du discours: Leçon inaugurale au Collège de France prononcée le 2 décembre 1970*. Paris: Gallimard.

———. 1979. *The Will to Knowledge, The History of Sexuality: Volume 1*. Translated by Robert Hurley. Penguin UK.

———. 1991. "Governmentality." In *The Foucault Effect: Studies in Governmentality*, 87–104. Chicago: University of Chicago Press.

———. (1975) 1995. *Discipline & Punish: The Birth of the Prison*. Translated by Alan Sheridan. 2nd edition. New York: Vintage Books.

———. (1976) 2003. *Society Must Be Defended. Lectures at the Collège de France, 1975-76*. Translated by David Macey. New York: Picador.

———. (1979) 2008. *The Birth of Biopolitics: Lectures at the Collège de France, 1978-1979: Lectures at the College De France, 1978-1979*. Edited by Arnold I. Davidson. Translated by Graham Burchell. 2008 edition. New York, NY: Palgrave Macmillan.

———. (1978) 2009. *Security, Territory, Population: Lectures at the Collège de France 1977--1978*. Edited by Michel Senellart. Translated by Graham Burchell. 1st ed. New York, NY: PICADOR.

———. 2016. *On the Government of the Living: Lectures at the Collège de France, 1979-1980*. Edited by Arnold I. Davidson. Translated by Graham Burchell. New York: Picador.

Friedman, Batya, and Helen Nissenbaum. 1996. "Bias in Computer Systems." *ACM Transactions on Information Systems* 14 (3): 330–47. https://doi.org/10.1145/230538.230561.

Fuchs, Christian. 2012a. "Capitalism or Information Society? The Fundamental Question of the Present Structure of Society." *European Journal of Social Theory* 16 (4): 413–34. https://doi.org/10.1177/1368431012461432.

———. 2012b. *Foundations of Critical Media and Information Studies.* London; New York: Routledge.

———. 2019. Rereading Marx in the Age of Digital Capitalism. London: Pluto Press.

———. 2020. *Communication and Capitalism: A Critical Theory.* London: University of Westminster Press.

Galloway, Alexander R. 2004. *Protocol: How Control Exists after Decentralization.* Leonardo. Cambridge, Mass: MIT Press.

———. 2006. "Language Wants To Be Overlooked: On Software and Ideology." *Journal of Visual Culture* 5 (3): 315–31. https://doi.org/10.1177/1470412906070519.

Gandy, Oscar, and Lemi Baruh. 2006. "Racial Profiling: They Said It Was Against the Law!" *University of Ottawa Law & Technology Journal* 3 (1): 279–327.

Garfinkel, Harold. 1984. *Studies in Ethnomethodology.* Cambridge, UK: Polity Press.

———. 2002. *Ethnomethodology's Program: Working Out Durkheim's Aphorism.* Edited by Anne Warfield Rawls. Lanham, Boulder, New York, Toronto, Oxford: Rowman & Littlefield.

———. 2006. Seeing Sociologically: The Routine Grounds of Social Action. Boulder, Colo: Paradigm Publishers.

Garfinkel, Harold, and D. Lawrence Wieder. 1992. "Two Incommensurable, Asymmetrically Alternate Technologies of Social Analysis." In *Text in Context. Contributions to Ethnomethodology,* edited by Graham Watson and Robert M. Seiler, 175–206. Newbury Park, London, New Delhi: SAGE Publications.

Geertz, Clifford. 1973. *The Interpretation Of Cultures.* New York: Basic Books.

Geiger, R Stuart. 2017. "Beyond Opening up the Black Box: Investigating the Role of Algorithmic Systems in Wikipedian Organizational Culture." *Big Data & Society* 4 (2): 2053951717730735. https://doi.org/10.1177/2053951717730735.

Gerlitz, Carolin, and Celia Lury. 2014. "Social Media and Self-Evaluating Assemblages: On Numbers, Orderings and Values." *Distinktion: Journal of Social Theory* 15 (2): 174–88. https://doi.org/10.1080/1600910X.2014.920267.

Giddens, A. 1984. *The Constitution of Society: Outline of the Theory of Structuration.* Outline of the Theory of Structuration. Cambridge: Polity Press..

Gilbert, Andrew Simon. 2018. "Algorithmic Culture and the Colonization of Life-Worlds." *Thesis Eleven* 146 (1): 87–96. https://doi.org/10.1177/0725513618776699.

Gillespie, Tarleton. 2014. "The Relevance of Algorithms." In *Media Technologies. Essays on Communication, Materiality, and Society,* edited by Tarleton Gillespie, Pablo J. Boczkowski, and Kirsten A. Foot, 167–94. Cambridge, London: MIT Press.

———. 2017. "Algorithmically Recognizable: Santorum's Google Problem, and Google's Santorum Problem." *Information, Communication & Society* 20 (1): 63–80. https://doi.org/10.1080/1369118X.2016.1199721.

———. 2018. *Custodians of the Internet: Platforms, Content Moderation, and the Hidden Decisions That Shape Social Media.* Yale University Press.

Gilpin, Leilani H., David Bau, Ben Z. Yuan, Ayesha Bajwa, Michael Specter, and Lalana Kagal. 2018. "Explaining Explanations: An Overview of Interpretability of Machine Learning." In *2018 IEEE 5th International Conference on Data Science and Advanced Analytics (DSAA),* 80–89. https://doi.org/10.1109/DSAA.2018.00018.

Girtler, Roland. 2003. *Randkulturen: Theorie der Unanständigkeit.* 3. Edition. Wien: Böhlau Wien.

———. 2004. *Der Strich: Soziologie eines Milieus.* Vienna, Berlin: LIT.

Gitelman, Lisa, ed. 2013. *"Raw Data" Is an Oxymoron.* Cambridge, Massachusetts: The MIT Press.

Goodwin, Charles. 2000. "Action and Embodiment within Situated Human Interaction." *Journal of Pragmatics* 32 (10): 1489–1522. https://doi.org/10.1016/S0378-2166(99)00096-X.

Graham, Stephen. 2005. "Software-Sorted Geographies." *Progress in Human Geography* 29 (5): 562–80. https://doi.org/10.1191/0309132505ph568oa.

Graham, Stephen, and Simon Marvin. 2001. *Splintering Urbanism: Networked Infrastructures, Technological Mobilities and the Urban Condition: Networked Infrastructures, Technological Mobilites and the Urban Condition.* London , New York: Routledge Chapman & Hall.

Grassmuck, Volker. 2014a. "Kollisionen Und Konvergenz." *Politik Und Kultur. Dossier: Der Öffentliche Rundfunk*, 20–21.

———. 2014b. "Von Daseinsfürsorge Zu Public Value: Für Einen Neuen Gesellschaftsvertrag Über Unsere Mediale Umwelt (From Daseinsfuersorge to Public Value: For a New Social Contract on Our Media Environment)." In *Überwiegend Neuland. Zwischenbilanzen Der Wissenschaft Zur Gestaltung Der Informationsgesellschaft*, edited by Dieter Klumpp, Klaus Lenk, and Günter Koch, 77–108. Berlin: edition sigma.

Greimas, Algirdas Julien. 1983. *Structural Semantics: An Attempt at a Method.* University of Nebraska Press.

Habermas, Jürgen. 1989. *Theory of Communicative Action, Volume 2: Lifeworld and Systems, a Critique of Functionalist Reason.* Cambridge: Polity.

———. 1991. "The Public Sphere." In *Rethinking Popular Culture. Contemporary Perspectives in Cultural Studies.* edited by Chandra Mukerji and Michael Schudson, 398–404. Berkeley: University of California Press.

———. 1997. Between Facts and Norms: Contributions to a Discourse Theory of Law and Democracy. Blackwell Publishers.

Hacking, Ian. 1990. *The Taming of Chance.* Cambridge, New York: Cambridge University Press.

Hagen, Wolfgang. 2013. "Die Verfassung, Der Rundfunk Und Das Netz. 14 Lemmatische Skizzen." In *Rundfunkpolitik Und Netzpolitik. Strukturwandel Der Medienpolitk in Deutschland.*, edited by Lutz Hachmeister and Dieter Anschlag, 266–82. Köln: Halem.

Haggerty, Kevin D., and Richard V. Ericson. 2000. "The Surveillant Assemblage." *The British Journal of Sociology* 51 (4): 605–22. https://doi.org/10.1080/00071310020015280.

Halavais, Alexander. 2017. *Search Engine Society.* 2nd ed. Cambridge, UK ; Medford, MA: Polity.

Hallinan, Blake, and Ted Striphas. 2016. "Recommended for You: The Netflix Prize and the Production of Algorithmic Culture." *New Media & Society* 18 (1): 117–37. https://doi.org/10.1177/1461444814538646.

Hammersley, Martyn, and Paul Atkinson. 2019. *Ethnography: Principles in Practice.* 4. Edition. New York: Routledge.

Haraway, Donna. 1988. "Situated Knowledges: The Science Question in Feminism and the Privilege of Partial Perspective." *Feminist Studies* 14 (3): 575–99. https://doi.org/10.2307/3178066.

Hargittai, Eszter. 2000. "Open Portals or Closed Gates? Channeling Content on the World Wide Web." *Poetics* 27 (4): 233–53. https://doi.org/10.1016/S0304-422X(00)00006-1.

Harkens, Adam. 2018. "The Ghost in the Legal Machine: Algorithmic Governmentality, Economy, and the Practice of Law." *Journal of Information, Communication and Ethics in Society* 16 (1): 16–31. https://doi.org/10.1108/JICES-09-2016-0038.

Hayles, Nancy Katherine. 1999. *How We Became Posthuman: Virtual Bodies in Cybernetics, Literature, and Informatics.* 74th ed. Chicago, Ill: University of Chicago Press.

———. 2005. *My Mother Was a Computer: Digital Subjects and Literary Texts.* Chicago: University of Chicago Press.

Helberger, Natali. 2011. "Diversity by Design." *Journal of Information Policy* 1: 441–69. https://doi.org/10.5325/jinfopoli.1.2011.0441.

———. 2015. "Public Service Media| Merely Facilitating or Actively Stimulating Diverse Media Choices? Public Service Media at the Crossroad." *International Journal of Communication* 9: 1324–40.

———. 2018. "Challenging Diversity—Social Media Platforms and a New Conception of Media Diversity." In *Digital Dominance: The Power of Google, Amazon, Facebook, and Apple*, edited by Martin Moore and Damian Tambini, 153–75. New York: Oxford University Press.

———. 2019. "On the Democratic Role of News Recommenders." *Digital Journalism* 7 (8): 993–1012. https://doi.org/10.1080/21670811.2019.1623700.

Helberger, Natali, Kari Karppinen, and Lucia D'Acunto. 2018. "Exposure Diversity as a Design Principle for Recommender Systems." *Information, Communication & Society* 21 (2): 191–207. https://doi.org/10.1080/1369118X.2016.1271900.

Helbing, Dirk. 2015. *The Automation of Society Is Next: How to Survive the Digital Revolution*. North Charleston, SC: CreateSpace Independent Publishing Platform.

Helbing, Dirk, Bruno S. Frey, Gerd Gigerenzer, Ernst Hafen, Michael Hagner, Yvonne Hofstetter, Jeroen van den Hoven, Roberto V. Zicari, and Andrej Zwitter. 2017. "Will Democracy Survive Big Data and Artificial Intelligence?" Scientific American. February 25, 2017. https://www.scientificamerican.com/article/will-democracy-survive-big-data-and-artificial-intelligence/.

Hoffmann, Anna Lauren. 2019. "Where Fairness Fails: Data, Algorithms, and the Limits of Anti-discrimination Discourse." *Information, Communication & Society* 22 (7): 900–915. https://doi.org/10.1080/1369118X.2019.1573912.

Honer, Anne, and Ronald Hitzler. 2015. "Life-World-Analytical Ethnography: A Phenomenology-Based Research Approach." *Journal of Contemporary Ethnography* 44 (5): 544–62. https://doi.org/10.1177/0891241615588589.

Hu, Yifan, Yehuda Koren, and Chris Volinsky. 2008. "Collaborative Filtering for Implicit Feedback Datasets." In *2008 Eighth IEEE International Conference on Data Mining*, 263–72. https://doi.org/10.1109/ICDM.2008.22.

Huckfeldt, Robert, Paul E. Johnson, and John Sprague. 2002. "Political Environments, Political Dynamics, and the Survival of Disagreement." *Journal of Politics* 64 (1): 1–21. https://doi.org/10.1111/1468-2508.00115.

Humphreys, Laud. 1976. *Tearoom Trade: Impersonal Sex in Public Places*. Chicago, Ill: Routledge.

Hunt, Robert, and Fenwick McKelvey. 2019. "Algorithmic Regulation in Media and Cultural Policy: A Framework to Evaluate Barriers to Accountability." *Journal of Information Policy* 9: 307–35. https://doi.org/10.5325/jinfopoli.9.2019.0307.

Introna, Lucas D. 2016. "Algorithms, Governance, and Governmentality: On Governing Academic Writing." *Science, Technology, & Human Values* 41 (1): 17–49. https://doi.org/10.1177/0162243915587360.

Introna, Lucas D., and Helen Nissenbaum. 2000. "Shaping the Web: Why the Politics of Search Engines Matters." *The Information Society* 16 (3): 169–85. https://doi.org/10.1080/01972240050133634.

Itō, Mizuko. 2008. "Introduction." In *Networked Publics*, edited by Kazys Varnelis, 1–14. Cambridge, MA: MIT Press.

Jamieson, Kathleen Hall, and Joseph N. Cappella. 2008. *Echo Chamber: Rush Limbaugh and the Conservative Media Establishment*. Oxford University Press.

Janssen, Marijn, and George Kuk. 2016. "The Challenges and Limits of Big Data Algorithms in Technocratic Governance." *Government Information Quarterly*, Open and Smart Governments: Strategies, Tools, and Experiences, 33 (3): 371–77. https://doi.org/10.1016/j.giq.2016.08.011.

Jaton, Florian. 2017. "We Get the Algorithms of Our Ground Truths: Designing Referential Databases in Digital Image Processing." *Social Studies of Science* 47 (6): 811–40. https://doi.org/10.1177/0306312717730428.

Jauert, Per, and Gregory F. Lowe. 2005. "Public Service Broadcasting for Social and Cultural Citizenship. Renewing the Enlightenment Mission." In *Cultural Dilemmas in Public Service Broadcasting*, edited by G. F. Lowe and P. Jauert, 13–33. Gothenburg: Nordicom.

Joas, Hans. 1997. *The Creativity of Action*. Translated by Paul Keast and Jeremy Gaines. Chicago: Univ of Chicago Press.

Johnson, J. Scott, and Leslie Paul Thiele. 1991. "Reading Nietzsche and Foucault: A Hermeneutics of Suspicion?" *American Political Science Review* 85 (2): 581–92. https://doi.org/10.2307/1963177.

Johnson, Jim. 1988. "Mixing Humans and Nonhumans Together: The Sociology of a Door-Closer." *Social Problems* 35 (3): 298–310. https://doi.org/10.2307/800624.

Jones, Rhianne, and Bronwyn Jones. 2019. "Atomising the News: The (In)Flexibility of Structured Journalism." *Digital Journalism* 7 (8): 1157–79. https://doi.org/10.1080/21670811.2019.1609372.

Joris, Glen, Frederik De Grove, Kristin Van Damme, and Lieven De Marez. 2020. "News Diversity Reconsidered: A Systematic Literature Review Unraveling the Diversity in Conceptualizations." *Journalism Studies* 21 (13): 1893–1912. https://doi.org/10.1080/1461670X.2020.1797527.

Just, Natascha, and Michael Latzer. 2017. "Governance by Algorithms: Reality Construction by Algorithmic Selection on the Internet." *Media, Culture & Society* 39 (2): 238–58. https://doi.org/10.1177/0163443716643157.

Kallis, Aristotle A. 2005. *Nazi Propaganda and the Second World War.* New York: Springer.

Kant, Immanuel. (1781) 2008. *The Critique of Pure Reason.* Translated by Marcus Weigelt. London: Penguin Books

Karppinen, Kari. 2013. *Rethinking Media Pluralism.* New York: Fordham University Press.

Kim, Young Mie. 2016. "Algorithmic Opportunity: Digital Advertising and Inequality in Political Involvement." *The Forum* 14 (4): 471–84. https://doi.org/10.1515/for-2016-0034.

Kim, Young Mie, Jordan Hsu, David Neiman, Colin Kou, Levi Bankston, Soo Yun Kim, Richard Heinrich, Robyn Baragwanath, and Garvesh Raskutti. 2018. "The Stealth Media? Groups and Targets behind Divisive Issue Campaigns on Facebook." *Political Communication* 35 (4): 515–41. https://doi.org/10.1080/10584609.2018.1476425.

Kitchin, Rob. 2014. "The Real-Time City? Big Data and Smart Urbanism." *GeoJournal* 79 (1): 1–14. https://doi.org/10.1007/s10708-013-9516-8.

Kittler, Friedrich A. 1990. *Discourse Networks 1800/1900.* Stanford, California: Stanford University Press.

———. 1995. "There Is No Software." *CTheory* a35: 147–55.

———. 1999. *Gramophone, Film, Typewriter.* Translated by Geoffrey Winthrop-Young and Michael Wutz. Stanford, Calif: Stanford University Press.

Kleinberg, Jon, Sendhil Mullainathan, and Manish Raghavan. 2016. "Inherent Trade-Offs in the Fair Determination of Risk Scores." *ArXiv:1609.05807 [Cs, Stat],* September. https://arxiv.org/abs/1609.05807.

Knoblauch, Hubert. 2005. "Focused Ethnography." *Forum Qualitative Sozialforschung / Forum: Qualitative Social Research* 6 (3). https://doi.org/10.17169/fqs-6.3.20.

Knoblauch, Hubert, and Theresa Vollmer. 2019. "Ethnographie." In *Handbuch Methoden der empirischen Sozialforschung,* edited by Nina Baur and Jörg Blasius, 599–617. Wiesbaden: Springer Fachmedien. https://doi.org/10.1007/978-3-658-21308-4_40.

Knorr-Cetina, Karin, Hannes Krämer, and René Salomon. 2019. "Die Ethnomethodologie umzirkeln: Karin Knorr-Cetina im Gespräch mit Hannes Krämer & René Salomon." *Forum Qualitative Sozialforschung / Forum: Qualitative Social Research* 20 (2): 30. https://doi.org/10.17169/fqs-20.2.3287.

Koliska, Michael, and Nicholas Diakopoulos. 2018. "Disclose, Decode, Demystify. An Empirical Guide to Algorithmic Transparency." In *The Routledge Handbook of Developments in Digital Journalism Studies,* edited by Scott Eldridge II and Bob Franklin. Routledge.

Koren, Yehuda, Robert Bell, and Chris Volinsky. 2009. "Matrix Factorization Techniques for Recommender Systems." *Computer* 42 (8): 30–37. https://doi.org/10.1109/MC.2009.263.

Kranzberg, Melvin. 1986. "Technology and History:" Kranzberg's Laws"." *Technology and Culture* 27 (3): 544–60.

Kreiss, Daniel, and Shannon McGregor. 2018. "Technology Firms Shape Political Communication: The Work of Microsoft, Facebook, Twitter, and Google With Campaigns During the 2016 U.S. Presidential Cycle." *Political Communication* 35 (2): 155–77. https://doi.org/10.1080/10584609.2017.1364814.

Kuhn, Thomas S. 1996. *Structure of Scientific Revolutions.* 3rd ed. Chicago, IL: University of Chicago Press.

Laat, Paul B. de. 2019. "The Disciplinary Power of Predictive Algorithms: A Foucauldian Perspective." *Ethics and Information Technology* 21 (July): 319–29. https://doi.org/10.1007/s10676-019-09509-y.

Lash, Scott. 2007. "Power after Hegemony: Cultural Studies in Mutation?" *Theory, Culture & Society* 24 (3): 55–78. https://doi.org/10.1177/0263276407075956.

Latour, Bruno. 1990. "Technology Is Society Made Durable." *The Sociological Review* 38 (S1): 103–31. https://doi.org/10.1111/j.1467-954X.1990.tb03350.x.

———. 1992. "Where Are the Missing Masses? The Sociology of a Few Mundane Artifacts." In *Shaping Technology/Building Society*, edited by W. E. Bijker and John Law, 151–80. Cambridge, Mass.: MIT Press.

———. 1993a. *The Pasteurization of France*. Cambridge, Massachusetts, London: Harvard University Press.

———. 1993b. *We Have Never Been Modern*. Cambridge, MA: Prentice Hall / Harvester Wheatsheaf.

———. 1994. "On Technical Mediation." *Common Knowledge* 3 (2): 29–64.

———. 1996. "On Interobjectivity." *Mind, Culture, and Activity* 3 (4): 228–45. https://doi.org/10.1207/s15327884mca0304_2.

———. 1999a. *Pandora's Hope: Essays on the Reality of Science Studies*. Cambridge, MA: Harvard University Press.

———. 1999b. "On Recalling ANT." In *Actor Network Theory and After*, edited by John Law and John Hassard, 15–26. Oxford England ; Malden, MA: Wiley-Blackwell.

———. 2004. "Why Has Critique Run out of Steam? From Matters of Fact to Matters of Concern." *Critical Inquiry* 30 (2): 225–48. https://doi.org/10.1086/421123.

———. 2005. *Reassembling the Social: An Introduction to Actor-Network-Theory*. Oxford; New York: Oxford University Press.

———. 2009. *The Making of Law: An Ethnography of the Conseil d'Etat*. Cambridge, UK ; Malden, MA: Polity.

———. 2013. *An Inquiry into Modes of Existence: An Anthropology of the Moderns*. Translated by Catherine Porter. Cambridge, Massachusetts: Harvard University Press.

Latour, Bruno, Pablo Jensen, Tommaso Venturini, Sébastian Grauwin, and Dominique Boullier. 2012. "'The Whole Is Always Smaller than Its Parts' – a Digital Test of Gabriel Tardes' Monads." *The British Journal of Sociology* 63 (4): 590–615. https://doi.org/10.1111/j.1468-4446.2012.01428.x.

Latour, Bruno, and Steve Woolgar. 1986. *Laboratory Life: The Construction of Scientific Facts*. 2nd ed. Princeton, N.J.: Princeton University Press.

Law, John. 1992. "Notes on the Theory of the Actor-Network: Ordering, Strategy, and Heterogeneity." *Systems Practice* 5 (4): 379–93.

———. 1994. *Organizing Modernity: Social Ordering and Social Theory*. Cambridge, MA: Wiley-Blackwell.

———. 2002. *Aircraft Stories: Decentering the Object in Technoscience*. Durham, NC: Duke University Press.

———. 2004. *After Method: Mess in Social Science Research*. London ; New York: Routledge Chapman & Hall.

Lee, Min Kyung, Daniel Kusbit, Evan Metsky, and Laura Dabbish. 2015. "Working with Machines: The Impact of Algorithmic and Data-Driven Management on Human Workers." In *Proceedings of the 33rd Annual ACM Conference on Human Factors in Computing Systems*, 1603–12. CHI '15. New York, NY, USA: Association for Computing Machinery. https://doi.org/10.1145/2702123.2702548.

Leese, Matthias. 2014. "The New Profiling: Algorithms, Black Boxes, and the Failure of Anti-Discriminatory Safeguards in the European Union." *Security Dialogue* 45 (5): 494–511. https://doi.org/10.1177/0967010614544204.

Leicht-Deobald, Ulrich, Thorsten Busch, Christoph Schank, Antoinette Weibel, Simon Schafheitle, Isabelle Wildhaber, and Gabriel Kasper. 2019. "The Challenges of Algorithm-Based HR Decision-Making for Personal Integrity." *Journal of Business Ethics* 160 (2): 377–92. https://doi.org/10.1007/s10551-019-04204-w.

Lenglet, Marc. 2019. "Algorithmic Finance, Its Regulation, and Deleuzean Jurisprudence: A Few Remarks on a Necessary Paradigm Shift." *Topoi*, May. https://doi.org/10.1007/s11245-019-09653-6.

Lessig, Lawrence. 1999. *Code: And Other Laws Of Cyberspace*. New York: Basic Books.

———. 2006. *Code: Version 2.0*. New York: Basic Books.

Lindemann, Gesa. 2019. *Strukturnotwendige Kritik*. Weilerswist: Velbrück Wissenschaft. https://doi.org/10.5771/9783845298887.

Liu, Nathan N., Evan W. Xiang, Min Zhao, and Qiang Yang. 2010. "Unifying Explicit and Implicit Feedback for Collaborative Filtering." In *Proceedings of the 19th ACM International Conference on Information and Knowledge Management*, 1445–48. CIKM '10. New York, NY, USA: Association for Computing Machinery. https://doi.org/10.1145/1871437.1871643.

Livingston, Eric. 1987. *Making Sense of Ethnomethodology*. London, New York: Routledge.

Loukissas, Yanni Alexander. 2017. "Taking Big Data Apart: Local Readings of Composite Media Collections." *Information, Communication & Society* 20 (5): 651–64. https://doi.org/10.1080/1369118X.2016.1211722.

Luhmann, Niklas. 1996. *Social Systems*. Translated by John Bednarz Jr and Dirk Baecker. Stanford, Calif: Stanford University Press.

———. 1997. *Die Gesellschaft der Gesellschaft*. Frankfurt am Main: Suhrkamp.

Lury, Celia, and Sophie Day. 2019. "Algorithmic Personalization as a Mode of Individuation." *Theory, Culture & Society* 36 (2): 17–37. https://doi.org/10.1177/0263276418818888.

Lynch, Michael. 2000. "Against Reflexivity as an Academic Virtue and Source of Privileged Knowledge:" *Theory, Culture & Society* 17 (3): 26–54. https://doi.org/10.1177/02632760022051202.

Lyon, David. 2003. "Surveillance as Social Sorting: Computer Codes and Mobile Bodies." In *Surveillance as Social Sorting: Privacy, Risk, and Digital Discrimination*, 13–30. London; New York: Routledge.

Lyotard, Jean-Francois. 1984. *The Postmodern Condition: A Report on Knowledge*. Manchester University Press.

Mackenzie, Adrian. 2005. "The Performativity of Code: Software and Cultures of Circulation." *Theory, Culture & Society* 22 (1): 71–92. https://doi.org/10.1177/0263276405048436.

———. 2006. *Cutting Code: Software and Sociality*. Peter Lang.

———. 2013. "Programming Subjects in the Regime of Anticipation: Software Studies and Subjectivity." *Subjectivity* 6 (4): 391–405. https://doi.org/10.1057/sub.2013.12.

———. 2015. "The Production of Prediction: What Does Machine Learning Want?" *European Journal of Cultural Studies* 18 (4–5): 429–45. https://doi.org/10.1177/1367549415577384.

———. 2017. *Machine Learners: Archaeology of a Data Practice*. Cambridge, MA: The MIT Press.

Mackenzie, Adrian, and Theo Vurdubakis. 2011. "Codes and Codings in Crisis: Signification, Performativity and Excess." *Theory, Culture & Society* 28 (6): 3–23. https://doi.org/10.1177/0263276411424761.

MacKenzie, Donald. 2006. *An Engine, Not a Camera: How Financial Models Shape Markets*. Cambridge, Mass: MIT Press.

———. 2019. "How Algorithms Interact: Goffman's 'Interaction Order' in Automated Trading." *Theory, Culture & Society* 36 (2): 39–59. https://doi.org/10.1177/0263276419829541.

Magalhães, João Carlos. 2018. "Do Algorithms Shape Character? Considering Algorithmic Ethical Subjectivation." *Social Media + Society* 4 (2): 2056305118768301. https://doi.org/10.1177/2056305118768301.

Mager, Astrid. 2012. "ALGORITHMIC IDEOLOGY. How Capitalist Society Shapes Search Engines." *Information, Communication & Society* 15 (5): 769–87. https://doi.org/10.1080/1369118X.2012.676056.

———. 2014. "Defining Algorithmic Ideology: Using Ideology Critique to Scrutinize Corporate Search Engines." *TripleC: Communication, Capitalism & Critique. Open Access Journal for a Global Sustainable Information Society* 12 (1): 28–39.

Malik, Sarita. 2018. "Diversity: Reflection and Review." In *A Future for Public Service Television*, edited by Des Freedman and Vana Goblot, 91–101. London: Goldsmiths Press.

Manovich, Lev. 2001. *The Language of New Media*. Cambridge, Mass: MIT Press.

———. 2013a. "There Is Only Software." In Doing Cultural Studies: The Story of the Sony Walkman edited by Paul du Gay, Stuart Hall, Linda Janes, Anders Koed Madsen, Hugh Mackay, and Keith Negus, 136–38. LA, London, New Delhi, Singapore, Washington DC: Sage.

———. 2013b. *Software Takes Command*. New York ; London: Bloomsbury Academic.

Marres, Noortje. 2007. "The Issues Deserve More Credit: Pragmatist Contributions to the Study of Public Involvement in Controversy." *Social Studies of Science* 37 (5): 759–80. https://doi.org/10.1177/0306312706077367.

———. 2012. *Material Participation: Technology, the Environment and Everyday Publics.* London: Palgrave Macmillan.

———. 2017. *Digital Sociology: The Reinvention of Social Research.* Malden, MA: John Wiley & Sons.

Martin, Kirsten. 2019. "Ethical Implications and Accountability of Algorithms." *Journal of Business Ethics* 160 (4): 835–50. https://doi.org/10.1007/s10551-018-3921-3.

Marvin, Carolyn. 1990. *When Old Technologies Were New: Thinking About Electric Communication in the Late Nineteenth Century.* Oxford ; New York: Oxford University Press.

Marx, Karl. (1867) 1990. *Capital: A Critique of Political Economy. Volume 1.* Translated by Ben Fowkes. London ; New York, N.Y: Penguin Classics.

———. (1844) 2010. "Comments on James Mill, Éléments d'economie Politique." In *Collected Works. Vol. 3, Marx and Engels: 1843-44*, edited by Karl Marx and Friedrich Engels, 211–28. Moscow, London: Lawrence & Wishart.

Mayer-Schönberger, Viktor, and Thomas Ramge. 2018. *Reinventing Capitalism in the Age of Big Data.* New York: Basic Books.

Maynard, Douglas W., and Steven E. Clayman. 1991. "The Diversity of Ethnomethodology." *Annual Review of Sociology* 17 (1): 385–418. https://doi.org/10.1146/annurev.so.17.080191.002125.

Mead, George Herbert. (1934) 1967. *Mind, Self, and Society: From The Standpoint Of A Social Behaviorist.* Chicago, Ill.; London: University of Chicago Press.

Méndez Fernández, Daniel, and Jan-Hendrik Passoth. 2019. "Empirical Software Engineering: From Discipline to Interdiscipline." *Journal of Systems and Software* 148 (February): 170–79. https://doi.org/10.1016/j.jss.2018.11.019.

Meraz, Sharon. 2009. "The Many Faced 'You' of Social Media." In *Journalism and Citizenship: New Agendas in Communication*, edited by Zizi Papacharissi, 121–47. New York ; London: Routledge.

Meteren, Robin Van, and Maarten Van Someren. 2000. "Using Content-Based Filtering for Recommendation." In *Proceedings of ECML 2000 Workshop: Maching Learning in Information Age*, 47–56.

Milan, Stefania, and Emiliano Treré. 2019. "Big Data from the South(s): Beyond Data Universalism." *Television & New Media* 20 (4): 319–35. https://doi.org/10.1177/1527476419837739.

Mill, John Stuart. (1861) 2020. Considerations on Representative Government John Stuart Mill: Classic Edition. Independently published.

Miller, Peter. 2008. "Calculating Economic Life." *Journal of Cultural Economy* 1 (1): 51–64. https://doi.org/10.1080/17530350801913643.

Mittelstadt, Brent, Chris Russell, and Sandra Wachter. 2019. "Explaining Explanations in AI." In *Proceedings of the Conference on Fairness, Accountability, and Transparency*, 279–88. FAT* '19. New York, NY, USA: ACM. https://doi.org/10.1145/3287560.3287574.

Mol, Annemarie. 2002. *The Body Multiple: Ontology in Medical Practice.* Durham, London: Duke University Press.

Möller, Judith, Damian Trilling, Natali Helberger, and Bram van Es. 2018. "Do Not Blame It on the Algorithm: An Empirical Assessment of Multiple Recommender Systems and Their Impact on Content Diversity." *Information, Communication & Society* 21 (7): 959–77. https://doi.org/10.1080/1369118X.2018.1444076.

Montfort, Nick, Batsy Baudoin, John Bell, Ian Bogost, Jeremy Douglass, Mark C. Marino, Michael Mateas, Casey Reas, Mark Sample, and Noah Vawter. 2012. *10 Print Chr$(205.5+rnd(1)); Goto 10.* Cambridge, MA; London, England: MIT Press.

Morozov, Evgeny. 2014. *To Save Everything, Click Here: Technology, Solutionism, and the Urge to Fix Problems That Don't Exist.* London: Penguin.

Morris, Jeremy Wade. 2015. "Curation by Code: Infomediaries and the Data Mining of Taste." *European Journal of Cultural Studies* 18 (4–5): 446–63. https://doi.org/10.1177/1367549415577387.

Mossberger, Karen, Caroline J. Tolbert, and Ramona S. McNeal. 2007. *Digital Citizenship: The Internet, Society, and Participation.* MIT Press.

Mouffe, Chantal. 2000. "Which Ethics for Democracy?" In *The Turn to Ethics*, edited by Marjorie Garber, Beatrice Hanssen, and Rebecca L. Walkowitz, 85–94. London; New York: Routledge.
———. 2005. *On the Political*. London ; New York: Routledge.
Müller, Peter, and Nikolaus Pöchhacker. 2019. "Algorithmic Risk Assessment als Medium des Rechts." *Österreichische Zeitschrift für Soziologie* 44 (1): 157–79. https://doi.org/10.1007/s11614-019-00352-5.
Mutz, Diana C. 2006. *Hearing the Other Side: Deliberative versus Participatory Democracy*. Cambridge: Cambridge University Press. https://doi.org/10.1017/CBO9780511617201.
Mützel, Sophie. 2015. "Facing Big Data: Making sociology relevant." *Big Data & Society* 2 (2): 2053951715599179. https://doi.org/10.1177/2053951715599179
Mützel, Sophie, Philippe Saner, and Markus Unternährer. 2018. "Schöne Daten! Konstruktion Und Verarbeitung von Digitalen Daten." In *Datengesellschaft: Einsichten in Die Datafizierung Des Sozialen*, edited by Daniel Houben and Bianca Prietl, 17:111–32. Bielefeld: transcript Verlag.
Napoli, Philip M. 1999. "Deconstructing the Diversity Principle." *Journal of Communication* 49 (4): 7–34.
Napoli, Philip M. 2011. "Exposure Diversity Reconsidered." *Journal of Information Policy* 1: 246–59. https://doi.org/10.5325/jinfopoli.1.2011.0246.
Nassehi, Armin. 2019. *Muster: Theorie der digitalen Gesellschaft*. 3rd ed. München: C.H.Beck.
Neuberger, Christoph, and Frank Lobigs. 2010. *Die Bedeutung des Internets im Rahmen der Vielfaltssicherung: Gutachten im Auftrag der Kommission zur Ermittlung der Konzentration im Medienbereich (KEK)*. Vol. 43. Schriftenreihe der Landesmedienanstalten. Berlin: Vistas.
Neyland, Daniel. 2015. "On Organizing Algorithms." *Theory, Culture & Society* 32 (1): 119–32. https://doi.org/10.1177/0263276414530477.
———. 2016. "Bearing Account-Able Witness to the Ethical Algorithmic System." *Science, Technology, & Human Values* 41 (1): 50–76. https://doi.org/10.1177/0162243915598056.
Neyland, Daniel, and Norma Möllers. 2017. "Algorithmic IF … THEN Rules and the Conditions and Consequences of Power." *Information, Communication & Society* 20 (1): 45–62. https://doi.org/10.1080/1369118X.2016.1156141.
Nissen, Christian S. 2006. "No Public Service without Both Public and Service - Content Provision between the Scylla of Populism and the Charybdis of Elitism." In *Making a Difference: Public Service Broadcasting in the European Media Landscape*, edited by Christian S. Nissen, 65–82. Eastleigh, UK : Bloomington, IN: John Libbey Publishing.
Nissenbaum, H. 2001. "How Computer Systems Embody Values." *Computer* 34 (3): 120–119. https://doi.org/10.1109/2.910905.
Noble, Safiya Umoja. 2018. *Algorithms of Oppression: How Search Engines Reinforce Racism*. New York: New York University Press.
Nygren, Katarina Giritli, and Katarina L. Gidlund. 2015. "The Pastoral Power of Technology. Rethinking Alienation in Digital Culture." In *Marx in the Age of Digital Capitalism*, edited by Christian Fuchs and Vincent Mosco, 396–412. Leiden ; Boston: BRILL.
O'Callaghan, Derek, Derek Greene, Maura Conway, Joe Carthy, and Pádraig Cunningham. 2015. "Down the (White) Rabbit Hole: The Extreme Right and Online Recommender Systems." *Social Science Computer Review* 33 (4): 459–78. https://doi.org/10.1177/0894439314555329.
O'Donnell, Mike. 2010. *Structure and Agency*. Four-Volume Set ed. Los Angeles: SAGE Publications Ltd.
O'Neil, Cathy. 2016. *Weapons of Math Destruction: How Big Data Increases Inequality and Threatens Democracy*. New York: Crown.
Papacharissi, Zizi. 2010. *A Private Sphere: Democracy in a Digital Age (Digital Media and Society)*. Cambridge: Polity Press.
Parikka, Jussi. 2012. *What Is Media Archaeology?* Cambridge, UK ; Malden, MA: Polity.
Parry, Geraint. 1989. "Democracy and Amateurism—the Informed Citizen." *Government and Opposition* 24 (4): 489–502.
Parsons, Talcott. 1954. *Essays in Sociological Theory*. Glencoe, Ill.: Free Press.
———. 1971. *The System of Modern Societies*. Englewood Cliffs, NJ: Prentice-Hall.

Pasquale, Frank. 2015. *The Black Box Society: The Secret Algorithms That Control Money and Information*. Cambridge: Harvard University Press.

Pasquinelli, Matteo. 2009. "Google's PageRank: Diagram of the Cognitive Capitalism and the Rentier of the Common Intellect." In *Deep Search: The Politics of Search beyond Google*, edited by Konrad Becker and Felix Stalder, 152–62. Innsbruck, Piscataway, N.J.: Studien Verlag, Austria.

Paßmann, Johannes, and Asher Boersma. 2017. "Unknowing Algorithms. On Transparency of Un-Openable Black Boxes." In *The Datafied Society. Studying Culture through Data*, edited by Karin van Es and Mirko Tobias Schäfer, 139–46. Amsterdam: Amsterdam University Press. https://doi.org/10.5117/9789462981362.

Passoth, Jan-Hendrik. 2019. "From Hardware to Software to Runtime: The Politics of (at Least) Three Digital Materialities." In *Discussing New Materialism: Methodological Implications for the Study of Materialities*, edited by Ulrike Tikvah Kissmann and Joost van Loon, 173–89. Wiesbaden: Springer Fachmedien Wiesbaden. https://doi.org/10.1007/978-3-658-22300-7_9.

———. 2021. Soziologie der Umstände: Entwurf einer symmetrischen Praxistheorie. Bielefeld: transcript.

Passoth, Jan-Hendrik, and Werner Rammert. 2019. "Fragmentale Differenzierung Als Gesellschaftsdiagnose." In *Berliner Schlüssel. Arbeiten Mit Werner Rammert*, edited by Cornelius Schubert and Ingo Schulz-Schaeffer. Wiesbaden: Springer.

Passoth, Jan-Hendrik, and Nicholas J. Rowland. 2010. "Actor-Network State: Integrating Actor-Network Theory and State Theory." *International Sociology* 25 (6): 818–41. https://doi.org/10.1177/0268580909351325.

Pazzani, Michael J., and Daniel Billsus. 2007. "Content-Based Recommendation Systems." In *The Adaptive Web: Methods and Strategies of Web Personalization*, edited by Peter Brusilovsky, Alfred Kobsa, and Wolfgang Nejdl, 325–41. Lecture Notes in Computer Science. Berlin, Heidelberg: Springer. https://doi.org/10.1007/978-3-540-72079-9_10.

Peirce, Charles S. (1902) 1976. *The New Elements of Mathematics, Vol. 4: Mathematical Philosophy*. Edited by Carolyn Eisele. The Hague: Mouton Publishers / Humanities Press.

———. (1900) 2010. "Logic as Semotic: The Theory of Signs." In *The Philosophy of Peirce: Selected Writings*, edited by Justus Buchler, 98–119. London: Routledge.

Pfadenhauer, Michaela. 2005. "Ethnography of Scenes. Towards a Sociological Life-World Analysis of (Post-Traditional) Community-Building." *Forum Qualitative Sozialforschung / Forum: Qualitative Social Research* 6 (3). https://doi.org/10.17169/fqs-6.3.23.

Pingaud, B. 1966. "Jean-Paul Sartre Répond." *L'Aarc* 30: 87–96.

Pöchhacker, Nikolaus. 2016. "Predictive Policing. Datenbasierte Verbrechensbekämpfung Und Eine Neue Geographie Des Risikos." *GeoAgenda* 2016 (4): 13–15.

Pöchhacker, Nikolaus, Marcus Burkhardt, Andrea Geipel, and Jan-Hendrik Passoth. 2017. "Interventionen in die Produktion algorithmischer Öffentlichkeiten: Recommender Systeme als Herausforderung für öffentlich-rechtliche Sendeanstalten." *kommunikation @ gesellschaft* 18: 25.

Poechhacker, Nikolaus, and Severin Kacianka. 2021. "Algorithmic Accountability in Context. Socio-Technical Perspectives on Structural Causal Models." *Frontiers in Big Data* 3.

Poechhacker, Nikolaus, and Eva-Maria Nyckel. 2020. "Logistics of Probability. Anticipatory Shipping and the Production of Markets." In *Explorations of Digital Cultures.*, edited by Marcus Burkhardt, K. Grashöfer, M. Shnayien, and B. Westerman. Lüneburg: Meson Press.

Porter, Theodore M. 1995. *Trust in Numbers*. Princeton, N.J: Princeton University Press.

Prey, Robert. 2018. "Nothing Personal: Algorithmic Individuation on Music Streaming Platforms." *Media, Culture & Society* 40 (7): 1086–1100. https://doi.org/10.1177/0163443717745147.

Puschmann, Cornelius. 2019. "Beyond the Bubble: Assessing the Diversity of Political Search Results." *Digital Journalism* 7 (6): 824–43. https://doi.org/10.1080/21670811.2018.1539626.

Quattrociocchi, Walter, Antonio Scala, and Cass R. Sunstein. 2016. "Echo Chambers on Facebook." *Harvard Law School Discussion Paper* 877: 1–15.

Raffetseder, Eva-Maria, Simon Schaupp, and Philipp Staab. 2017. "Kybernetik und Kontrolle: Algorithmische Arbeitssteuerung und betriebliche Herrschaft." *PROKLA. Zeitschrift für kritische Sozialwissenschaft* 47 (187): 229–48. https://doi.org/10.32387/prokla.v47i187.143.

Ranciere, Jacques. 2005. *Disagreement*. Translated by Julie Rose. Minneapolis: Univ Of Minnesota Press.

Rawls, Anne Warfield. 2009. "An Essay on Two Conceptions of Social Order: Constitutive Orders of Action, Objects and Identities vs Aggregated Orders of Individual Action." *Journal of Classical Sociology* 9 (4): 500–520. https://doi.org/10.1177/1468795X09344376.

Rawls, John. 2005. *Political Liberalism*. New York: Columbia University Press.

Reith, John Charles Walsham. 1924. *Broadcast over Britain*. London: Hodder and Stoughton.

Renn, Joachim. 2006. Übersetzungsverhältnisse. Perspektiven einer pragmatistischen Gesellschaftstheorie. Weilerswist: Velbrück Wissenschaft.

Reviglio, Urbano. 2019. "Serendipity as an Emerging Design Principle of the Infosphere: Challenges and Opportunities." *Ethics and Information Technology* 21 (2): 151–66. https://doi.org/10.1007/s10676-018-9496-y.

Ribes, David. 2019. "STS, Meet Data Science, Once Again." *Science, Technology, & Human Values* 44 (3): 514–39. https://doi.org/10.1177/0162243918798899.

Ribes, David, Andrew S Hoffman, Steven C Slota, and Geoffrey C Bowker. 2019. "The Logic of Domains." *Social Studies of Science* 49 (3): 281–309. https://doi.org/10.1177/0306312719849709.

Ricaurte, Paola. 2019. "Data Epistemologies, The Coloniality of Power, and Resistance." *Television & New Media* 20 (4): 350–65. https://doi.org/10.1177/1527476419831640.

Ricci, Francesco, Lior Rokach, Bracha Shapira, and Paul B. Kantor, eds. 2011. *Recommender Systems Handbook*. Springer US. https://doi.org/10.1007/978-0-387-85820-3.

Rieder, Bernhard. 2017. "Scrutinizing an Algorithmic Technique: The Bayes Classifier as Interested Reading of Reality." *Information, Communication & Society* 20 (1): 100–117. https://doi.org/10.1080/1369118X.2016.1181195.

Rieder, Gernot, and Judith Simon. 2016. "Datatrust: Or, the Political Quest for Numerical Evidence and the Epistemologies of Big Data." *Big Data & Society* 3 (1): 1–6. https://doi.org/10.1177/2053951716649398.

Roberts, Stephen L. 2019. "Big Data, Algorithmic Governmentality and the Regulation of Pandemic Risk." *European Journal of Risk Regulation* 10 (1): 94–115. https://doi.org/10.1017/err.2019.6.

Rogers, Richard. 2009. "Post-Demographic Machines." In *Walled Garden*, edited by A. Dekker and A. Wolfsberger, 29–39. Amsterdam: Virtueel Platform.

Rogers, Richard, Konrad Becker, and Felix Stalder. 2009. "The Googlization Question, and the Inculpable Engine." In *Deep Search: The Politics of Search Engines beyond Google*, 173–84. Edision, NJ: Transaction Publishers.

Rose, Nikolas. 2012. *Powers of Freedom: Reframing Political Thought*. Cambridge: Cambridge University Press.

Rosenblat, Alex. 2018. *Uberland: How Algorithms Are Rewriting the Rules of Work*. Oakland, California: University of California Press.

Rossiter, Ned. 2016. Software, Infrastructure, Labor: A Media Theory of Logistical Nightmares. New York: Routledge.

Rouvroy, Antoinette. 2011. "Technology, Virtuality and Utopia: Governmentality in an Age of Autonomic Computing." In *Law, Human Agency and Autonomic Computing. The Philosophy of Law Meets the Philosophy of Technology*, 119–40. Abingdon, Oxon; New York: Routledge.

———. 2013. "The End(s) of Critique: Data-Behaviourism vs. Due-Process." In *Privacy, Due Process and the Computational Turn: The Philosophy of Law Meets the Philosophy of Technology*, edited by Mireille Hildebrandt and Katja De Vries, 1st ed., 143–68. Abingdon, Oxon, England; New York: Taylor & Francis Ltd.

Sacks, Harvey. 1984. "Notes on Methodology." In *Structures of Social Action: Studies in Conversation Analysis*, edited by John Heritage and Paul Atkinson, 21–27. Cambridge, UK: Cambridge University Press.

Sadowski, Jathan, and Frank Pasquale. 2015. "The Spectrum of Control: A Social Theory of the Smart City." *First Monday* 20 (7). https://firstmonday.org/ojs/index.php/fm/article/view/5903.

Sandvig, Christian, Kevin Hamilton, Karrie Karahalios, and Cedric Langbort. 2016. "Automation, Algorithms, and Politics | When the Algorithm Itself Is a Racist: Diagnosing Ethical Harm in the Basic Components of Software." *International Journal of Communication* 10 (October): 4972–90.

Saussure, Ferdinand de, and Roy Harris. (1916) 1998. *Course in General Linguistics*. LaSalle, Ill: Open Court.

Schmidt, Manfred G. 2010. *Demokratietheorien. Eine Einführung*. 5th ed. Wiesbaden: VS Verlag Für Sozialwissenschaften.

Schumpeter, Joseph A. (1942) 2008. *Capitalism, Socialism, and Democracy: Third Edition*. New York: Harper Perennial Modern Classics.

Schutz, A. 1976. *Collected Papers II: Studies in Social Theory*. The Hague: Martinus Nijhoff.

Schütz, Alfred. (1932) 1993. *Der sinnhafte Aufbau der sozialen Welt. Eine Einleitung in die verstehende Soziologie*. 6th ed. Frankfurt am Main: Suhrkamp Verlag.

Schütz, Alfred, and Talcott Parsons. 1978. *Theory of Social Action: Correspondence of Alfred Schutz and Talcott Parsons*. Edited by Richard Grathoff. Bloomington: Indiana University Press.

Schwartz, Morris S., and Charlotte Green Schwartz. 1955. "Problems in Participant Observation." *American Journal of Sociology* 60 (4): 343–53.

Schwarz, Ori. 2019. "Facebook Rules: Structures of Governance in Digital Capitalism and the Control of Generalized Social Capital." *Theory, Culture & Society* 36 (4): 117–41. https://doi.org/10.1177/0263276419826249.

Scott, J.C. 1998. *Seeing Like a State: How Certain Schemes to Improve the Human Condition Have Failed*. Series / Institution for Social and Policy Studies at Yale University. Yale University Press.

Seaver, Nick. 2012. "Algorithmic Recommendations and Synaptic Functions - EScholarship." *Limn* 1 (2). https://escholarship.org/uc/item/7g48p7pb.

———. 2017. "Algorithms as Culture: Some Tactics for the Ethnography of Algorithmic Systems." *Big Data & Society* 4 (2): 2053951717738104. https://doi.org/10.1177/2053951717738104.

———. 2019. "Captivating Algorithms: Recommender Systems as Traps." *Journal of Material Culture* 24 (4): 421–36. https://doi.org/10.1177/1359183518820366.

Segura, María Soledad, and Silvio Waisbord. 2019. "Between Data Capitalism and Data Citizenship." *Television & New Media* 20 (4): 412–19. https://doi.org/10.1177/1527476419834519.

Shani, Guy, and Asela Gunawardana. 2011. "Evaluating Recommendation Systems." In *Recommender Systems Handbook*, edited by Francesco Ricci, Lior Rokach, Bracha Shapira, and Paul B. Kantor, 257–97. Boston, MA: Springer US. https://doi.org/10.1007/978-0-387-85820-3_8.

Sheehey, Bonnie. 2019. "Algorithmic Paranoia: The Temporal Governmentality of Predictive Policing." *Ethics and Information Technology* 21 (1): 49–58. https://doi.org/10.1007/s10676-018-9489-x.

Shor, P.W. 1994. "Algorithms for Quantum Computation: Discrete Logarithms and Factoring." In *Proceedings 35th Annual Symposium on Foundations of Computer Science*, 124–34. https://doi.org/10.1109/SFCS.1994.365700.

Simmel, Georg. (1900) 2004. *The Philosophy of Money*. Revised Edition. London ; New York: Routledge.

———. (1908) 2009. *Sociology: Inquiries into the Construction of Social Forms*. Translated by Anthony J. Blasi, Anton K. Jacobs, and Mathew Kanjirathinkal. Leiden, Boston: Brill.

Smith, Brent., and Greg Linden. 2017. "Two Decades of Recommender Systems at Amazon.Com." *IEEE Internet Computing* 21 (3): 12–18. https://doi.org/10.1109/MIC.2017.72.

Sørensen, Jannick Kirk. 2019. "Public Service Media, Diversity and Algorithmic Recommendation. Tensions between Editorial Principles and Algorithms in European PSM Organizations." In *CEUR Workshop Proceedings*, 2554:6–11. Copenhagen. http://ceur-ws.org/Vol-2554/paper_01.pdf.

Sørensen, Jannick Kirk, and Jonathon Hutchinson. 2018. "Algorithms and Public Service Media."
In RIPE@ 2016 Conference Proceedings . Antwerpen: Nordicom.

Sørensen, Jannick Kirk, and Jan-Hinrik Schmidt. 2016. "An Algorithmic Diversity Diet? Questioning Assumptions behind a Diversity Recommendation System for PSM." In RIPE@2016 Conference Proceedings. Antwerpen: Nordicom.

Spiekermann, S., and F. Pallas. 2006. "Technology Paternalism – Wider Implications of Ubiquitous Computing." *Poiesis & Praxis* 4 (1): 6–18. https://doi.org/10.1007/s10202-005-0010-3.

Srnicek, Nick. 2016. *Platform Capitalism*. 1st ed. Cambridge, UK ; Malden, MA: Polity.

Staab, Philipp. 2019. Digitaler Kapitalismus: Markt Und Herrschaft in Der Ökonomie Der Unknappheit. Berlin: Suhrkamp.

Star, Susan Leigh, and James R. Griesemer. 1989. "Institutional Ecology, `Translations' and Boundary Objects: Amateurs and Professionals in Berkeley's Museum of Vertebrate Zoology, 1907-39." *Social Studies of Science* 19 (3): 387–420. https://doi.org/10.1177/030631289019003001.

Stark, Luke. 2018. "Algorithmic Psychometrics and the Scalable Subject." *Social Studies of Science* 48 (2): 204–31. https://doi.org/10.1177/0306312718772094.

Steen, Marc. 2015. "Upon Opening the Black Box and Finding It Full: Exploring the Ethics in Design Practices." *Science, Technology, & Human Values* 40 (3): 389–420. https://doi.org/10.1177/0162243914547645.

Suchman, Lucille Alice. 2007. *Human and Machine Reconfigurations: Plans and Situated Actions*. 2nd ed. Cambridge: Cambridge University Press.

Sunstein, Cass R. 2009. *Republic.Com 2.0*. Princeton, N.J: Princeton University Press.

Sztompka, Piotr. 2014. *Agency and Structure: Reorienting Social Theory.*. Routledge.

Taylor, Charles. 2004. *Modern Social Imaginaries*. Durham, London: Duke University Press.

Ten, Chin Liew 1998. "Democracy, Socialism, and the Working Classes." In *The Cambridge Companion to Mill*, edited by John Skorupski, 372–95. Cambridge Companions to Philosophy. Cambridge: Cambridge University Press.

Terranova, Tiziana. 2004. *Network Culture: Politics for the Information Age*. London, Ann Arbor, MI: Pluto Press.

Thomas, William Isaac, and Dorothy Swaine Thomas. 1928. *The Child in America: Behavior Problems and Programs*. New York: Alfred A. Knopf.

Thorson, Kjerstin, Kelley Cotter, Mel Medeiros, and Chankyung Pak. 2021. "Algorithmic Inference, Political Interest, and Exposure to News and Politics on Facebook." *Information, Communication & Society* 24 (2): 183–200. https://doi.org/10.1080/1369118X.2019.1642934.

Thrift, Nigel, and Shaun French. 2002. "The Automatic Production of Space." *Transactions of the Institute of British Geographers* 27 (3): 309–35. https://doi.org/10.1111/1475-5661.00057.

Torrance, John. 1995. *Karl Marx's Theory of Ideas*. Cambridge University Press.

Totaro, Paolo, and Domenico Ninno. 2014. "The Concept of Algorithm as an Interpretative Key of Modern Rationality." *Theory, Culture & Society* 31 (4): 29–49. https://doi.org/10.1177/0263276413510051.

Tufekci, Zeynep. 2014. "Engineering the Public: Big Data, Surveillance and Computational Politics." *First Monday* 19 (7). https://doi.org/10.5210/fm.v19i7.4901.

Unkel, Julian. 2019. *Informationsselektion Mit Suchmaschinen*. Baden-Baden: Nomos Verlagsgesellschaft mbH & Co. KG. https://doi.org/10.5771/9783748901037.

Upchurch, Martin, and Phoebe V. Moore. 2018. "Deep Automation and the World of Work." In *Humans and Machines at Work: Monitoring, Surveillance and Automation in Contemporary Capitalism*, edited by Phoebe V. Moore, Martin Upchurch, and Xanthe Whittaker, 45–71. New York, NY: Palgrave Macmillan.

Van den Bulck, Hilde, and Hallvard Moe. 2018. "Public Service Media, Universality and Personalisation through Algorithms: Mapping Strategies and Exploring Dilemmas." *Media, Culture & Society* 40 (6): 875–92. https://doi.org/10.1177/0163443717734407.

Vargas, Eduardo Viana, Bruno Latour, Bruno Karsenti, Frédérique Aït-Touati, and Louise Salmon. 2008. "The Debate between Tarde and Durkheim:" *Environment and Planning D: Society and Space*, January. https://doi.org/10.1068/d2606td.

Varnelis, Kazys, ed. 2008. *Networked Publics*. Cambridge, MA: MIT Press.

Veale, Michael, and Reuben Binns. 2017. "Fairer Machine Learning in the Real World: Mitigating Discrimination without Collecting Sensitive Data." *Big Data & Society* 4 (2): 2053951717743530. https://doi.org/10.1177/2053951717743530.

Vioulac, Jean. 2009. *L'époque de La Technique. Marx, Heidegger et l'accomplissement de La Méta-physique.* Paris: Presses Universitaires de France.

Wachter, Sandra, Brent Mittelstadt, and Chris Russell. 2017. "Counterfactual Explanations without Opening the Black Box: Automated Decisions and the GDPR." *Harvard Journal of Law & Technology (Harvard JOLT)* 31: 841–88.

Wacquant, Loïc. 2004. *Body & Soul: Notebooks of an Apprentice Boxer.* Oxford, New York: Oxford University Press.

Warren, Mark. 1992. "Democratic Theory and Self-Transformation." *American Political Science Review* 86 (1): 8–23. https://doi.org/10.2307/1964012.

Weber, Max. (1922) 1978. *Economy and Society: An Outline of Interpretive Sociology.* Edited by Guenther Roth and Wittich Claus. Berkeley, Los Angeles, London: University of California Press.

Wieder, D. Lawrence. 1974. *Language and Social Reality: The Case of Telling the Convict Code.* The Hague, Paris: Mouton.

Willson, Michele. 2014. "The Politics of Social Filtering." *Convergence* 20 (2): 218–32. https://doi.org/10.1177/1354856513479761.

———. 2017. "Algorithms (and the) Everyday." *Information, Communication & Society* 20 (1): 137–50. https://doi.org/10.1080/1369118X.2016.1200645.

Winner, Langdon. 1980. "Do Artifacts Have Politics?" *Daedalus* 19 (1): 121–36.

Wirth, Niklaus. 1975. *Algorithms + Data Structures = Programs.* New Delhi: Prentice Hall India.

Wong, Pak-Hang. 2020. "Democratizing Algorithmic Fairness." *Philosophy & Technology* 33 (2): 225–44. https://doi.org/10.1007/s13347-019-00355-w.

Yadav, Naina, Rajesh Kumar Mundotiya, Amil Kumar Singh, and Sukomal Pal. 2020. "Diversity in Recommendation System: A Cluster Based Approach." In *Hybrid Intelligent Systems: 19th International Conference on Hybrid Intelligent Systems (HIS 2019) Held in Bhopal, India, December 10-12, 2019,* edited by Ajith Abraham, Shishir K. Shandilya, Laura Garcia-Hernandez, and Maria Leonilde Varela, 113–22. Cham: Springer Nature.

Yeung, Karen. 2017. "'Hypernudge': Big Data as a Mode of Regulation by Design." *Information, Communication & Society* 20 (1): 118–36. https://doi.org/10.1080/1369118X.2016.1186713.

———. 2018. "Algorithmic Regulation: A Critical Interrogation." *Regulation & Governance* 12 (4): 505–23. https://doi.org/10.1111/rego.12158.

Zarsky, Tal. 2016. "The Trouble with Algorithmic Decisions: An Analytic Road Map to Examine Efficiency and Fairness in Automated and Opaque Decision Making." *Science, Technology, & Human Values* 41 (1): 118–32. https://doi.org/10.1177/0162243915605575.

Zhu, Haiyi, Bowen Yu, Aaron Halfaker, and Loren Terveen. 2018. "Value-Sensitive Algorithm Design: Method, Case Study, and Lessons." *Proc. ACM Hum.-Comput. Interact.* 2 (CSCW): 194:1-194:23. https://doi.org/10.1145/3274463.

Ziewitz, Malte. 2016. "Governing Algorithms: Myth, Mess, and Methods." *Science, Technology & Human Values* 41 (1): 3–16. https://doi.org/10.1177/0162243915608948.

———. 2017. "A Not Quite Random Walk: Experimenting with the Ethnomethods of the Algorithm." *Big Data & Society* 4 (2): 2053951717738105. https://doi.org/10.1177/2053951717738105.

Zuboff, Shoshana. 2019. *The Age of Surveillance Capitalism: The Fight for a Human Future at the New Frontier of Power.* New York: PublicAffairs.

www.ingramcontent.com/pod-product-compliance
Lightning Source LLC
LaVergne TN
LVHW051118180726
843512LV00012B/867